THE ORDEAL OF HEGEMONY

THE ORDEAL OF HEGEMONY

The United States and Latin America

Guy Poitras

Westview Press
BOULDER, SAN FRANCISCO, & OXFORD

Copyright © 1990 by Westview Press, Inc.

Published in 1990 in the United States of America by Westview Press, Inc., 5500 Central Avenue, Boulder, Colorado 80301, and in the United Kingdom by Westview Press, Inc., 36 Lonsdale Road, Summertown, Oxford OX2 7EW

Library of Congress Cataloging-in-Publication Data
Poitras, Guy E., 1942–
  The ordeal of hegemony : the United States and Latin America / Guy Poitras.
    p. cm.
  Includes bibliographical references (p.   )
  ISBN 0-8133-7627-0
  1. Latin America—Foreign relations—United States. 2. United States—Foreign relations—Latin America. 3. Latin America—Politics and government—1948–   . 4. Latin America—Economic conditions—1945–   . 5. Debts, External—Latin America. 6. Latin America—Dependency on the United States. I. Title.
F1418.P66 1990
327.7308—dc20   90-11939
                                                                               CIP

Printed and bound in the United States of America

The paper used in this publication meets the requirements of the American National Standard for Permanence of Paper for Printed Library Materials Z39.48-1984.

10   9   8   7   6   5   4   3   2   1

Contents

List of Tables   vii
Preface   ix

1   The U.S. Century in the Western Hemisphere   1

Prelude to Hegemony, 3
The Rise of U.S. Power, 7
The U.S. Century Begins, 9
Policies of Hegemony, 10
Summing Up, 19

2   U.S. Power in Latin America   21

A New Consensus? 22
Perspectives as Prologue, 26
Hegemony, 29
Five Theses About U.S. Decline, 31
The Argument, 41

3   Farewell to Hegemony   43

The State of Hegemony, 46
Hegemony in Latin America, 51
No Farewells to Hegemony, 66

4   Participation Crisis in Central America   67

Alternative Perspectives, 68
Crisis and Participation, 71
Three Life Signs, 74
Crisis, Democracy, and the United States, 81

5   The Containment of Central America   83

Strategies of Containment, 83
Containment of the Left, 84

Containment of Conflict, 87
Containment of Counterrevolution, 92
The End of Exclusivity, 96

6   Security   99

Interests and Threats, 101
Security of the Hegemonic State, 102
Security of Latin America, 107
Security and Military Power, 110
Military Endowments, 115
Military Transfers, 117
Security Issues, 120
Securing the Americas or Securing Hegemony? 126

7   Economics and Debt   129

Hegemony and Debt, 130
The Roots of Crisis, 131
Aftermath, 136
The "Lost" Decade of Debt, 143
Dimensions of Debt, 144
Ravages of Debt and Debt Adjustment, 146
Crisis and Hegemonic Decline, 152
The Bottom Line for Hegemony, 152
The "Lost" Decade and Hegemony, 154

8   Hegemony and Intervention   157

Sharing Losses, Dividing Gains, 158
The Empire Strikes Back, 160
The Battleground, 161
The Reagan Doctrine, 162
The Latins React to the Doctrine, 170
In Tune or at Odds? 171
Esquipulas II, 172
Making Peace, 175

9   Beyond Hegemony   179

Cooperation After Hegemony, 181
Discord, 185

Notes   191
Bibliography   201
Index   205

Tables

3.1 GDP and GDP per capita growth rates in Latin America, 1950–1982   52

3.2 GDP of selected countries as a percentage of United States GDP, 1950, 1960, 1970, 1977, 1982   54

3.3 GDP of Western Hemisphere countries as a percentage of United States GDP, 1970, 1977, 1982   56

3.4 Share in world exports of Latin American states, the United States, and selected other countries, 1950–1980   60

3.5 Shares of exports from Latin America and selected countries to the United States and Latin America, 1948–1983   62

6.1 Force levels in the Americas   100

6.2 Comparative military spending, 1982   112

6.3 Comparative military capabilities   116

6.4 Latin American defense   118

6.5 Latin American military treaties, 1946–1975   121

7.1 Changes in terms of trade and in current accounts for the Western Hemisphere, 1967–1986   133

7.2 Net change in real GDP and in GDP per capita for Latin America, 1980–1984   138

7.3 Distribution of Latin American trade   140

7.4 Latin America's share of U.S. direct investment abroad, 1979–1985   141

7.5 U.S. direct investment position abroad in Latin America, 1980–1985   142

7.6 U.S. and Soviet economic aid to Latin America, 1954–1984   143

7.7 Foreign debt of the regional Big Four and of other Latin American countries   146

7.8 Growth in real GNP, 1970–1985   153

Preface

The fate of the United States as a great power has energized academic debate like few issues within recent memory. The "declinists" in economics, political science, and history argue that U.S. hegemony is on the wane, challenging its leadership and the stability of the liberal economic order in the world. A small, but persuasive, group of skeptics take exception to this view of U.S. power in the world. Like Mark Twain's falsely rumored death, the death or even the decline of hegemony has been exaggerated.

The Ordeal of Hegemony owes a great deal to both sides of this prolonged discussion. Extending the debate to regional hegemony in the Western Hemisphere, this book attempts to build three bridges. The first is between international relations theory and the realities of U.S.–Latin American relations. Rather than chronicle the latest and intriguing developments in the unfolding drama of inter-American relations, I have synthesized bodies of literature that may enrich our understanding of the North and the South.

A second bridge links the realist school of international relations with questions of power and change in the Western Hemisphere. Dependency as well as strategic and other perspectives have added to our understanding of U.S.–Latin American relations. In adopting a modified realist view of intraregional ties, I have aimed to see what an eclectic view of hegemony might have to offer rather than to argue that other perspectives are exhausted and no longer useful.

Finally, the book attempts a reappraisal of U.S. power in Latin America, a risky venture in times of indeterminate change and divergent thinking. Although realist hegemony theory is our chosen route, it is not always the most direct path to follow. To understand how U.S. power in the Americas has changed, one must be willing to acknowledge the deficiencies of any approach. Failing that, the enigmas and complexities of the region will remain as difficult to understand as they have been in the past.

My thanks go to Susie DuBose for her diligence in preparing the manuscript.

Guy Poitras
San Antonio, Texas

1

The U.S. Century in the Western Hemisphere

It is the peculiar fate of Latin America to share a continent with and live in the shadow of the foremost world power of the twentieth century. This is not necessarily either a beneficent or malevolent destiny. Rather, it is simply an intriguing and inescapable reality that shapes U.S.–Latin American relations to this day. Assuming a relatively surprise-free future, the United States will wield its great influence in the Americas for decades to come, but this does not mean that U.S.–Latin American relations have calcified. Change will continue to characterize the power relations of states throughout the Americas.

The United States and Latin America share the ordeal of living in a hemisphere that is significantly transformed with every passing decade. During most of the nineteenth century, the Americas went through a difficult period in which new nations were being forged within a Eurocentric world. Then, as the United States strode to the forefront of regional and global leadership in the late nineteenth and early twentieth centuries, the nature of the ordeal itself changed. At the beginning of the twentieth century, the challenge facing Latin America was to live with the ascent of a robust, powerful young nation capable of making itself felt throughout much of Latin America.

Today, as the twentieth century draws to a close, the ordeal of hegemony is to live with and adjust to the slow, relative, incomplete, uneven, and complex decline in U.S. power and the sometimes agonizing effect this has on relations between the United States and Latin America. Unfortunately, this fading hegemonic order has not been replaced by a new, coherent arrangement for managing conflict, dealing with pressing problems, or simply relating as mature partners. The modern ordeal of hegemony, then, involves the uneasy coexistence of unequal neighbors who have yet to find a way to cope with the travails of interdependence in an era of U.S. decline.

In examining the ordeal of hegemony, we must answer several critical questions. What is hegemony? How did the United States ascend to hegemony in the Americas? What does the third quarter of the twentieth century reveal about the relative decline of U.S. power? How do domestic and international dimensions of the Central American crisis help us understand why U.S. power is on the decline? And how does this important change in the hemisphere affect the security, economics, and management of the Americas?

Hegemony is a *preponderance* of power of one state over other states. It is far more than mere inequality among states. The power is derived from economic and military resources, and it is coupled with the ability to use these resources for specific purposes. When a great power like the United States is hegemonic, its share of the economic and military resources is so preponderant that it can control international and even domestic outcomes of a region to suit itself. Furthermore, it can stabilize the economic and political relations between states to its own benefit and to help those who have cast their lot with it.

As the last hegemonic power, the United States has held an overwhelming advantage in economic, military, and political power resources in the hemisphere for more than a century. It has had far and away the largest and most dynamic economy that fostered important technological innovations. Its rapid economic growth enabled it to take on the mantle of regional and even world leader and, by the end of the nineteenth century, it enjoyed a domestic political consensus that enabled it to manage hemispheric affairs to its own liking. In subsequent years, it used these economic and political advantages to build a military to contain Soviet expansion and to soothe the intermittent disturbances in its own hemisphere. Coupled with its will to use these resources, the United States was not only hegemonic (i.e., dominant) in the Americas but so preeminent that no other center of power in the Americas could dare challenge it.

The United States now presides over a peculiar hemisphere, with a distinctive asymmetry that makes the Americas unique. Some have called it an exclusive zone or sphere of influence; others simply refer to the "backyard" of the United States. What has been clear, at least until recently, is that what the United States wants in Latin America, it usually gets. It has made the rules, enforced the rules, and, when it chose, changed the rules. This is what it means to have a preponderant power base and a will to use it to achieve preeminence.

Of course, U.S. hegemony within the hemisphere began earlier and lasted far longer than its hegemony in the world, even as important changes in the international system have percolated through the region. Major industrial powers in the world had become important challengers to U.S. dominance. A more multipolar world had eroded the uncomplicated era of U.S. leadership of the 1950s. As a result, the United States has remained influential but has not been able to hold on to an unrivaled supremacy in the changing global system.

This decline of U.S. world hegemony has not occurred exactly the same way in the Western Hemisphere. Despite the evolution of Brazil and Mexico as regional players, no major challenge has yet redistributed economic power in the Americas; in Latin America, the United States has found no comparable rival. Power is less concentrated than it once was in the Americas, but clearly U.S. hegemony has not eroded to the extent that it has at the global level. If the United States is no longer preeminent in Latin America, it is still preponderant. Its influence has changed, but it has not dissipated and it still plays a decisive, even critical role in some countries in the Caribbean and Central America. Yet its ability to control other countries in Latin America has been weakened. The great irony is that the United States finds it increasingly arduous to dictate events even in the absence of any serious regional challenger. Unlike its position in the early twentieth century, the United States today falls short of having an "empire without colonies" in the Caribbean.[1]

Prelude to Hegemony

The maturation of the adolescent power in the north was a slow process. But economic growth in the United States and a domestic political consensus to use its new power heralded the onset of the U.S. century during the waning years of the 1800s. The nation's hegemonic vigor was first expressed in policies of imperialism and accommodation. Hegemony was not so much grand strategy as it was an almost inevitable condition of a lopsided hemisphere. U.S. preeminence is the modern history of power and change in the Western Hemisphere, and its rise was due to the uneven development of the Americas. The Industrial Revolution fostered disparities in the Western Hemisphere just as it did in the world during the nineteenth century. For example, between 1825 and 1910, the annual average rate of per capita economic growth of the United States was 1.6 percent, far surpassing that of Latin America.[2] This imbalance had a great deal to do with the shift of relative economic power to the north, and it reflected the growing preponderance of the industrial and economic power base in the United States. Yet the ascendancy was also due to the wielding of power, not just the unequal accumulation of power. The United States was preeminent in influencing the direction of the hemisphere because it was dominant in power resources *and* because it used them to get its way.

The evolution of the state in the nineteenth century planted the seeds of hegemony. While Latin America experienced frustration, neglect, and powerlessness, the United States moved toward becoming a "strong state." The outcome of the Civil War laid the foundation for national unity, and, buoyed by a strong sense of nationalism, U.S. policymakers were not shy about promoting U.S. interests in Latin America and especially in Central America. Public and private interests in U.S. foreign policy toward Latin America generally converged at the beginning of the U.S. century, yet the interests of the state prevailed over private ones whenever the latter failed to serve the goal of building a system of U.S. domination.[3] A strong state in the north and weak states in the south reinforced the disparities that signaled the onset of U.S. ascendancy.

For the greater part of the nineteenth century, the United States had neither the power nor the policy to underwrite hegemonic ambitions in Latin America. Early on, it sought to avoid a direct confrontation with European colonial powers. Cautious about supporting the wars of independence yet sympathetic to liberation from colonial rule, the United States clung to neutrality. Neither did the U.S. leaders embrace intimate relations with the newly independent states. Although Latin America sought political and military alliances, the United States did not respond warmly to these overtures.[4] Of course, this disinterest ebbed first with respect to the Caribbean. A "Caribbean consciousness" gradually emerged in the late nineteenth century. When the United States eventually began to wield some influence, it was used only in the region where it was likely to bear fruit, only where immediate national interests were most affected, and only where those of European powers were residual. The actual practice of U.S. policy coincided with its power base or power capabilities in the early decades of Latin American independence.

In the first half of the nineteenth century, the United States harbored great power aspirations, but it was constrained by regional realities for many years. The underlying goal was to secure the Western Hemisphere and in so doing ensure U.S. interests. This, in turn, entailed a commitment to exclude European influence, nurture the foundations of U.S. leadership, and bolster the political stability of Latin American states, goals that have endured from one century to the next. What has changed is the way power has been distributed in the region and the way the U.S. has used *its* power to realize these goals.

In the beginning, the regional reality was, for the most part, a post-colonial hegemony imposed by the world leader of the day, Great Britain. Even if the United States had wanted to assert itself, it was in no position to throw down the gauntlet to British domination. The

Monroe Doctrine epitomized the chasm between hegemonic aspirations and regional realities at the time. In 1823, when Monroe declared the Americas off-limits to European recolonialization and intervention, it was abundantly apparent to one and all (especially the Europeans themselves) that the United States did not yet have a hemisphere to itself, as Thomas Jefferson had wished; in Central America and elsewhere, "the United States could proclaim the Monroe Doctrine, but Britannia's fleet and investors wrote their own rules."[5] The pronouncement was unilateral, precocious, and unenforceable, but it did serve notice on Britain and Latin America about what the United States wanted for the hemisphere and for itself in the hemisphere.

A hollow proclamation for years, the Monroe Doctrine nevertheless anticipated the gradual rise of U.S. power later in the century. It advanced the Western Hemisphere idea. The new nations of the Americas were "essentially different" from Europe and must therefore seek isolation from European involvement. Promising to abandon intervention itself, the United States offered a reciprocal policy to Europe: mutual non-intervention in the affairs of the old and new worlds. However, implementation did not follow declaration, and European intervention in Latin America in the early 1800s was sometimes overlooked in the United States. Because Great Britain was the power with the most to gain from the breakup of colonialism and the guarantor of Latin American security, the fulfillment of the Monroe Doctrine had to await the outcome of the Anglo-U.S. rivalry in the hemisphere. Only when British power was shoved aside toward the end of the nineteenth century did U.S. policy in the Americas bear any close resemblance to the doctrine.

The implications behind the Monroe Doctrine were not lost on the Latin Americans. A self-declared redeemer from their own hemisphere could imperil their fragile independence just as the Europeans might have done earlier. As the possibility of European recolonialization waned after the Napoleonic Wars, the Spanish Caribbean in particular felt the threat, rather than the security, of the U.S. embrace. For most Latin Americans, the doctrine was a "handy shield" for U.S. expansion.[6] It was "an expression of United States hegemony employed to justify that country's own intervention."[7]

What happened between the end of colonialism and the ascent of U.S. hegemony is open to interpretation. One view is that British hegemony bridged the two eras in Latin America, as Spanish colonialism dissolved in favor of British domination of trade with Latin America.[8] Some countries, like Peru, escaped this fate, but, for the most of the region, the forerunner of U.S. preeminence had a British accent.

The other view is that British hegemony was a mirage and that Latin America actually enjoyed a respite from foreign domination in the mid-

1800s.[9] The economic ties between Latin America and Europe were thin and brittle, and, except for Brazil and Cuba, the states of the region were not oriented toward raw material exports to the world economy. Not only was Latin American trade "unimportant" and "stagnant" in the colonial and post-colonial periods but the region also stood outside the world of finance. And although Britain was the main exporter to Latin America at this time, the export market of Latin America was hardly an important one to Britain. In fact, it was not until the mid and late nineteenth century that the world economy began to intrude in this region—in limited ways and only in some countries.

The United States was not "first among equals" in the Americas in the first half of the nineteenth century. Without the fear or respect it would later acquire in the region, it was only a pretender to regional leadership at this point. But even in this prehegemonic era, the United States did assert itself, however cautiously and deliberately, into Latin America. Rather than challenge external powers where they were strongest, it pursued narrow national interests close to home where the involvement and the resistance of foreign countries were minimal. For example, its quest for continental expansion led to intervention in Mexico and the Caribbean countries. The goal was to control some regions of Latin America, rather than to defend all of it against foreign intrusion. In that way, the United States could pursue "manifest destiny" without risking a premature confrontation with Great Britain.

By the mid-nineteenth century, the United States was in a better position to rival British power in the Americas, particularly in the Caribbean and Central America. (In fact, the British presence in Central America may actually have stimulated U.S. involvement there.) U.S.-Anglo rivalry at this time was centered on the slave trade and trans-isthmian traffic, and nourished by mutual interest in constructing a canal. Thus, U.S. efforts to secure canal rights in Honduras, Nicaragua, and Colombia (Panama) were made in response to British plans to seek the same privilege. In 1850, the Clayton-Bulwer treaty led to a temporary agreement calling for the United States and Great Britain to jointly build a canal. In effect, the United States endorsed the continued role of Great Britain in Central America.

The two powers were also commercially competitive in the region during the last half of the century. But U.S. investors concentrated in certain economic activities, and British investors tended to focus on others. By the 1890s, U.S. economic influence came from investments in the production of cash crops such as coffee and bananas; British businessmen favored utilities and securities. Elsewhere in the region, British commercial interests were rather modest, primarily confined to

Cuba and Mexico. Consequently, it was the defense of these interests, rather than their magnitude, which complicated the generally amicable competition between Britain and the United States in this part of Latin America. Toward the end of British influence in the waning years of the century, the United States became the policeman of commercial interests in this region—both British and U.S. (although Great Britain would have preferred to defend its own).

But, at midcentury, the United States was still in no position to act like a great power or become the preeminent leader. It refrained from taking steps against Spain in its failed attempt to recolonize what is now the Dominican Republic. And, distracted by its own civil war, the United States did little to expel the French occupiers in Mexico. It was the exhaustion of colonialism, perhaps as much as U.S. policy, that served the purposes of Monroe's doctrine.

The Rise of U.S. Power

The U.S. century in the Western Hemisphere did not arrive until the 1800s were about to come to a close. But, changes in the last half of the nineteenth century were critical to the development of U.S. hegemony in the Americas. It was only after the Civil War in the United States, for example, that a "strong state," powered by a rapidly expanding industrial base could offer credible leadership in the hemisphere. Similarly, the accumulation of national power in the last half of the century was a prerequisite for the growing asymmetry in hemispheric relations. With a semifeudal social structure and an economic organization still largely based on subsistence and raw materials exports, Latin America could only fall farther behind the growing colossus to the north.

As economic growth and political healing in the United States set the stage for U.S. preeminence in the decades to come, its foreign policy was moving from traditional isolationalism to rudimentary internationalism. During the late nineteenth century, this transition was reflected in a reawakened interest in the Caribbean and in Latin America, despite the fact that economic relations were skeletal. Secretary of State James Blaine was perhaps the foremost advocate of closer ties with the south in this era. Although his principal legacy was the Pan American Union, Blaine advanced the idea that it was the United States and not Great Britain that was the "natural protector" of Latin America. (Despite such altruistic proclamations, Latin American suspicions of U.S. motives grew as U.S. power did.) By the 1890s, U.S. interest in the region had grown considerably. The stage was set for active involvement.

What were the underlying motives and intent of the United States as its influence in the hemisphere expanded? Of course, the stated goal was to ensure a stable region devoid of outside meddling. But though the North American state was by now a relatively strong one, it was buffeted by controversy over its proper role. The U.S. Congress generally maintained that the purpose of its foreign policy should be to defend the hemisphere against foreign intruders—that is, U.S. intervention and imperialism could be justified if they preempted *European* intervention. But the presidency and the executive branch as a whole advocated something else, something more intrusive: Resources permitting, it should be the policy of the United States to control the hemisphere and "press for further advantages."[10] The unchallenged premise in the United States was that the Western hemisphere was an official possession of an unofficial empire. However, there was no grand strategy to make this a reality. Rather, predispositions, opportunities, and evolving policies eventually forged the hegemonic role of the United States.

By this point, the United States had assumed two roles—protector and imperialist—and one was occasionally used to excuse the other. Spain's control of Cuba and Britain's dispute with Venezuela in the 1890s were cases in point. In the official U.S. view, dispatching Spain from the Western Hemisphere was one thing; annexing Cuba was quite another. The Congress therefore settled for the Platt Amendment, which imposed control without official annexation. Congress had also resisted earlier executive pressures to annex what is now the Dominican Republic, yet it allowed the purchase of the Virgin Islands from the Dutch. Similarly, the growing rivalry with the British led to hegemonic involvement without actual colonization. The border dispute between Venezuela and Great Britain in 1896 provoked the secretary of state to threaten the use of U.S. power in the name of the Monroe Doctrine. He virtually demanded international arbitration of the dispute. Then, after the British conceded, the secretary of state effusively claimed that the United States was the new sovereign of the region.

Whether to defend Latin America or to control it was a hegemonic dilemma even before the United States had any major economic interests to advance in the region. Trade between North and South in the Western Hemisphere was slow to develop. Blaine did advocate more trade relations through a policy of reciprocity, but Latin Americans were uninterested; they were too preoccupied with U.S. expansionism to seek closer economic ties and they believed that trade reciprocity simply furthered U.S. domination. In his own way, Blaine would have agreed. He argued against the dominance of protectionism in the U.S. trade policy by claiming that the United States would reap the most from reciprocity.

Ostensibly, U.S. intervention was intended to protect Latin America by preempting European intervention. Thus, British and German interference in Venezuela during Roosevelt's term led to a U.S. policy to deal with debt collection. The corollary's "preventive intervention" was intended to head off foreign collection, but neither European nor U.S. intervention to collect debts was palatable to Latin Americans. They sought to secure an agreement to renounce the use of force to collect debts and employ international arbitration instead. This agreement, called the Drago Doctrine, was meant to disarm the United States as constable of the region, but Roosevelt would only accept the doctrine under the condition that, if the debtor nation refused to accept arbitration, then force could be used to collect debts.[11] This was clearly unacceptable to Latin Americans. As a result, the United States continued to be both a constable and a collection agency.

The policy of direct intervention established during the Roosevelt years set the course for U.S. hegemony for more than a decade. Something more ambitious, however, could be inferred from Roosevelt's aggressive stance in the hemisphere. He hoped that U.S. assertiveness would signal to the world something more far reaching: The United States had not only regional ambitions, it had global ones, too. An adviser to Roosevelt, Brooks Adams, candidly reflected upon what this might mean for the future. For Adams, the 1898 war with Spain was a "turning point." This "first taste" of power in the Caribbean region was the "sweetest." It was also a harbinger of things to come. "I do believe," he said, "that we may dominate the world."[12]

Interventionism, gunboat diplomacy, and the "big stick" were trademarks of Theodore Roosevelt. But rather than abandon them, subsequent presidents built upon them and modified them to suit the changing circumstances facing hegemonic policy. In the Taft administration, for example, coercion and the military option still had their place; commercial and economic power were merely added to the arsenal.

The deepening of U.S. direct control did not signify the subjugation of state interests to private ones in the United States, although dollar diplomacy had quite another intent and outcome. The primary goal of state interests remained the security of the Caribbean and especially of the Panama Canal. Dollar diplomacy served the interests of a "strong state" bent upon stability in the region. Therefore, state and private interests were actually compatible. The policy was designed to extend benefits to U.S. business in Latin America and to use coercive diplomacy to help it, but U.S. business did not dictate the policy. Military intervention would protect U.S. commercial interests, but this was also supportive of broader goals. Whereas Roosevelt saw treaties and political deals in the region as an alternative to intervention, Taft placed his

But domestic and international constraints on U.S. trade policy in the prehegemonic era sustained protectionism over reciprocity. Economic and trade relations were therefore secondary to security and hegemonic interests at the end of the nineteenth century.

The U.S. Century Begins

U.S. preeminence in Latin America may have been inevitable. Yet, it was not until the late nineteenth century and the early twentieth that U.S. power and the domestic will to sustain leadership came together to herald the advent of U.S. hegemony in Latin America. Fundamentally, it was the will to exercise power and influence rather than the industrial and military strength alone which was so crucial for initiating this new era. And the dramatic involvement of the United States in the Caribbean region at this time quite clearly signaled the dawning of the U.S. century.

The will to use power was first apparent in the Spanish-American War. Until then, the United States had restrained its involvement to areas of Latin America that were of marginal interest to the European powers but of great interest to its own goal of "manifest destiny." Cuban efforts to gain independence from Spain afforded the United States the opportunity to apply manifest destiny to Latin America by using the economic, political, and military means at its disposal. The Cuban situation also stimulated changes in, and corollaries to, the Monroe Doctrine: Not only would European colonizers be prevented from reestablishing empire in the Americas but the United States would see to it that foreign interests would be expelled and replaced. As U.S. power and assertiveness grew, the goals of control and regional stability began to supplant foreign exclusion as the main interests of the United States. Furthermore, it was not only in the national interest to control Latin America, it was also the presumed right of the United States to do just that.

The remnants of British influence disppeared in the face of the growing influence of the United States. Although retaining some colonies and protectorates, Britain withdrew from a more commanding role: It no longer sought to preside over the region. Although it had previously retained naval bases and fueling rights in the Caribbean, after 1896 it seemed less willing to keep them in the face of changing realities, and by 1903, it had abandoned its Caribbean bases altogether. In surrendering its traditional role as the maker and enforcer of the rules in the region, Britain turned over to the United States the prerogative of political tutelage under which British economic interests themselves would flourish or languish. And yet there was no explicit pact between the United States and Great Britain about this transition at the beginning of the twentieth century.

In the early years, this new hegemony was more political than economic. It was deemed more important to use political power and military acumen to control events than it was to place the United States at the very center of inter-American economic relations. In fact, except in Cuba, North American investment in the Caribbean or in Latin America as a whole was relatively insignificant. What was of prominent concern was establishing a system of control through which U.S. security goals could be guaranteed, even before the United States had substantial economic interests to protect. Thus, the creation of a hegemonic system was the real issue in the early twentieth century. The United States used military power to foster the new rules of the game in the Caribbean. Intervention either imposed tutelage directly through protectorates and intimidation or it established the guidelines by which the small states of the region would have to act in this new century.

Policies of Hegemony

The basic goals of the United States changed very little with its rise to hegemonic grandeur in the Americas. It had always embraced the nineteenth-century ideal of an isolated, stable hemisphere in which the United States would remain secure and preeminent, and the ascent to hegemony merely placed these objectives within reach. What had changed at the inception of the hegemonic era was the capability and will of the North American state. By the early 1900s, the United States had become a world power, endowing it with the status only a few European countries had ever achieved. Although still unable and unwilling to carry the burden of world leadership and thereby supplant British hegemony, the United States had, by the turn of the twentieth century, clearly signaled that it was ready and willing to make the Western Hemisphere its "sphere of influence."

Latin America became the first region in the world to feel U.S. power. U.S. policies and doctrines radiated with confidence; the United States, if it wanted, could shape the hemisphere to its liking. The primary issue within the United States was just how this was to be accomplished. The nation was more or less of one mind about its domination of Latin America; what was in dispute was just how to do it. For example, how best to exclude foreign powers and to control the hemisphere was not self-evident, even in these simpler times. The policies of hegemony established during the early twentieth century were variations on this central theme—the Roosevelt corollary to the Monroe Doctrine, dollar diplomacy, gunboat diplomacy and "pecuniary intervention." The con-

sensus over the U.S. mission in the hemisphere used mor[e]
an iron fist.

Indeed, the policies of hegemonic control in Latin America
between two tendencies. The first was *imperialism*—direct,
interventionist. Between 1898 and 1928, such imperialism was
visible expression of the hegemonic vision and it was also the
tendency in U.S. policy. Imperialism enforced the hegemonic
forth by the United States. It relied upon coercion or the thre[at]
and it went so far as to dictate the parameters of internal gov[ernment]
within the states of the Caribbean region. The second tenden[cy]
accommodation—subtle, cooperative, and reciprocal. As impe[rialism]
became a liability in the late 1920s, accommodation found a pl[ace]
the hegemonic system, although, after decades of intervention, a[ccom]
modation was perhaps destined to be both negative and positive[.]
United States forsook its more egregious practices: It now pro[mised]
not to do something. But accommodation also extended benefit[s]
promising trade and economic inducements. Accommodation end[ured]
from 1928 until 1954. Since then, neither tendency has prevai[led]
Instead, military, economic, and diplomatic tools of hegemony h[ave]
been employed, with mixed results. But, whether imperialist or [ac]
commodationist, the intent of U.S. policy has remained constant.

Imperialism

After U.S. hegemony first crystallized in the form of imperialism[,]
the first significant policy innovation was President Theodore Roosevelt'[s]
modification of the Monroe Doctrine. His corollary, proclaimed in 1904,
was a defense of U.S. preeminence. Under the doctrine, Europe was
denied the right to intervene in Latin America; under the corollary,
the United States reserved to itself the very right that it denied foreign
powers. The United States took on the duty of an "international police
force" in cases of "wrongdoing or impotence." It could intervene in
lieu of foreign powers and creditors or even in the absence of foreign
meddling. Not only had the corollary proclaimed U.S. preeminence but
the United States had defined the rules and had anointed itself the
enforcer of those rules.

It was not long before the corollary was put to its first important
test. A year after its proclamation, it was applied to the Dominican
Republic. And then, from 1905 until 1909, the United States, sending
in U.S. Marines, ruled Cuba directly. In Nicaragua, which like Cuba
would undergo a major revolution later in the twentieth century, U.S.
Marines wielded the powers of state off and on for almost twenty years.
By 1962, there had been nearly 100 incidences of direct U.S. intervention,
primarily in the Caribbean region.

faith in capitalism as a stabilizing influence. Dollar diplomacy assumed that a large U.S. commercial presence in the region would hold foreign interests at bay and cultivate political stability in the Caribbean.

The power of the dollar was not a lone pillar in U.S. policy. In the case of Nicaragua, dollar diplomacy took on a more coercive appearance. Hoping to install a more cooperative government, Taft backed a successful rebellion with U.S. Marines. A new, more pliant government accepted U.S. economic control through loans and customs receivership. Certainly, Dollar diplomacy was an extension of past policy, but at the same time it was also a refinement of it. Protectorates, receiverships, and intervention simultaneously advanced both U.S. strategic *and* commercial goals in Latin America.

Regional stability and U.S. control were cherished by Wilson just as they had been by his predecessors. And, for all his public doubts about dollar diplomacy and interventionism, he found himself doing, for "noble" reasons, what he had chastised his predecessors for doing. Wilson was consumed by a "missionary" mentality; he was the moral imperialist who would teach the Latins about democracy and capitalism, impart the rules of democracy, and instruct them on how to "elect good men." The tutelage of the powerful became a Wilsonian refinement of hegemonic policy, as the United States became the hegemonic redeemer of the Americas.

Wilson was innovative, and under his administration hegemony had acquired the cloak of a legitimating ideology. Order and stability were to be sought within a legitimate political order based on constitutional, "good" government—one that was good for Latin America and, of course, good for everyone. In his declaration on Latin America, he quite clearly expressed the view that democratic principles, such as consent of the governed, were fundamental rules to live by. Further, he believed the mission of the United States was to see to it that Latin America practiced what he preached. This ideological refinement planted the seeds for the accommodationist tendency in U.S. hegemony that would emerge a decade later. But at the time, it meant that interventionism would proceed as it had in the past. A number of Latin American countries felt the indignity of U.S. intervention. A bilateral treaty established Haiti as a U.S. protectorate in 1915. U.S. troops occupied the Dominican Republic after the country refused a customs receivership. In Cuba, "constitutional reform" was the excuse to send in 2,600 marines to quell a revolt over an election. Minor territorial ambitions of the United States in Nicaragua were legalized in the Bryan-Chamorro Treaty of 1916. And U.S. interference in the Mexican Revolution is something many U.S. citizens do not remember but most Mexicans cannot forget.

Wilson had refined past policies, but his missionary quest for "good government" also anticipated the future. If stable, good governments came to power, then intervention would be unnecessary. But, to make good government possible and intervention outmoded, the foundation of stability would have to rest on coalitions within Latin American countries that would defend the interests of hegemonic rule. U.S. business interests, military governments, and the oligarchy would become the coalition to subdue instability and "bad" government. Thus, Wilson had, perhaps unintentionally, suggested a new form of hegemonic control.

The 1920s were a decade of transition in the still young century of U.S. hegemony. Interventionism had engendered ill will and had begun to pollute inter-American relations. In the Latin American view, even cooperation under the guise of Pan-Americanism was a form of complicity with U.S. domination, and regional resentment of U.S. policy had become palpable. Protectorates, interventionism, and dollar diplomacy had seen their day.

There were other reasons to justify a reappraisal, as well. After World War I, the Americas had ended European hopes for resurgence in the region. The war had, in fact, sped up the Americanization of the Americas. Of course, this meant that intervention had lost much of its legitimacy. Intervention no longer was "needed" to protect the hemisphere—it was no longer needed to protect the hemisphere. Rather, it became a blatant, counterproductive expression of hegemonic ambitions. Hegemony was now ready for a swing toward a more hospitable tendency.

Accommodation

Accommodation had taken a backseat to imperialism in the very early years of U.S. hegemony. But as the economic reach of the United States into Latin America became more impressive, U.S. influence assumed a more subtle character. The economic dimensions of U.S. hegemony were added to, but did not entirely replace, the imperialism of direct military intervention. President Cleveland had advanced the idea of greater trade with Latin America; Secretary of State Blaine championed reciprocity in U.S. trade with the hemisphere. During the early years of the U.S century, U.S. foreign commerce and investment gradually expanded far and wide. However, the United States remained reluctant in the early twentieth century to underwrite a policy of free trade. Instead, it insisted on a "free ride" from British trade policy as late as 1909.

Once again, Wilson added a new ingredient by advocating the economic dimension. He believed that the economic strength of the

United States and its changing relations with the world clearly called for changes in tariff policy. Although U.S. foreign economic policy slowly adapted to the nation's growing economic power, it was clear by the 1920s that U.S.–Latin American relations would be more affected by U.S. economic power than by its military advantage. By the late 1920s, President Hoover had arrived at the same judgment: Intervention was a very mixed blessing. Hegemony would wear a new mask.

The preponderance of economic strength in the north signaled the evolution of hegemonic domination of Latin America. The early years of the twentieth century witnessed a pronounced asymmetry in U.S.– Latin American economic relations. By the 1920s, the United States had become far more important to Latin America than vice versa, as the volume of U.S. investment and trade in the region indicated. By 1930, the United States dominated foreign investment virtually everywhere in the hemisphere. Trade figures confirmed this growing economic presence. Latin American imports from the United States grew from 24 per cent of all imports in 1913 to 39 per cent of all imports in 1929. On the other hand, Latin American exports to the United States rose from 30 per cent to 34 per cent of all exports during the same period.[13] The pillar of economic asymmetry became more important to U.S. hegemony in Latin America than the pillar of military intervention. Yet growing U.S. economic power, along with military intervention, had fed a growing sense of unity among most Latin American states.

The abandonment of military intervention was neither sudden nor complete. However, the Hoover administration became convinced that overt coercion was less viable. With no tangible European threat and with the growing economic power emanating from the United States, intervention had become devalued. Hoover specifically jettisoned the Roosevelt corollary while retaining the Monroe Doctrine and the right of intervention itself. In 1928, the Clark memorandum advanced the view that intervention was justified to preserve U.S. interests in the face of internal and external threats, even if the Europeans themselves were nowhere to be found. Although reserving the right to resuscitate imperialism, the United States had discarded its practice for a time. Marines left Haiti, customs receiverships ended, and protectorates were given up, all in the name of a new policy—the policy of a "good neighbor." The use of power had changed and matured even before U.S. hegemony had reached its zenith at the middle of the twentieth century.

A policy of accommodation with Latin America was prudent and even unique. By pledging itself to be a good neighbor and forgo the policy of intervention, the United States had invented a more subtle policy. It agreed not to use force or to intervene in the internal affairs of twenty republics, a policy that endured for two decades. It gave up its right under the Platt Amendment to interfere in Cuban affairs. Yet accommodation was possible because there was a mutuality of interests within the hemisphere during the 1930s. The United States and Latin America shared an abhorrence of the disturbing trends in European politics; hemispheric isolationism was generally embraced in the south as well as the north.

The "good neighbor policy" relied upon accommodation and co-alitions. Instead of using marines, the United States would ensure control through an implicit alliance with domestic elites. This was Wilsonian theory with a twist. The United States would dictate the nature of "domestic hegemony" in countries like Nicaragua, and co-alitions of U.S. bankers and businessmen, dictators, and the oligarchy would control instability in the Caribbean region. But, contrary to one view, the Good Neighbor was no enemy of dictators[14]—order, not democracy, was top priority. In fact, the economic dependence of autocratic elites in small countries was part of a system of control that would work as long as the few could dominate the many within Central America and elsewhere. This alliance of "dollars and dictators" proved to be a potent innovation in U.S. hegemony.

The political component of the good neighbor policy stressed restraint and was arguably more successful than its economic counterpart. Nonintervention was a political means to a hegemonic end. It entailed *not* doing something. Even for a hegemonic state, forbearance is easier to practice than action. And as the United States committed itself to self-restraint, the Latin Americans applauded this shift. In fact, the United States proved willing to do something that Latin America had been unable to do: harness U.S. military power. Furthermore, curbing interventionism was domestically useful because it allowed the hege-monic state to pay attention to acute economic distress at home and to the rumblings of disequilibrium and instability in Europe and elsewhere during the 1930s.

The economic aspects of the good neighbor policy, however, fared less well. For one thing, economic asymmetry in the Western Hemisphere limited the ability and willingness of the governments to pursue common economic goals. For another, the economic crisis of the 1920s and 1930s made it more difficult to practice the good neighbor policy on an economic level. Finally, an economic good neighbor policy engen-dered wariness and mistrust throughout much of Latin America, as was all too evident on the issue of reciprocal trade.

Relative to the economic strength of other great world leaders, the United States was as powerful at the end of World War II as it was at the end of World War I. Yet during the interwar years, it shrank from a role as world leader. It did not aspire to replace Great Britain on a global level. To the regret of some Europeans, the United States continued to practice the economic nationalism of a second-rate power. It was financially tightfisted in the world economy, seemed hostile to truly free trade, and refused to take its place among the world leaders by declining to join the League of Nations. The United States could have led, but it chose not to.

The situation in the Western Hemisphere was different, up to a point. In the early years of the good neighbor policy, the power and policy of the United States made hegemonic leadership far more tempting. Even so, the United States could not bring itself to practice the foreign economic policy of a full-fledged hegemonic leader. What it sought was liberal and reciprocal trade with Latin America. It did not agree to free trade, without conditions, which would give Latin America an edge.

The United States remained unwilling to carry the economic burdens of hegemony. Rather, it adopted a trade policy as if it were on an economic par with Latin America. More liberal trade with Latin America was meant to help the United States; it was not meant to construct a liberal economic order in the region. The good neighbor policy was economic nationalism in the guise of mutual interests and shared benefits. There was, however, at least one spokesman for an alternative. Cordell Hull, secretary of state under Franklin Roosevelt, was a tireless advocate of free trade for Latin America. He not only believed that this internationalized version of the New Deal would help the United States export more but that it would equally help Latin America increase and diversify its exports.[15] Yet reciprocal trade policy was indeed the centerpiece of economic accommodation with Latin America.

The Reciprocal Trade Agreements Act of 1934 was enacted to promote U.S. trade. It called for unconditional most favored-nation treatment, tariff bargaining through bilateral trade agreements and safeguards of countervailing duties for subsidized imports. For Cordell Hull, it was a vast improvement over the high tariffs and neomercantilism enshrined in the Smoot-Hawley Act. Reciprocal trade was the vindication of the strong state, not the triumph of commercial over state interests. The State Department defended reciprocal trade in the broadest strategic terms. It would do nothing less than prevent "the subversion of the political economies of Latin America by foreign powers."[16] By bargaining hard with Latin American governments and those of other regions, reciprocal trade would serve the self-interests of everyone.

Although a departure for the United States, reciprocal trade confirmed its strong economic position: Only a strong industrial nation could afford reciprocity and most favored nation treatment. For this very reason, it was greeted with mixed responses. There were few supporters in Latin America as the suspicion became widespread that this reciprocity would help the United States more than Latin America by solidifying economic domination by the United States over the region. The fear was that U.S. trade policy would bring with it "industrial and commercial hegemony" rather than mutual prosperity, and would reinvigorate trends toward asymmetry in the hemisphere. The opponents of trade reciprocity in Latin America saw insidious motives behind Hull's program. They believed that, instead of promoting mutual interests, reciprocity was a "subtle maneuver" to retard industrialization and self sufficiency. In sum, then, Latin America saw U.S. trade policy as a refinement of economic domination.

The goodwill earned from nonintervention was depleted over the failure to arrive at a plan to deal with the economic asymmetry in the Americas. And ultimately, it was not a plan from Washington that revived Latin American economies and exports in the late 1930s. Rather, global war did more to bolster economic relations and to legitimize U.S. leadership of the hemisphere than almost anything done in the name of the good neighbor policy.

The impact of the war was most significant. The demand for Latin American commodities grew tremendously, and the United States became an eager importer of raw materials needed for the war effort. The war also encouraged both trade diversification and incipient industrialization in Latin America. More generally, it brought the United States and Latin America closer together. In exchange for more trade and credit from the United States, Latin America practiced price restraint on its primary exports and even joined the alliance against the Axis. Consequently, at war's end, Latin America had become even more dependent upon the U.S. economy. The enduring impact of the good neighbor policy and the war combined to enhance U.S. control over Latin American economies.

By 1945, the U.S. century in the Western Hemisphere had reached a critical juncture. In five decades or so, the United States had accumulated vast power and at times wielded it politically, militarily, and economically in Latin America. It had taken a special interest in the Caribbean region and in Central America, but it also aspired to hegemonic leadership of the whole region. Its power was indeed preeminent.

How this power was used reflected changes over the decades in the willingness of the North American state to blend military intervention with economic domination. Its priorities in the region were those of a "strong state" in which security and strategic considerations were given top priority. Particularly in Central America, where U.S. control at this time was quite thorough, the willingness to use power, rather than the power itself, was decisive. As Kurth argues, the "political and economic logics" of the hegemonic power itself held the key to the ascent of hegemony in the region.[17] During the first half of the U.S. century, its regional hegemony or spheres of influence had become well entrenched. Military alliances were forged, economic dependence deepened, foreign intervention was intermittently used (even after the good neighbor policy) and system stability continued to be the constant preoccupation of the United States.

With its ascent to world leadership after World War II, the United States sought to prolong the U.S. century in the Western Hemisphere. Its basic goals in the region remained unchanged or had changed very little. Yet the challenges in the Western Hemisphere called for new policies. These policies put Latin America low on the global agenda. The hemisphere was to be protected from a new threat. Consequently, in the late 1940s, the Rio Pact and the Organization of American States were erected as bullwarks against new forms of external threat and as new means to Pan Americanize the control of the United States over the region. The United States also began the dismantling of the good neighbor policy. In 1954, self-determination and nonintervention were shoved aside in Guatemala in the face of geopolitical fears about communism. The political, ideological, and strategic solidarity of the Western Hemisphere under U.S. leadership became an overriding goal. The policies of the past in the hemisphere would have to be resuscitated, or abandoned, to fulfill the ambitions and responsibilities of a world superpower.

Ironically, just as U.S. power in Latin America reached the pinnacle of preeminence, the United States found it increasingly difficult to maintain the system it had constructed over the first half of the twentieth century. During the two decades following World War II, the United States reached its peak as a world and regional leader. Yet even as its resources grew, so too did the burdens and difficulties of leadership. The U.S.-led coup in Guatemala in 1954 was therefore misleading: The ease with which the United States deposed Arbenz's leftist government was by no means an accurate indicator of how difficult it would be in general to rule Latin America even at the height of U.S. power at the mid-point of the twentieth century. Only later would the ordeal of hegemony and change become far more evident to all Americans.

Summing Up

Political and economic change in the late nineteenth and early twentieth centuries transformed hemispheric relations. The uneven growth of economic and industrial power in the Americas not only tilted in favor of the United States but was mainly responsible for creating a regional hegemonic system. From the 1890s to the mid-twentieth century, the United States became an awesome presence in the Western Hemisphere. Its economic prowess not only elbowed a fading Britain from the hemisphere but enabled it to exercise great influence over the foreign and domestic affairs of its hemispheric neighbors. The United States was preeminent.

The growth of the U.S. power base, especially in economic terms, was just beginning. Hegemony also required (1) an elite consensus, (2) policies of hegemony, and (3) a willingness to adapt these policies to changing circumstances arising from economic growth and political change in the hemisphere and elsewhere. Uneven growth and the shift in power to the north led to occasional conflict and fissures. But the United States, in its dominant position, was able to use its power to tranquilize the region. Its hegemonic role in the Americas was assumed to be the essential definition of U.S.–Latin American relations during this time.

Although debate raged in the United States about the U.S. role in Latin America, the ordeal of ascendancy was a successful test of a youthful hegemonic state and its ability to make the hemisphere a place where its interests were secure and expanded. But, for the Latin Americans, the ordeal was seen differently. Some U.S. interests dovetailed with Latin ones, but others did not. The uneven growth of power that led to the hegemonic system would for decades diminish their own control over their affairs. Consequently, for Latin America, the U.S. century in the Western hemisphere was an ordeal of living with a patronizing, adolescent, yet powerful neighbor who at times would do things *for* Latin America but more often than not would do things *to* Latin America.

2

U.S. Power in Latin America

The ordeal confronting the Americas during the late twentieth century differs substantially from that experienced in the early part of the 1900s. Almost a century ago, the central issue was how to live with the rise of U.S. power. But, as the twentieth century comes to a close, the issue is how to live with diminished U.S. power. Since the middle of the twentieth century, there has been a consensus about U.S. power in Latin America: The United States dominates, indeed prevails, in the Western Hemisphere. The "hovering giant" cast a long shadow over both the small and mid-sized countries. And the United States prevails precisely because it is dominant.[1]

Until recently, this consensus held firm. The U.S. economy was ten times larger than that of Latin America combined in 1950. It absorbed almost one-half of the region's trade and more than half of the trade of many Caribbean countries. As a result, Latin America had become dependent upon the economic juggernaut to the north. Militarily, the United States was even more supreme in the Americas than it was in the world at large. It erected regional alliances (the Rio Pact and CONDECA) and made the Latin American military establishments a part of its security policy. From time to time, it even resorted to armed intervention (the Dominican Republic in 1965; Grenada in 1983; Panama in 1989). Finally, the United States was the occasional gendarme—U.S. hegemony and regional peace were not coincidental. In fact, there were no conventional armed conflicts among Latin American states between 1942 and 1981. The absence of interstate conflict in the region, due in part to U.S. hegemony and domestic and global security problems as well as to a lack of national and regional integration, also made Latin America relatively peaceful. Fundamentally, then, the United States was able to fashion its own version of a sphere of influence, and its presence assured relative tranquility. Latin America was generally stable, secure, and friendly, sealed off from contamination by the global adversaries of the United States.

But even during the heyday of U.S. domination, the preoccupations of the great power became more global and less regional. Although it was overwhelmingly preeminent, the United States did not always use its power to shore up its domination. The 1954 intervention against the Arbenz government in Guatemala and the 1965 intervention in the Dominican Republic belied the fact that U.S. policymakers abandoned a regional approach in favor of a global approach to Latin America and Latin America was more often than not put on the back burner. More subtle was the very gradual shift in material power resources. Although still unipolar, relations between the United States and Latin America were becoming defined less by the supremacy of the North and more by the development of the South.

A New Consensus?

Today, the old, midcentury consensus on U.S. preponderance has been badly shaken—and deservedly so. No longer is a U.S. wish a command for Latin America. It is premature to speak of the end of hegemony in the Americas, but this hegemony has certainly changed and even eroded to some extent, requiring the building of a new consensus about U.S. power in its own hemisphere.

Such a new consensus must take into account the significant changes of the last few decades. The United States is still dominant to a degree and even may be able to prevail in some circumstances. Yet neither the United States, Latin America, nor the world at large are what they once were. The Americas are more multipolar than they have been for decades; they are more interdependent with the world than ever before, and the familiar strengths of hegemonic leadership in the Americas suffer from a growing debility. Even when U.S. leaders decide to do something in Latin America, such as support insurgencies in Central America, they have great difficulty in making things come out the way they want. Sandinista Nicaragua and Noriega's Panama prove that even Lilliputians can stand up against U.S. power much longer than they ever could in the early twentieth century.

Although the extent of the decline is arguable, the erosion of U.S. hegemony in Latin America is itself undeniable and even paradoxical. The paradox is that the United States is more powerful in absolute terms than ever before, yet it cannot prevail as readily as it once did. It has far more economic and military capabilities than it did at the end of World War II yet, in relative terms, it is less preponderant than it was at midcentury. Instead of being the only actor in a theater of spectators, the United States is now the lead protagonist in a regional drama with a large cast of actors, most having speaking parts to play.

A new consensus on U.S. power must confront three daunting issues. First, why is the decline taking place? The role of the United States as a great power is being eclipsed much like Great Britain and others were in the past. But though some of the reasons for U.S. decline reside in larger historical forces that faced its unfortunate predecessors, they also arise from within the Americas and not just from changes in the world or within the United States itself. Second, how far advanced is this erosion of power? This is not easy to answer at either the global or regional level. Skeptics think that the decline is overstated, that the power of the United States remains unfazed, and that U.S. consensus on how to use its power may be the root of the problem. For their part, "declinists," on the other hand, insist that U.S. power is ebbing, although perhaps not as fast nor as much in the Americas as in the world. Finally, what does decline, if it is occurring, mean for the Americas? The twilight of hegemony might mean chaos, instability, and conflict, but it could just as well lead to peace, interdependence, and cooperation.

It is hard to envision a ready consensus on the extent and meaning of hegemonic decline being formed in the near future. Those who think the decline of the United States as a hegemonic power and world leader is well underway believe this bodes ill for the stability of global peace and prosperity. With the inevitable shift in economic and military resources away from the United States, they argue, its capacity and its resolve to maintain the global economic order and to manage crises have atrophied.[2] The decline of U.S. power, legitimacy, and leadership therefore darkens the future.

Others, however, contend that the issue of U.S. decline has been exaggerated. Much like the premature announcement of Mark Twain's death, they say, claims about the end of U.S. hegemony are unwarranted; the basis of U.S. global hegemony has not yet vanished.[3] Despite the fact that U.S. power capabilities have declined relative to Japan, Western Europe, and even some Third World countries, this gradual erosion may not yet have crippled the United States. While U.S. voters and leaders may wring their hands over the decline of the United States, others see the it as formidable and destined to remain so for some time.[4] They offer some specific issues to illustrate their point. In trade, economic productivity, and global monetary issues, the United States has fared quite well. As Keohane concludes:

> The United States remains the most important state in the world political economy, although it is less predominant than before. Hegemony by the standards of the 1950s has disappeared, but the United States is not yet an "ordinary country."[5]

The debate over the fate of U.S. hegemony in Latin America specifically also reflects agreement and divergence. Some believe the United States has lost its hegemony in the Caribbean Basin and not learned to cope with this reality due to a shift of basic power resources within the hemisphere.[6] The new realities point to the fact that U.S. hegemony is no longer overwhelming; its power is weaker and the United States as a model in the region is tarnished. Likewise, Wesson echoes the refrain of U.S. decline in its southern backyard, although he believes its ability to sway the Caribbean was never as overwhelming as was widely thought.[7]

Understanding the extent and causes of decline requires a more prudent appraisal of U.S. power in Latin America. After all, to say that hegemony has been "lost" in the Americas is hyperbole; to say that it is in decline merely initiates the debate. In reality, the economic and military asymmetries in the Americas remain stark and impressive, and these extremes in material power resources have softened the blow to U.S. power. In the final analysis, Latin America is still part of an unofficial empire.

Expansive claims about decline are hazardous. Time and again, when aroused, the United States can still be a fearsome presence. This typically occurs during a crisis in which extrahemispheric intruders become involved. According to Dominguez, the United States defends its "hegemonial preeminence" in the face of Soviet alliances with regional actors or to uphold international capitalism.[8] As Wesson sees it, maintaining hegemony is deceptively simple in one sense—keeping major powers from competing with the United States in hemispheric affairs.[9]

Hegemony is sometimes equated with old-style interventionism. Although U.S. Marines and mercenaries no longer work as well as they once did, the restrained use of force in Grenada and Panama shows that it has hardly been discarded altogether. Clearly then, the barrel of a gun still has a place in inter-American quarrels, but it is surprisingly ineffective in achieving broadly political goals, such as defending the hegemonic system itself.

When all is said, the issue of decline of U.S. power in Latin America is about how power is used and not just about power itself. Hegemony certainly depends on material power capabilities (i.e., economic productivity and military endowments), but it also depends upon will and leadership. If a political will to act like a leader still exists in the United States, it can continue to influence events in Latin America.

Currently, a peaceful, stable, isolated, and friendly hemisphere is under siege and so, too, is the power of the United States to deal with it. One test is the renewed susceptibility of the region and especially of the Caribbean Basin to strategic conflict. The Soviet-Cuban presence in the U.S. backyard remains, as do the tensions between the United States and its adversaries. Central America has become a stake in the conflict.

The second challenge is the growing uncertainty about security issues in general. For example, the Malvinas/Falklands War of 1982 between Argentina and Great Britain sorely tested the solidarity of Rio Treaty members on issues of security that are facing the hemisphere. In taking the side of the British, the United States confirmed its globalist security priorities and minimized its regionalist ones.

The third test is economic interdependence. The United States is actually dependent upon rather than insulated from the economic changes in the world and hemispheric economies. The oil shocks of the 1970s, for example, eroded U.S. leadership in its regional sphere of influence.

The fourth test is revolution. The Nicaraguan insurrection of 1979 against a client regime of the United States further challenged U.S. ability to dominate the region. It raised doubts about the ability of the United States to "prevail" and to bring about preferred outcomes, even in small corners of its informal empire. In other words, the Nicaraguan Revolution was a breach of hegemony that occurred despite tremendous U.S. advantages in material power resources. It was the *use* of these very resources, however, that forced the revolutionaries from power through elections.

Economic interdependence, revolution, adversarial intrusions, and disarray within regional security and economic systems have blemished the image of the United States. Although, a hegemonic state able to use its power and its control over international agenda can stifle challenges to its predominance, this is getting harder for the United States to do with each passing decade.

The case for minimizing the decline of the United States has its points, too. On this side of the ledger, the United States has secured some victories in the 1980s. Nicaragua bolted from U.S. domination, but the revolution was battered by a proxy war and economic pressure, leading to a victory for anti-Sandinista leaders in 1990. The United States still holds sway over much of the Caribbean Basin, and, as the "rescue mission" in Grenada and Operation Just Cause in Panama showed, the interventionist impulse was far from dead. U.S. policy toward El Salvador has been unable to secure a victory against the Left, but it has forestalled if not immunized a strife-torn country against a takeover from the Left. Countries in Central America, other than Nicaragua, have become more closely tied to U.S. goals, if not always to U.S. policy. Costa Rica and Honduras, client states in Central America, struggle to side with the United States without surrendering to its every whim.

In the simple win-loss calculation of strategic chess, the United States has suffered no clear "losses" since 1979, which may be merely good fortune or continuity with the past. The rise of elected governments in Latin America was hailed as a fortuitous trend, and the "democratic transition" in Latin America during the 1980s, while troubled, has served more than harmed U.S. interests. Economically, the global recession of the early 1980s has left a legacy of foreign debt and economic difficulties. In a departure from the past, the United States actively intervened in the international debt problems of the region, helping to stave off the more fearsome potential in the crisis of 1982–1983. But the "U.S. first" policies of the Reagan administration did more for the United States than for its client states in the south. They extricated the United States from the recession of the early 1980s, but the outlook for Latin America remains less promising, as illustrated by economic riots by Argentine workers in 1989.

Perspectives as Prologue

To understand U.S.–Latin American relations, we must, to begin with, rely on *perspectives*. Major perspectives on inter-American relations do several things: They attempt to explain or at least put into context the fascinating interplay of a large superpower in the north with the aspiring, mid-sized powers and many, small states in the south. More often than not, these perspectives are U.S.-oriented—they seek to explain inter-American relations by looking at the United States. This is perhaps an understandable bias. After all, a preponderance of power will attract a preponderance of attention. Yet, an explanation of U.S. policy or explaining inter-American relations in terms of the United States alone must eventually fall short because power and change are derived from many levels and sources. To understand power and change, we must also look at Latin America and the world beyond its borders with which it interacts.

Two basic ideas are imbedded in perspectives on U.S.–Latin American relations: (1) interstate power is asymmetric, but not frozen, and (2) the United States and Latin America are interdependent. These two ideas are combined into the term *asymmetric interdependence*. Major perspectives try to shed light on both the unequal power resources and growing ties among states and other actors in inter-American relations.

Two perspectives have been used to explain U.S.–Latin American relations and especially U.S. policy in this arena: the first is the *strategic perspective* and the second is the *dependency perspective*. The strategic view underscores the concepts of state and power in international relations. The state is seen as the central, if not the sole actor in world politics. Why states do what they do is determined by the rational choice of leaders confronted with external constraints. In a world of near-anarchy, the strategic perspective puts the security of the state ahead of other values. On the other hand, the dependency perspective, grounded in earlier *dependencia* theories, explains the structure of inter-American relations in terms of the economic domination of the center, or core, over the periphery. Classes within and across states are seen to be more important than the states themselves for explaining the exploitation and domination of the hemisphere by U.S. capitalism. Both perspectives are ideologies more than scientific theories.

The strategic and dependency perspectives are opposite sides of the same coin. For both, the structure of power at the international level determines what states and others do. Both stress and are even obsessed with the overwhelming power of the United States in shaping inter-American relations—it appears to be the only important actor in the hemisphere. And Latin American states are seen as subjects or victims of the system. Dependency particularly underestimates the vulnerability of the hegemonic state.

However, important differences emerge over the essential motive of domination and the role of the state. The strategic perspective harks back to the classic realist view of world politics: Inter-American relations is the search for security and power among unequal but autonomous states. But the dependency perspective, even in its unorthodox form, regards U.S.–Latin American relations through a distinctive prism: Structure and policy in a U.S.-dominated region are shaped by economic exploitation, not state security, and it is a struggle of classes, not of states. The strategic realists also regard the state as having interests of its own, which it pursues autonomously from private interests. The dependency and neodependency perspectives, however, portray the state as a tool of private (capitalist) interests. It has no interests of its own, except perhaps to defend the entire system of imperialism. Meanwhile, class interests compete for control of the state, and states make up the rules of the international market to favor class interests at home and abroad.

Strategic and dependency perspectives are ambitious—and consequently flawed. At their worst, both are mere caricatures of inter-American realities.[10] What is more, both rely upon dubious premises. The strategic perspective is vulnerable on several counts. It makes too much of the state as a monolithic and "rational egoist." In fact, the rise of the state in Latin America is tempered by territorial quarrels and political illegitimacy, and there is far less internal unity than meets the eye, even within the U.S. policymaking process. Furthermore, the strategic imperative can too easily be exaggerated. It also makes more sense to speak of security and strategic thinking in some parts of the region rather than it does in others. Thus, the exercise of U.S. power in the Caribbean Basin may indeed be motivated by largely strategic and security concerns, but these are less compelling motivations for U.S. policy toward more stable and economically developed states farther to the south.

This state-centric perspective also glosses over the rich complexity of the Americas. In so doing, it points us toward the asymmetry of power but not toward the dynamics or paradoxes of the region. For example, actors other than states have leading roles in the Central America drama; such non-state actors are vital to understanding how Nicaragua broke away from the traditional hegemonic system erected by the United States in the early twentieth century. And though revolution in Latin America proves that the state may be both a target and an instrument of change, it also shows that other political contenders, outside forces, and social classes can vitally influence this region.

Dependency is an influential perspective that emerged from Latin American intellectual circles in the 1950s. Since then, it, too, has gone through some revisions. Neodependency, for example, takes dependency one step further, stating that domination may destroy rather than perpetuate dependency because foreign domination fosters domestic poverty and injustice that in turn precipitates crisis. Neodependency theorists believe that economic domination of Central America has made revolution inevitable. However, the alternative is just as plausible: Uneven economic growth, rather than the lack of it, has sparked revolution. A single-factor theory, dependency has been stretched to explain domination in an entire hemisphere.

Just as the strategic perspective may be guilty of exaggerating the role of the state, dependency makes too little of it. In this perspective, economics, rather than political and strategic interests, are the crux of inter-American relations, and class, not state, interests prevail. Latin America is therefore described as the region of the "vanishing state." This, of course, is debatable. In both the North and South, the state is sometimes embattled; it may even be disunited and is not always "rational." Yet it no doubt remains at the center the ordeal of power and change for both the United States and Latin America. State interests do prevail over private ones, especially when large issues are at stake. And states are far more than an automatic and servile tool of multinational corporations or of ruling social sectors. Indeed, "states can act in inter-

American affairs, autonomous both from foreign countries and from social and economic class and group pressures."[11]

The two perspectives, different as they are, are valuable, but they should not be taken too far. To regard inter-American relations as a system of states or of transnationally organized classes sheds little light on how policy may affect inter-American relations. So, at some point, we must go beyond the regional structure of relations between states and classes and look within the states themselves to make sense of the behavior of states to understand why states act the way they do.

Inter-American relations must also be understood in terms of what is being done by whom. Take interstate conflict, for example. Noting that the structural bases of conflict have changed very little in Latin America since World War II, Grabendorff stresses domestic determinants. "Generally, internal factors have caused the growing heterogeneity within the region and the resulting new patterns of conflict."[12] Disenchantment with structure among states sets in, leading Pastor to argue for an "interactive" approach.[13] And not only do countries and economic forces in Latin America affect the United States and vice versa but internal crisis may become internationalized because of the interplay of domestic and international actors.

Hegemony

Hegemony takes two forms: *pure* and *eclectic*. Earlier, hegemony was defined as the preponderance of power among states. This is hegemony in its pure form, where the material resources of the hegemonic state are compared with those it dominates. This may require the measurement of "share capabilities." For example, to what extent does one state control raw materials, sources of capital, and markets for imports? For others, it may suggest looking at the hegemonic state's share of the world's gross national product (GNP) or even its relative control over the productivity of manufactures and world trade. Essentially, though, pure hegemony focuses on the distribution of material resources between states and on what states have, rather than how they use what they possess. But hegemony has a broader interpretation as well. The eclectic version goes beyond the emphasis on distribution of material power resources among states and stresses that both having *and* using power are important.

Eclectic hegemony departs from pure hegemony in several ways. First, it assumes that the asymmetry of material resources alone is not enough to ensure predominance because interdependence may dilute hegemonic leadership. Therefore, even if the United States is still overwhelming in resources, it may be too dependent upon the outside world to act unilaterally to achieve its own ends. Second, as mentioned above, hegemony depends upon what states do and not just upon their material resources. In trade policy, this may mean considering policies of free trade and relative openness to imports. In military matters, this may mean using resources to intervene in or to underwrite client states. The United States can use its position to help itself more than others, or it may use its resources to pay costs of stability from which others benefit almost as much as it does itself. Thus, such factors as national will and policies may enrich a pure view of hegemony.

For the most part, coercion lurks underneath both versions of hegemony. But preponderance of power does at least imply the use of coercion. Material resources and the use of these suggest that the powerful do something *to* the weak. And in fact, coercion and force have been used from time to time to secure U.S. control. Few Latin Americans need be reminded of the element of coercion in their relationship with the United States during the first half of this century. And even fewer have to be reminded of the revival of coercion during the 1980s. What makes U.S. hegemony in Latin America intriguing, however, is not that coercion exists but that it has been used so sparingly.

Intrusive, active coercion is unnecessary much of the time because there is more to hegemony than force. Hegemony can survive if it is accepted by those who are affected by it; it need not be imposed. Compliance does not always rely on the unilateral exercise of preponderant power or overwhelming force. Such *subjective* hegemony can take different forms. One example is the Gramscian notion of *cultural* hegemony which is important in inter-American relations. The cultural influence of the United States has permeated Latin America and done a good deal in the past to rationalize and even legitimize U.S. hegemony in the hemisphere. U.S. culture, diffused widely throughout Latin America, has shored up the influence of the United States and has even diluted the impact of the more recent hegemonic decline.

Ideological hegemony, which involves the acceptance of U.S. control, is also subjective, but in a unique way. Latin American leaders may be more or less willing to accept hegemony, given the options and opportunities they may have at any one time. It may even be in their self-interest to "play ball" because cooperation with the United States can have its rewards for them personally and even for the broader national community they claim to represent. The United States may extend its protective umbrella over a beleaguered regime; it may create inducements for Latin American states to stay in the liberal economic order it has created; it has also devised a system of beliefs or myths about hemispheric unity.

However, ideological hegemony, more so than cultural hegemony, faded in much of Latin America during the 1970s and 1980s. It clashed with nationalism and antiinterventionism, and in the process, the legitimacy of hegemony in Latin America clearly lost ground. As distasteful as General Noriega's regime was to many in the hemisphere, Latin American leaders were put off by the Bush administration's invasion to oust him from power.

Five Theses About U.S. Decline

Why has U.S. influence declined in Latin America? Has there been a fundamental shift in power in the world and within the Americas, as theory of pure hegemony would suggest? Have changes within the states of the region had anything to do with hegemonic decline, as the advocates of eclectic hegemony would argue? Has the United States shrunk from its responsibilities of leadership even as Latin American states seek more control over their own fate?

Explaining change is an important but hazardous undertaking. But though hegemony theory cannot fully explain what has happened, it can point us toward some theses about change in the Americas. Moreover, the theory of pure hegemony—that which looks at shift in power among states in the Americas—must be modified if it is to help explain anomalies in U.S.–Latin American relations. For example, how can it explain the fact that the United States is often unable to control events in the Caribbean Basin where the power asymmetries most highly favor the United States?

There are five theses about the decline of U.S. power in Latin America: (1) the diffusion of power; (2) strategic intrusion; (3) revolutionary defection; (4) the rise of the Latin American state; and (5) the "will" of U.S. policymakers.

Some of the theses owe more to pure hegemonic theory than do others. For example, the diffusion of power thesis describes power in terms of material resources or capabilities, but the national will thesis is more concerned with how those capabilities are mobilized and used. The theses on the diffusion of power and strategic intrusion stress the changing relations *between* states; the theses on revolutionary defection, the rise of the Latin American state, and U.S. will emphasize what happens *within* states. Some, even most, take a long-term look at power, largely immune from the short-term decisions of leaders. Others (national will, again) are absorbed by the here and now. Each thesis seeks to enlighten us about U.S. power in Latin America in its own way. The critical thing to keep in mind is that none of them is entirely convincing on its own but each stresses something about U.S.–Latin American relations that bears consideration before trying to comprehend U.S. power in the hemisphere.

The Diffusion-of-Power Thesis

Simply stated, the diffusion-of-power thesis asserts that power has ebbed away from the United States in a relative sense. This has been most evident in the global system but it has affected U.S.–Latin American relations, too. Although the United States is now wealthier and more robust than ever before, the status of others has risen, due to a shift of *relative* power resources. The United States enjoyed an "artifically predominant status" at the end of World War II.[14] Since then, its descent from predominance has been due more to the rejuvenation of other centers of power in the world. Thus, although U.S. power capabilities have, in fact, grown in absolute terms since the war's end, its *share* of the world's material resources or capabilities has shrunk gradually. The rise of its once prostrate allies, who were helped along by hegemonic largesse in the 1940s and 1950s, eventually challenged U.S. hegemony. And others have also risen quickly. Europe, Japan, OPEC, and the Communist bloc experienced strong and even more rapid economic growth than the United States from the 1950s through the 1970s. With twenty-twenty hindsight, this leveling of material power resources seems natural, even predestined.

Diffusion of power could eventually lead to multiple power centers at the international level. Managing the world economy from one center becomes unrealistic because this diffusion of power broadens and pluralizes the effective management of interdependence. In the meantime, with its capabilities diminished to a degree by this power diffusion, the United States must now rely on others more than it once did. But a world composed of countries with more equal capabilities has risks and uncertainties, and, in such a world, it is more difficult to prevent or deal with economic crises. Economic turmoil has most certainly done little for U.S. prestige as a great power. In fact, the crisis in the world economy, the transnational movement of capital, and the perverse behavior of prices in the 1980s have signaled the decline, if not the end, of U.S. management of a liberal world order. The emperor still has clothes, but they appear a little tattered.

What has happened at the global level is extremely pertinent to U.S. power in Latin America. First, the United States by itself no longer sets the rules nor is it the only superstar in the game. Europe, Japan, OPEC, the Communist bloc, and the semi-industrialized periphery now have markets, capital, and exports in Latin America. The loss of U.S. influence to its global rivals is most apparent in the patterns of trade and investment with Latin America. The Western Hemisphere idea—which holds to the tradition that the Americas is a special and unique sanctuary insulated from world politics—is dying as an economic reality, just as it died strategically with Castro's ascent to power in 1959. Second, the hegemonic state's economic rivals and strategic adversaries now have a foothold and a stake in Latin America. The decline of U.S. power has coincided with the formation of commercial, cultural, and economic relations between Latin America and Europe, Japan, and the Middle East. There is even speculation about Latin American reliance on Europe rather than on the United States. Third, the United States cannot separate its leadership role in the hemisphere from its role in the rest of the world. Consequently, the position of the United States in the world at large has significant implications for its future in Latin America; U.S.–Latin American relations are simply some of the threads in a larger global fabric. And inter-American relations are becoming more like international relations on the global level, with greater diffusion, competition, conflict, and cooperation.

There has been a diffusion of power within the Americas as well. However, the shift in power from north to south in the Western Hemisphere has been less dramatic than that in U.S. relations with major world powers. Certainly, impressive asymmetries still exist in inter-American relations and the economic crises of the 1980s may have deepened them. Yet over the years, the relative power of Latin America has increased at the same time that the power of the United States to prevail in the South has ebbed. The gap between the hegemonic state and the region has shrunk.

Without doubt, the redistribution of power in the Americas has altered the reality of U.S.–Latin American relations. But what does this portend for U.S. power? The United States retains an impressive advantage in material resources, but this does not bestow upon the United States a halo of invincibility in the Americas. The redistribution of power to Latin America was a blow for a more egalitarian (though not a *very* egalitarian) hemisphere. It also may have encouraged some Latin American states, such as Mexico and Brazil, to be more assertive. The United States is confronted with its own dependence on Latin America.

The Strategic-Intrusion Thesis

The strategic-intrusion thesis contends that outside powers have punctured the hegemonic exclusivity of Latin America for the United States. That is, U.S. power has declined because other great powers now have their own interests and stakes in the region and the Americas are no longer a backyard only for the North Americans. It had always been a measure of U.S. hegemony that the United States could keep Latin America beyond the reach of global adversaries, world politics, and the cold war. In particular, the United States sought to make the Caribbean Basin a sphere of influence where it prevailed exclusively and from which other major powers were excluded. But even though the United States is still the most important state in the Americas, it is not powerful enough to purge or even contain outsiders. Consequently, it is less preeminent because it must share the regional stage with friendly rivals and strategic adversaries alike. The unipolar simplicity of hegemony has largely dissolved.

The strategic perspective favored among policymakers in the United States portrayed Latin America as a prize in the East-West conflict. This view was revived during the early 1980s as a new "strategic reality" for reversing the decline of U.S. hegemony, and Soviet subversion and aggression are the causes of the crisis in the Caribbean Basin. After all, the Soviets and the Cubans are rising powers in the Caribbean; Cuba has been thoroughly "Sovietized"; the Soviet blue-water navy is present in the south Atlantic; the wars in Central America have been internationalized; and Nicaragua stands between the two crumbling strategic blocs. These and other changes account for the decline of U.S. domination in the Caribbean Basin. Meanwhile, the United States vainly seeks to hem in or expel this foreign threat altogether.

A strategic view of U.S. power in the hemisphere as seen from Latin America puts the threat in a different light. Instead of an East-West perspective, Latin American leaders lean more toward a North-South one. And as always, the principal concern of these leaders has been to limit U.S. intervention. The agitation expressed by the United States over Soviet involvement has made Latin Americans anxious about the potential response from the north. But neither the East-West nor the North-South perspective has altered much since the early days of hegemonic ascent. Just as the United States has found it difficult to curb strategic threats in the region, Latin America has always found it difficult to curb the threat of unilateral U.S. intervention.

The interplay of interests and threats further illuminate the decline of U.S. power in this strategic perspective. In the north, U.S. security interests come first and these interests rest on cherished premises. For example, there is little doubt that the Caribbean Basin is vital to the defense of the United States. This premise is also wedded to another— that the threat is great. According to Robert Pastor, a former national security adviser for Latin America, the strategic imperative in the United States is so important that the threat may *define* U.S. interests.[15] With interests bonded to threats, the United States cannot sit back and allow others to dictate events: It must "do something" if it intends to restore and ensure its security interests.

Even so, the strategic-intrusion thesis is hardly euphoric about the possibility of protecting these interests in the face of the threats because U.S. options are amazingly meager. The United States might resort to traditional proconsularism and try to run the domestic affairs of a country directly; it might try to reach an understanding with the Soviet Union about spheres of influence, perhaps trading agreement on one regional conflict for another; it might pursue a broad, multilateral strategy involving key countries; it might adopt a developmental view of Caribbean security; or it might revive gunboat diplomacy, even if only theatrically as in the case of military manuevers in Honduras. However, these options fail to match limited means with the grand strategic goals of a declining hegemonic power. In fact, enlarged threats and interests call even more attention to the limits of U.S. power. And the strategic-intrusion thesis cannot offer any ironclad plan for strategic expulsion.

Power entails more than resources or capabilities; it is also a matter of credibility. Thus, the meddling of outsiders calls into question the credibility of the United States: Can it truly do what it wants, when it wants, anywhere it wants? Hegemony and credibility are dual motives of U.S. power in Latin America. Consequently, "events in Latin America at times [are] treated as tests of U.S. global credibility . . . not as mere challenges of U.S. hegemony in a neighboring country."[16]

The power and position of the United States in Latin America can subjectively influence its power and position in the world because prestige and image are accorded great weight, perhaps even more so when the reality of hegemonic power is in doubt. In this game of mirrors, where credibility as well as threats can define interests, the hegemonic state sets a near-fatal trap for itself. If the United States stakes its reputation on Central America, it might indeed suffer because any decline in hegemony in Central America could be interpreted as a loss of U.S. credibility.

The Defection Thesis

The defection thesis holds that U.S. power in Latin America has occasionally been diminished by what happens *within* countries. Instead of stressing a shift of material resources in the Americas or the meddling of outsiders, the thesis focuses on structural changes within countries like Cuba and Nicaragua that have redistributed power to new groups, redefined participation, and tried to deal with development problems in a manner unappreciated by the hegemonic state. Such radical experiments sever the bonds of hegemony that were personified by the prerevolutionary leaders of Fulgencio Batista in Cuba and the Somoza dynasty in Nicaragua. And by according more importance to social and economic factors within countries than to broad shifts in power among states, the defection thesis is the reverse of the first and second theses. It serves as a counterweight to pure hegemony with its emphasis on structural changes in the international system of states.

Domestic changes within Latin American states may chisel new cracks in the hegemonic system. Therefore, it has become the crucible of U.S. policy in the Caribbean Basin to "arrest the decay of the region's sociopolitical fabric."[17] Genuine revolutions are rare in Latin America, but they are home-grown and arise ultimately from poverty, injustice, uneven growth, political suppression, and the like. And although international factors clearly have their place, it is also evident that the presumed allies of revolution, such as the Soviet Union, were largely irrelevant to the actual process of bringing revolution to power in Cuba and Nicaragua.

This thesis cannot stand alone, however. Ironically perhaps, the United States best exemplifies this point. It has, at times, actually fostered revolutionary movements by propping up repressive systems tied to its own control over certain countries. Indeed, "the lessons of the past are that U.S. attempts to mold Central American and Caribbean politics often produced regimes that in recent years have been the causes of revolutions."[18]

Revolution, of course, is anathema to U.S. goals in Latin America. And the policy toward revolution is a test of its power to prevent, undo, or weaken radical states. How well has it done? It has generally proven to be ineffectual in reversing the defection of a radical state once the revolutionaries come to power. The security and development doctrines of the 1960s placed the United States squarely against "people's war" and "guerrillas of the poor." Yet some rebels have been too popular to ignore or to isolate. Consequently, broad-based insurgencies against unpopular and sclerotic dictatorships have been treated differently. The United States has, as a result, maintained some flexibility toward rebels in hopes of minimizing influence of the Left and the Soviets by strengthening the moderate and democratic elements among the insurgents. Failing that, it has tried to launch counterrevolutionary assaults on the unrepentant radicals who come to power.

The eventual triumph of the rebels usually brings a change of heart and policy. Two broad policy options are open, once the insurgents attain power. The first is reconciliation; the second is suppression.[19] Which path is followed largely depends upon the chances for satisfactory relations and the likelihood that the new government could become a pawn of a great power hostile to the United States. Having come full circle, the defection thesis meets the strategic-intrusion thesis.

Defection from the U.S. to the Soviet orbit is not solely up to the leaders of the new radical state, of course. The Soviets have been cautious opportunists in Latin America; they have been reluctant to embrace radical regimes too quickly. The United States also has an important if not decisive voice in the direction of the new, revolutionary state. However, U.S. patience and tolerance usually give way to implacable opposition. For example, by taking the path of conciliation, the United States has moderated revolutions in Mexico and Bolivia, but by following the path of suppression it may have helped to radicalize revolutions in Cuba and Nicaragua. Entrenched, radical regimes are usually seen in Washington within a larger context, not an expression of nationalistic forces, and the presence of such regimes is perceived as threatening to the global power and prestige of the United States.

Counterrevolution in Guatemala (1954) and Chile (1973) restored friendly if not entirely savory regimes. The U.S. success in Chile is instructive. The Allende government may have aligned itself eventually with the Soviet bloc but Nixon and Kissinger took no chances in their efforts to prevent a full-fledged domestic and international defection. Allende's democratic socialism was bad enough, but the possibility that he might align Chile with the Soviet Union was intolerable. This lesson was not lost on the Latin Americans themselves. According to Molineu, "Washington's interference in Chile confirmed Latin perceptions of U.S. hegemony and of their countries as mere pawns in the game of great power politics."[20] There is another lesson here, as well: Failing to prevent or reverse defection may in fact help create the outcome to be prevented—a decline of U.S. power vis-à-vis an entrenched radical state aligned with the Soviet bloc.

The Active-State Thesis

Like the defection thesis, the active-state thesis minimizes the concern of pure hegemonic theory about shifting power resources among states, and it, too, looks *within* Latin America to understand the decline of U.S. power. But unlike the defection thesis, with its emphasis on the political convulsions inherent in social and economic crisis, this thesis underscores the rise of relatively stable, strong, and confident states in Latin America. The defection thesis points to countries like Cuba and Nicaragua; the active-state thesis cites countries like Brazil and Mexico.

It may be tempting to dismiss this thesis from the start. After all, Latin America appears, at first glance, to be nearly ungovernable at times. Events in Central America during the 1980s readily come to mind, such as the splintering of domestic orders in Nicaragua and El Salvador that presented severe challenges to the state. Problems of governance in this region are indeed formidable.

However, just as economic growth has unevenly blessed (and cursed) Latin America, so, too, has more capable government. In relative terms, the state in some Latin American countries has emerged as a potent force, and this has helped to strengthen the region's relations with the United States. For one thing, the state has created institutions to manage conflict and formulate policy, thereby introducing a semblance of stability and permanence not found in the more personalistic systems of the past. For another, the eternal struggle between "ins" and "outs" has been muted in some countries. The opposition has been silenced, coopted, or integrated into the domestic political order. Also, some states have more to work with and are willing to put these assets to work. A few countries in the region are endowed with fairly substantial resources, natural and otherwise. Reliant upon on a statist, corporatist tradition, Latin American countries are inclined to use these resources to achieve desired ends both at home and abroad. As Roett has made clear, "the Latin American state has become, and will remain, a principal—perhaps the principal—arbiter of power."[21]

The active state in Latin America is a player, not just a spectator, in inter-American relations. Active and interventionist at home, the state has also had an impact beyond its borders. Such assertiveness became a trademark of Latin American foreign policy during the 1970s. Some states diversified their foreign relations; others even aspired to Third World leadership. Many cast their lot with their neighbors, forming regional associations such as the Caribbean shipping firm (NAMUCAR) and the Latin American Economic System (SELA). The ferment of the 1970s signaled the dawning of the active state in foreign affairs.

Why did the active state appear on the scene? Dominguez believes that a combination of international and internal factors help explain this emergence.[22] First, the distribution of power and resources in the international system afforded greater opportunities to Latin American states. Second, the ideology—and, one might add, the new nationalism—of the state and its leaders was important. Unwilling to defer to the United States as before, Latin American states forged more independent foreign policies, even as the structure of inter-American relations remained tilted toward the United States. Third, the activism of the Latin American state in world affairs was affected by growing state resources and the learning needed to use these more effectively. Finally, the state had become relatively independent; the active state was more autonomous from both domestic and international influences. As long as it did not offend the United States (by switching sides in the great power rivalry or by directly threatening its economic interests in the region), the active state could chart a course more to its own liking.

The United States must cope with the active state in Latin America, but it has not yet found a formula for doing so. In fact, U.S. leaders sometimes assume that independent and assertive Latin American states are less threatening than the current turmoil in Central America. Although U.S. interests may coincide at times with the interests of the active state, there is no easy and automatic mutuality of interests between the United States and Latin American states, whatever their ideology. If Stephen Krasner's view of North-South relations is correct, then the United States and Latin America will collide over the question of power itself. The South wants more than economic growth and wealth; if it sought only economic benefits, it would have behaved differently.[23] Likewise, the Latin American state seeks growth, but, more than that, it seeks power—the power to control its domestic situation and the power to control its international environment. It wants new principles, norms, rules, and procedures. It wants a more regulated and authoritative regime in the Americas. In this ultimate sense, then, the hegemonic state in the North is on a collision course with the active Latin American state.

The Loss-of-Will Thesis

The loss-of-will thesis attributes the decline of U.S. power in Latin America to a lack of national will. Changes in U.S. relations with Latin America or changes within Latin America itself pale in comparison to the reluctance of the United States to act as it once did and to commit resources as it once had to bolster its hegemony. Thus, it was a lack of will rather than a lack of resources or capabilities that caused the retrenchment of U.S. world leadership in the 1970s. In the words of Wesson, "Much of the decline of U.S. influence . . . may be laid to the flagging of will and attention."[24]

But what has happened to U.S. will? Why does the United States act less like the leader of days gone by? A diminished international position is one explanation. Leveling of capabilities and growing interdependence may make it too costly to sustain leadership. Yet the loss-of-will thesis looks more to domestic consensus, institutional policymaking, and self-confidence within the United States than it does to such long-term factors as loss of relative ability to pay the costs of leadership. The will to lead (or dominate) is often seen, then, as a deliberate decision to use capabilities to meet national and global interests, and power is a direct reflection of the will to use resources boldly to achieve grandly defined interests of a truly hegemonic state.

However, the U.S. will to exercise hegemony in Latin America is tempered by domestic constraints. First of all, an internal consensus on U.S. foreign policy has yet to be revived, following the debacle over Vietnam. Although Americans might yearn for a revitalized pax Americana in the Western Hemisphere, they are at odds over just what their country should do to bring peace, order, and democracy to the region. For example, the cold-war internationalists embrace tough talk and limited interventionism against Soviet action in the Third World. The post–cold-war internationalists, for their part, downplay the Soviet threat but advocate extensive global leadership. And the semiisolationists reject the cold war and interdependence, and cling to retrenchment, that is, a scaling back of both interests and commitments to fit more modest resources.[25]

The memory of Vietnam haunts the United States even now. Its peoples want their country to *have* power, but they are hesitant to give their leaders a free hand to *use* it. The fear is that direct military intervention will entrap the United States in another quagmire, this time closer to home. Even cold-war internationalists like President Reagan argued for U.S. involvement in Central America in order to *prevent* the commitment of U.S. troops. Both interventionists and noninterventionists alike live with the Vietnam Syndrome, wherein the desire for control is weighed against the fear of entrapment. Those who stand generally opposed to U.S. policy in Central America may argue for intervention in the interests of justice and human rights. For example, one senator opposed the contra war against Nicaragua but favored the campaign against Panama's "narcomilitarist," Manuel Antonio Noriega, but a few "cautious realists" forswear any intervention, regardless of the target, and maintain that intervention does more harm than good for U.S. policy.

The will to be hegemonic is also diluted by other constraints, some of them foreign in nature. For example, the will to reassert dominance is blunted by the realization that the use of force and technological wizardry of the hegemonic state is at times inappropriate. To complicate matters even more, much of U.S.–Latin American relations is conducted through private, rather than state, channels. Pluralism also affects the policymaking process in the United States, with elements in Congress and in the foreign policy bureaucracy resistant to change. As a result, a president bent upon the restoration of will may have one hand tied behind his back. Finally, the costs of national will are not cheap. Many are economic, to be sure, but they also are political and even military. National will, if it is more than theatrics and rhetoric, can be expensive in a subtle and even hidden way.

One would think that a diminished national will could somehow be restored by a visionary leader. Although some things are beyond the control of a president, national will would seem more malleable in the hands of a persuasive, popular leader. However, as the Reagan years proved once again, subjective and political factors in leadership can be formidable obstacles. Stirring rhetoric may stimulate a temporary sense of national self-confidence, but it is not an enduring substitute for cutting domestic consumption that may be needed to increase foreign aid, military assistance, and similar programs that shore up U.S. power in Latin America. In essence, the people of the United States would rather feel good about their country without paying the price of hegemony to act out their nostalgia for the days when U.S. hegemony produced a compliant and tranquil hemisphere.

The Argument

The ordeal of hegemony in the Western Hemisphere is tied to the issues of power and change, and both the United States and Latin America have featured roles in this regional drama. The ordeal first centered on the rise of the United States; today, it focuses on the problematic decline of U.S. influence. This ordeal has impacted the entire hemisphere in profound ways, and each state has been affected according to its unique conditions and its place within the hegemonic system.

The ascent of the United States defined the basic structure of inter-American relations for half a century, but the complex descent of the United States promises changes that are just as far reaching for the hemisphere. The United States has tried to play the hegemonic role longer than it could realistically be sustained. It tends to rely on worn-out, maladaptive responses to critical and fundamental shifts of power in the hemisphere. And, for Latin America, the problems it confronts with the decline of U.S. power are just as serious as those it faced when the United States was ascendant.

Hegemony is a useful concept for discussing power relations among states. In its pure form, it refers to the preponderant *distribution* of power among states. The concept of pure hegemony is straightforward: the preponderance of material resources dictates the nature of hegemony, and when a shift in such resources takes place, hegemony declines.

Problems become apparent, however, when we try to understand *why* U.S. power has declined. The five theses about U.S. decline strongly imply that the concept of pure hegemony shows us only one perspective on this important issue. The fact is that U.S. power has declined not just because of a diffusion of power among states but because of changes within states and within the world at large.

To this point, the main concerns of this volume have been to explain the concepts of hegemony, to describe the ascent of the United States, and to explore reasons why power has ebbed and flowed in the Americas. It is abundantly clear that U.S. power in Latin America has changed. Less clear is the *extent* to which the United States is still predominant or hegemonic. Those who claim that the decline has advanced quite far are disputed by those who believe the case for decline has been overstated. I will tackle this issue in Chapter 3.

The ordeal of hegemony in the Americas lies not only in the past but in the present, not only in why hegemony has declined but what it means for understanding what is happening on vital issues affecting inter-American relations. I will therefore advance and hope to deal with the following questions:

1. How much has U.S. hegemony, seen in terms of diffusion of economic power, actually declined in Latin America? (Chapter 3)
2. How does Central America illustrate the defection thesis regarding domestic upheaval and its relationship to the erosion of U.S. control over these small states? (Chapter 4)
3. How has U.S. hegemony in Central America been changed due to the conflicting foreign policies of the United States and of countries within and outside the region? (Chapter 5)
4. How are inter-American security issues dealt with in an era of declining U.S. hegemony? (Chapter 6)
5. How are inter-American economic issues, especially public foreign debt, dealt with in an era of declining U.S. hegemony? (Chapter 7)
6. How was U.S. intervention used to attempt a restoration of hegemony and what was the Latin American response to this strategy? (Chapter 8)
7. Finally, what are the prospects for managing conflict through cooperation in an era of declining hegemony? (Chapter 9)

3

Farewell to Hegemony

If the United States is no longer preeminent, certainly it is not just another country in the hemisphere. Somewhere between these two extremes lies the reality about U.S. power in Latin America today. There is more than one way to get at this central issue in U.S.–Latin American relations, and each is tied to a reason for the decline of U.S. power. In this chapter, I will examine the diffusion of power thesis as a way of determining how much U.S. hegemony has declined.

Power in the Americas can be defined by how many material resources the states have relative to each other, which is the idea of power rooted in the "pure" view of hegemony. Naturally then, a greater diffusion of these material power resources means a greater decline in the status of the United States as a hegemonic power. But though the hemisphere's great power has, without doubt, experienced a decline, it has not been a precipitous fall from hegemonic grandeur. Instead, seen in terms of material resources, the decline has been gradual, uneven, and incomplete. In some areas, it has not even happened at all.

The *theory of hegemonic stability* is an offshoot of the theory of hegemony as a preponderance of material resources. Taken together, they are initially alluring. The first points to the decline in U.S. power relative to the power of other states in the hemisphere, and the second argues that the decline of U.S. power has led to growing instability in inter-American relations on economic and security matters. That is, diffusion of power hastens instability in the backyard of the besieged hegemonic state.

These two theories have significantly influenced thinking about U.S.–Latin American relations. Lowenthal, for example, tied the decline of U.S. hegemony to a shift of basic power resources among the states of the Western Hemisphere, and suggested that this decline, a long time in coming, may not be reversible.[1] As he notes, the rapid pace of growth in key material resources or capabilities in Latin America during the third quarter of the twentieth century narrowed the asymmetry between the north and the south in the Americas.

Of course, others have gravitated to different views, which I will examine in detail later. For these observers of the Americas, hegemony is not just the relative shifts of material power resources among states. They believe it is possible to look for shifts, but at the same time they speak of subjective hegemony and how that too has declined. For example, Greene sees U.S. hegemony as not just economic but ideological and cultural dominance. The concept of relative economic decline of the United States in the world and in the Americas is, of course, retained, but the Gramscian notion of hegemony injects subjectivity and legitimacy as well. Thus, the United States is seen to be on the wane both globally and regionally.[2] This makes hegemony less simple to understand in the Americas, but it helps to explain the inability of pure hegemony to account for the decline of U.S. preeminence where a shift of material resources from the United States to small states like those in Central America has not been sufficient to explain instability.

The diffusion of power thesis strongly implies inevitability. In this view, the die is cast, and nothing can be done consciously to change it. In the Americas, as in the world, this may turn out to be true, but it would be premature to entomb the corpus before the patient has actually succumbed. As I will argue later, hegemonic decline in the Americas was halted for a time in the mid-1980s; in the future, the decline may be arrested if not reversed with respect to foreign debt in the Americas. Moreover, hegemony is a matter of using resources, not just possessing them. Renewed U.S. involvement in the Americas during the 1980s invokes this very idea. Consequently, U.S. policy in the early 1980s was an attempt to restore hegemony. Attempt is not accomplishment, of course, but policy, then, has its place. It may not cancel out long-term shifts in power, but, in the meantime, it may have a great impact on some countries in the Americas. For them, a policy of resisting decline may be futile, even harmful. Some believe the United States should forego its hegemonic role as the "delineator of acceptable behavior by others" in Latin America.[3]

The concept of hegemony as the preponderance of material power resources has its uses. It helps us to map out the shift in these material resources and to explain what is going on. Yet it must struggle against daunting obstacles. Take "power," for example. First, pure hegemonic theory dwells on what states have and how much of it they have relative to others. This idea of an inventory of resources takes us over some of the distance we wish to traverse, but it is less helpful for understanding instability and change from within Latin America and for those countries that are on the bottom of the new hierarchies of power in the Western Hemisphere.

The theory of hegemonic stability ties the fate of the hegemonic state to that of world stability. A hegemonic power sustains a stable, liberal world economic order; nothing else can. Great Britain and the United States certainly illustrate this point. But if the hegemonic power is fading, then it cannot and will not sustain the free market, free trade, and openness of a liberal world economy. If the hegemonic power declines, its commitment to the values of liberal economic relations will weaken, leading to greater instability in economic relations (including financial and debt questions), a trend towards trade protectionism, and greater self-centered nationalism. If its dominance declines, the hegemonic power is less willing to act as a stabilizer, to limit conflict, to manage crisis, to facilitate agreement, and generally to rule the roost as the arbiter of economic and security relations among states.

As U.S. economic power relative to Latin America has gradually declined, the U.S. commitment to openness and liberal trade for Latin America has also ebbed. The decline of U.S. hegemony generally also coincides with growing instability *within* Latin America, although not all of this ferment can be laid at the feet of the dwindling giant to the north. When the United States was preeminent, security and economic relations were arranged in a predictable and orderly fashion. But the subsequent decline of the United States has brought with it security and economic relations which could be more colorfully portrayed as increasingly "deranged" rather than "arranged." The job of the hegemonic power is to maintain its hegemonic system and to manage crises in that system. However, the United States is having a hard time doing either of those two things very well in Latin America. It has, though, handled regional security and debt problems in a way that has prevented a total collapse of the hegemonic system.

Although initially appealing, the theory of hegemonic stability is not entirely convincing. U.S. decline and regional instability have taken place—that much is true. But has the decline caused the instability? Some think so, but others are not so certain. What is really going on in Latin America does not always square with the theory. For example, the theses about U.S. decline that stress internal change, such as revolutionary defection or the rise of the active state, may help to explain some of the instability in inter-American relations. This is especially true for Nicaragua and other such challenges to hegemony. Furthermore, though the theory leads us to expect the instability of economic and security relations in the hemisphere, the management of instability and crisis may be possible without hegemony (if not without the United States). The Contadora process and the Central American peace plan of the 1980s may signal the rudimentary beginnings of posthegemonic management of hemispheric instability. Another possibility is that the U.S. decline has not been very great, which explains why the entire fabric has not come unraveled. Finally, the great myth of looking at power in the inter-American drama is that every change or development is caused by what the United States does or does not do, but this myth is becoming even more detached from reality with every passing decade.

Another myth is that Latin America is one cohesive entity. But when these countries are viewed separately rather than lumped together, we see that the decline of U.S. hegemony in Latin America is not uniform, universal, or even complete. This deflates any number of rash claims about the end of hegemony or that hegemonic decline is well advanced in all corners of the hemisphere. It also suggests that U.S. power in the Americas is perhaps different from its power in relation to Europe, Japan, and major Communist powers.

Although weakening the hold of the United States on the lion's share of the hemisphere's resources is important, it is not the only significant issue. U.S. power and hemispheric shifts in power may be tied to changes in U.S.–Latin American relations generated from *national* and even *subnational* forces. For example, domestic weariness in the hegemonic state and convulsive changes within Latin America may transform interstate relations, especially in the short term. And, again, power is more than what one has to work with; it is subjective, too. This may be why the decline of *ideological* hegemony in the hemisphere outpaces the decline of material hegemony. As a result, dictating the rules, events, and outcomes may have as much to do with the struggle over legitimacy as it does with changes in material resources.

The State of Hegemony

As the hegemonic state goes, so goes the state of hegemony. This is essential to the idea that U.S. decline stems from the diffusion of power resources. During the ascent of hegemony, the state of hegemony was different. A vibrant great power casts a lengthy shadow over the global system for a time. Thus, the United States once had an innovative, market-oriented economy so robust and so well endowed with resources, ideology, and global legitimacy that it could do all that was necessary to sustain a liberal world economic order. Its productivity and relative economic power were such that it could afford to provide a liberal and open trading regime to one and all; it could underwrite a stable international currency; at times, it could even provide for international security. Its control over resources was so great that no other state was able to challenge its leadership. In sum, it was willing to allot enough of this bounty to lead (or dominate) the world economy.

Power

Fundamentally, what *is* power or, more to the point, hegemonic power? Some would say that the power of the hegemonic state is "economic efficiency." This means that the United States has the power to be hegemonic if it can outperform all competitors by a very wide margin. Others agree but prefer the term of "relative productivity" for the same idea.[4] Comparison is important because, since a hegemonic state has more power than all the others, its dominance actually stems from its *relative* advantage in mobilizing and transforming resources into valued goods and services. The most powerful country may simply have the "lead economy," one that outperforms all the others and gives the state a special place in the world. Global leadership is powered by an economic base that makes it a given country the front-runner and its economy is fueled by very high levels of productivity and technology. Sustaining such an advantage takes more than just bountiful material resources; it also calls for "political innovation."[5] Ultimately, the advantage comes down to the matter of "relative economic influence." revealed in the share of world trade the hegemonic state is able to dominate.[6]

Thus, hegemonic power can be defined as relative advantage in material power. Keohane regards the power of the hegemonic state as its comparative advantage over its rivals. It produces higher value added, yielding both high wages and high profits. He offers the straightforward view that the power of a hegemonic state lies in its "preponderance of material resources."[7]

Change

History tells many tales and one is especially clear: The state of hegemony and the hegemonic state are forever buffeted by significant change because the hegemonic system is inherently unstable. It loses its will, gets frustrated with those who rise faster than it does by taking what it has to give, and eventually loses its relative influence. The irony is that the liberal economy so prized by the hegemonic state is its own undoing because such a market system transforms itself by diffusing power away from the hegemonic state itself.

Of course, this long-term change is gradual and at times barely perceptible. This is particularly true in the Western Hemisphere. The descent of the United States from unchallenged preeminence to dubious dominance has not been steep or briskly paced. But change raises the specter of conflict and uncertainty. Power diffuses throughout the international system, bringing about a yawning gap between what *is* and what is *coming to be*. The transition can be traumatic and sudden, as in a global war. Or hegemony can be dealt a fatal blow after lingering for decades. In the interwar years, for example, British hegemony suffered from gradual but terminal decline. World War II simply administered the *coup de grace*. By contrast, the gradual U.S. decline confers on the United States the distinction of being possibly the last hegemonic power.

The loss of the hegemonic advantage also leads to the loss of hegemonic commitment. In the era of ascendancy, the expansion of U.S. power was based on its relative efficiency, and early on, the costs of leadership relative to the benefits of hegemony were affordable. However, as time went on, the balance tipped the other way, as the costs relative to benefits mounted. Leaders of the hegemonic state were forced to rethink priorities. In the final analysis, it is not so much that the hegemonic state cannot afford hegemony any longer but that the balance between benefits and costs are less rewarding. The hegemonic state is then faced with two choices: it can cut its losses and protect its own interests or it can try to carry greater burdens for the good of everyone, even if this helps its closest economic rivals.

The first choice is the more likely. The power and the will to be hegemonic have eroded along with the stability of the liberal world economy. Financial, trade, and security arrangements (called regimes) begin to flounder under the strain. The relative advantages of hegemony change, too, and rivals of the hegemonic state take advantage of the "free ride." Under such conditions, the incentive to be Atlas and carry the world on its shoulders is sharply reduced, making hegemonic leadership "self-liquidating." Consequently, the hegemonic state, hounded by competitors who are not that far behind any longer, may have less to gain from its support of a liberal world economy.

In time, the hegemonic state comes to a crossroads and must decide whether to embark on a policy of *restoration* or one of *retrenchment*. The instinct is to shore up a sagging economic position in the world with a temporary burst of commitment to military and other resources, but history shows that either policy leads to decline eventually. The United States arrived at such a crossroads in the third quarter of the twentieth century. And despite the self-serving boasts of the 1980s that "America is standing tall" once again, past experience indicates that, in the long haul, full restoration will not materialize. A temporary resurgence of influence is, however, possible.

Retrenchment is the more expedient course of action. To find a better balance between commitments and resources, the hegemonic state cuts down on the commitments dedicated to a stable, free market system to match relatively more scarce resources. And because it is unable or unwilling to pay the costs of hegemony by continuing to expose its own domestic market to unrestrained competition, it is tempted to act more like its less powerful rivals.

But if the hegemonic state seeks to enhance its own position by increasing its economic growth, it must act like a hegemonic state by keeping itself open to competition from its economic rivals, regardless of what they do because it will thereby maximize its own returns.[8] Yet to keep or regain lost advantage over the others, it must adopt a policy of closure to imports from its competitors regardless of what they do.

Kindleberger believes that a stable, liberal economic world order is impossible in the absence of a hegemonic state committed to it.[9] Without the United States in charge and underwriting the costs of international peace and prosperity, discord and disarray could overtake and even bring about the collapse of the international financial system, the world trading system, the monetary system, and the global security regime. Nothing can substitute for the international stability secured by the hegemonic state.

How persuasive is this view of hegemonic decline and international instability? The decline of U.S. power certainly had unsettling effects on the informal global regime in the international oil trade during the 1970s. It is also true that the coordination of efforts by major industrialized powers to replace the old regime of the substitution account in the world monetary system previously underwritten by the United States proved futile.

But the glass may be half full, rather than half empty. In other words, both stability *and* turmoil have been experienced since the decline of the United States. In fact, there has been more stability than the decline would lead us to expect. For example, Lake has shown that a "mutual supportership" between the United States and the Federal Republic of Germany was able to stabilize to some extent international economic relations in the late 1960s.[10]

A critic of hegemonic stability theory, Keohane remains unconvinced of its basic premise: decline necessarily leads to instability. For one thing, he argues that the decline of hegemony and its impact on international arrangements or regimes created during the hegemonic era are incomplete and uneven.[11] The regimes in trade and finance constructed under ascendant hegemony, for example, did not evaporate altogether. Therefore, some degree of cooperation is possible even in the aftermath of hegemonic decline.

How well does the theory of hegemonic stability fit the Americas? At a very general level, it works fairly well. After all, instability in economic and security relations has increasingly been a part of inter-American relations with the decline of U.S. power. But when we look a little closer at what is going on, the theory of hegemonic stability appears to be somewhat rough around the edges because it places too much emphasis on the U.S. relations with Latin America and not enough on Latin America itself.

The Latin American Exception

Let us return to the idea that Latin America is actually a diverse, complex grouping of large and small states, rather than an undifferentiated lump of very similar units. Latin America can be considered as two regions: the Caribbean Basin and South America. The Caribbean Basin is made up a diverse collection of rather small and historically unstable states. South America is as diverse, but is made up of larger and more developed states. Unfortunately, hegemonic stability theory cannot deal very easily with these intrinsic regional differences.

The shifts in power between the United States and the Caribbean Basin have been less dramatic than have those between the United States and the larger, more developed states of South America. And yet, U.S. relations with the Caribbean Basin have been more unstable. Further, instability within the Basin runs across the board, and security and economic changes there have threatened to unhinge the hegemonic system. But the situation in South America is not the same. There, where power in a realist sense has shifted most, the instability is less acute and relations between the United States and South America are less volatile. In this region, it is economic and debt problems rather than security issues that most imperil long-term stability. The paradox is that, where instability is the greatest and most wide ranging, i.e., in the Basin, the United States retains a preeminent advantage in material resources, and the long-term challenge comes, instead, from the rise of the large, more stable regional powers, such as Brazil. Thus, analyzing U.S. decline is not always the best way to understand inter-American instability.

Diffusion of economic power is one of the most important developments of the twentieth century. As Lowenthal makes clear, Latin America is "demographically, economically, and politically far more consequential than it was. The power of the *major* Latin American nations has exploded, the influence in Latin America of extrahemispheric countries has steadily increased, and the relative position of the United States has inevitably diminished."[12]

Uneven economic growth rates and the relative shift in resources such as population, gross domestic product (GDP), trade, and industrial output had narrowed the gap between U.S. power in the north and Latin American power in the south. Today, the gap is still wide but not as wide as before.

The decline of U.S. economic power was evident in economic growth rates and in U.S.–Latin American trade over several decades. According to Bitar, the delinkage of trade between the United States and Latin America partially reduced the traditional imbalance in trade relations, thereby curbing U.S. influence on the region at the same time that Latin American economies were becoming more interdependent with the international system as a whole.[13]

But the decline must not be exaggerated either. U.S. banks still dominate private international lending to Latin America. And U.S. security interests, aggressively advanced during the 1980s, may have temporarily arrested the trend toward greater autonomy for some countries, although economic troubles forced several small nations to look elsewhere for bilateral assistance. Whatever the countervailing impact of economic crises during the 1980s, though, Latin America is destined to move toward autonomy and away from U.S. economic control in the years ahead.

Hegemony in Latin America

The central issue is: How much has U.S. hegemony declined since the mid-twentieth century? With regard to material resources specifically, to what extent has power declined in terms of gross domestic product and in trade within the Americas?

To track the decline of U.S. economic power through time, we must evaluate changes in both the rate of growth and changes in the shares of the total GDP or trade by year and/or by groups of years, as shown in Table 3.1. These provide a window on the changes in the Americas for much of the second half of the twentieth century. We may also detect the decline of hegemony in U.S. policy towards trade with the hemisphere.

What emerges from this analysis of both economic factors of hegemonic decline is significant.

1. U.S. economic power in an absolute sense has grown enormously since 1950, but that of Latin America as a whole has grown even faster, contributing to a significant though still modest erosion of

TABLE 3.1 GDP and GDP per Capita Growth Rates in Latin America, 1950--1982

	1950--1960		1960--1970		1970--1975		1976--1982	
	GDP	GDP/c	GDP	GDP/c	GDP	GDP/c	GDP	GDP/c
Argentina	3.0	1.4	4.2	2.4	2.9	1.3	-0.2	-1.7
Bolivia	0.2	-2.1	5.0	3.1	5.8	4.5	-0.1	-2.7
Brazil	6.2	3.1	6.2	3.2	10.4	7.7	3.8	0.9
Chile	3.6	1.2	4.2	2.0	-2.2	-3.9	3.9	2.2
Colombia	4.6	1.2	5.2	2.3	6.1	3.1	4.5	0.5
Costa Rica	6.6	2.6	5.9	2.6	6.0	3.4	1.5	-0.9
Dominican Republic	5.9	2.2	5.1	2.1	9.0	5.7	3.8	1.0
Ecuador	5.0	1.9	4.9	1.6	11.4	7.7	4.9	1.4
El Salvador	4.4	1.6	5.6	2.1	5.5	7.7	-2.4	-5.5
Guatemala	3.8	0.7	5.5	2.2	5.6	2.1	3.1	-0.0
Haiti	--	--	0.8	-0.8	3.8	2.2	2.6	0.8
Honduras	3.5	0.4	5.0	1.3	2.3	-0.9	4.6	0.9
Mexico	5.6	2.4	7.0	3.4	6.5	3.0	6.1	3.1
Nicaragua	5.4	2.5	6.9	3.4	5.1	1.7	-2.4	-6.6
Panama	4.8	1.9	7.9	4.8	4.7	1.5	5.5	2.6
Paraguay	2.7	0.4	4.4	1.6	6.7	3.4	9.2	5.8
Peru	4.7	2.6	5.6	2.5	5.5	2.6	1.4	-1.4
Uruguay	0.0	-1.5	1.6	0.8	1.6	0.8	1.3	0.8
Venezuela	7.3	3.5	6.1	2.6	4.9	1.7	1.6	-1.3

Sources: World Bank, World Tables 1976 (Baltimore: The Johns Hopkins University Press, 1976), p. 396; OAS, Statistical Bulletin of the OAS (Washington, D.C.: Organization of American States, 1983), Table A-2, pp. 22--25.

relative U.S. power. The erosion here was less marked, however, than it was with the industrialized rivals of Europe and Japan.

2. The decline of U.S. economic power is *uneven,* reflecting distinct patterns of growth in the Americas and especially within Latin America itself. In both GDP and trade, a handful of states in the region account for most of the change and therefore for most of the diffusion of economic power from the United States to Latin America.

3. The hegemonic commitment to an open trade system, the hallmark of hegemony at its most vibrant, is *weakening.* It is almost as if the uneven diffusion of economic power has been factored into U.S. policy. A blend of openness and closure in U.S. policy greets Latin American states according to the threat their economic power poses to the U.S. economy. Though Latin American states were once unequal partners with the United States, some, such as Brazil, have now emerged as unequal rivals.

Economic Growth and Change

U.S. economic power has grown in absolute terms but shrunk in relative terms. As Table 3.2 shows, U.S. GDP relative to that of Latin America declined between 1950 and 1980, as did U.S. labor productivity relative to Latin America's. This shift in power continued until the 1980s, with Latin American economic growth rates surpassing those of the United States.

But the United States is still formidable, even in relative terms. In fact, its position in relation to some states in Latin America has not changed very much over three decades. For example, small, less de-veloped states that are closer to the United States have not seen much change in the relationship unless they experienced tempestuous quarrels with the superpower, such as Cuba and Nicaragua. Another point to consider is the "loss of strength" gradient.[14] The more distant the Latin American states are from the United States, the greater diffusion of economic power. Therefore, the "loss" of hegemony is, at most, selective.

Uneven economic growth sets the stage for a decline in U.S. economic preeminence, and differential growth rates in GDP give a very important clue about what happened over the decades. Between 1960 and 1980, Latin American economic growth rates were about 6 percent annually. Those of the United States were 3.5 percent.[15]

Shares of economic activity suggest changes, too. Bitar examined both shares of GDP and shares of production in manufactures and found that Latin America's GDP share has grown larger compared to that of the United States. In 1950, the economy of Latin America was

TABLE 3.2 GDP of Selected Countries as a Percentage of United States GDP, 1950, 1960, 1970, 1977, 1982

	1950*	1960	1970	1977	1982
Latin America (total)	10.8	12.9	15.5	22.6	28.3
Argentina	2.7	2.4	2.5	2.7	2.2
Brazil	2.1	3.4	4.7	9.4	9.9
Mexico	2.0	2.3	3.4	4.3	8.2
Venezuela	0.5	1.5	1.2	1.9	2.3
Subtotal	7.3	9.6	11.8	18.3	22.6
Japan	---	8.5	20.6	36.1	39.3
West Germany	---	14.2	18.8	27.2	28.2
France	---	11.9	14.2	20.2	19.6
United Kingdom	---	14.1	12.3	13.2	18.0
Subtotal	---	48.7	65.9	96.7	105.1
Western Hemisphere (total)	---	---	16.1	23.7	29.2

*1950 data calculated in GNP 1970 dollars.

Sources: Adapted from the following sources: For 1950 data, James W. Wilkie, Statistics and National Policy, Supplement 3 (Los Angeles: UCLA Latin American Center, 1974), table 5, p. 400; for 1960, United Nations, Statistical Yearbook 1981 (New York: UN Publishing Service, 1983), pp. 152--153; for the remaining years, United Nations, World Statistics in Brief, 8th ed. (New York: UN Publishing Service, 1983).

10 percent of the U.S. economy. In 1960, it was 13 percent; in 1980, it was 26 percent.[16] During these three decades, the industrial capacity of Latin America improved, reducing the once formidable advantage of the United States. In one thirteen-year period, for example, U.S. production in manufactures went from 6.4 times greater than Latin America's down to 3.9 times greater than Latin America's.

The earlier gains of Latin America eclipsed the later ones. The highest growth rates in the region occurred during the first half of this period, and, although Latin America's growth rates remained fairly high in the 1960s and 1970s, they did not equal the earlier ones.

The different rates of growth in U.S. and Latin American economies have fostered the diffusion of economic power from the north to the south. Yet there is more to it than that. Growth *within* Latin America has been uneven, and the shift in economic power has affected individual states differently. Furthermore, high growth rates mean less for small states than for large ones. Therefore, the concept of a relative decline in U.S. economic power applies in some areas of Latin America more than others.

Studying the shifts in economic growth between the United States and Latin America sheds some light on the diffusion of power in the Americas, but the asymmetry among states within Latin America may even be more helpful for understanding the uneven and incomplete decline of U.S. power. Between 1960 and 1982, seven countries in Latin America accounted for 92 percent of the growth (or change) in Latin American GDP. The regional Big Four (Mexico, Brazil, Argentina and Venezuela) accounted for 80.7 percent of all the economic growth among twenty one countries of the region, and Brazil and Mexico alone accounted for 65.9 percent of the change in Latin American GDP. Thus, shifts in relative power within the region, in the case of growth rates, point to a differential process of change.

Hegemonic decline in Latin America is modest when compared with global hegemonic decline. The U.S. position relative to the regional Big Four is stronger than it is for the global Big Four (Japan, West Germany, France, and the United Kingdom). The combined economies of the regional Big Four are only about one-fifth the size of the U.S. economy, but the global Big Four exceed it. And between 1977 and 1982, the combined productivity of Japan, West Germany, France, and the United Kingdom surpassed that of the United States.

Only the regional Big Four and a few somewhat smaller economies carry much weight in the Americas. As the figures in Table 3.3 show, the Big Four together equaled 22.6 percent of the U.S. economy in 1982, adding in Colombia and Chile boosts that number by another 2.4 percent. Including all the others (excluding Canada) only brings

TABLE 3.3 GDP of Western Hemisphere Countries as a Percentage of United States GDP, 1970, 1977, 1982

Rank (1982)	Country	1970	1977	1982
1	Brazil	4.7	9.4	9.9
2	Mexico	3.6	4.3	8.2
3	Venezuela	1.2	1.9	2.3
4	Argentina	2.4	2.7	2.2
5	Colombia	0.7	1.0	1.3
6	Chile	0.8	0.5	1.1
7	Peru	0.7	0.7	0.8
8	Cuba	0.5	0.5	0.5
9	Uruguay	0.2	0.2	0.4
10	Guatemala	0.2	0.3	0.3
11	Bolivia	0.1	0.2	0.2
	Costa Rica	0.1	0.2	0.2
	Dominican Republic	0.2	0.2	0.2
	Trinidad & Tobago	0.0	0.1	0.2

12	Paraguay	0.1	0.1	0.1
	El Salvador	0.1	0.1	0.1
	Honduras	0.1	0.1	0.1
	Jamaica	0.1	0.2	0.1
	Nicaragua	0.1	0.1	0.1
	Panama	0.1	0.1	0.1
13	Bahamas	0.1	0.0	0.0
	Barbados	0.0	0.0	0.0
	Belize	0.0	0.0	0.0
	Grenada	0.0	0.0	0.0
	Haiti	0.0	0.0	0.0
	Surinam	0.0	0.0	0.0
	Dominica	0.0	0.0	0.0
	LATIN AMERICA	15.5	22.6	28.4
	WESTERN HEMISPHERE	16.1	23.6	29.2

Source: Calculated from United Nations, _World Statistics in Brief_, 8th ed. (New York: UN Publishing Service, 1983).

the total to 29.2 percent. It is crystal clear that a few countries count for quite a lot and a great many count for very little in this kind of inventory of economic power in the Americas.

In sum, although economic power has shifted, it has done so unevenly; it has gone to the large, not to the small, and to a few, rather than to the many. U.S. hegemony has eroded somewhat, but not in every nook and cranny of the hemisphere. In fact, for most countries, U.S. hegemony in terms of relative productivity remains largely undiminished.

The Hegemony of Trade

During the ascent of hegemony, the United States came close to monopolizing Latin American trade. In an unequal exchange of primary raw materials, food stuffs, and light consumer goods, the United States sold both capital and consumer goods to Latin America, and the rise of its hegemony was associated with a tighter trade relationship.

The state of inter-American trade, then, is one way to gauge the state of hegemony in the Americas. If hegemony in trade is declining, then Latin America is, relatively speaking, less linked to U.S. markets than it once was. Trade shares with Europe, Latin America, Japan, and the planned economies of the Soviet bloc would be expected to rise as trade shares with the United States, Latin America's traditional trading partner, go down. This is, in fact, what has happened. Indeed, U.S.–Latin American trade is in a state of mutual decline. Not only has U.S. influence over the region's foreign commerce diminished since the midcentury mark but Latin America has also become a less important trading partner for the United States.

Nonetheless, a perusal of trade confirms what economic growth did: Hegemonic decline is complex and uneven. Trade relations within Latin America reflect a diversity of experiences. (See Table 3.4.) Some countries have reduced their reliance on U.S. markets, others have not—or at least not significantly. But though the decline in trade between north and south is uneven, no Latin American states have appreciably raised their trading relationship with the United States to new heights.

What new directions, then, do we see in Latin American exports? Among other trends, we see changes in who trades with the United States, as well as the emergence of alternatives to the United States as a trading partner.

The regional Big Four once again account for much of the change in U.S.–Latin American economic relations. Argentina, Brazil, and Venezuela fall far *below* the regional average for share of trade with the United States, and since the mid-1950s, Argentina has been the least dependent upon the U.S. market for its exports. Mexico is, as usual, the exception. Despite its status as a large, semideveloped economy, Mexico's exports to the United States are still high, despite some slippage with time; they constitute more than half of all its exports. (See Table 3.5.)

The United States is the predominant market for the exports of several Latin American countries. However, just under one-half of them export more to other industrialized countries than they do to the United States. As one would expect, the delinkage of trade is not far advanced in the Caribbean Basin, and four out of five countries that trade more with the United States than they do with other industrialized countries are in the Basin.

The United States and alternative trading partners for Latin America share the large and growing market in the South, but none dominates the region's exports across the board. During the late 1970s and early 1980s, it was apparent that both the United States and the industrialized states heavily imported Latin American manufactures and primary products, although the global recession of the early 1980s curbed the demand in these affluent markets. However, the United States was preeminent in trade with more countries than were the other industrialized countries. Despite this, U.S. preeminence in export shares fell as low as 16.1 percent of all Western Hemisphere states during one year, although it rose as high as 32.2 percent of the states in 1983. In other words, the United States consumed one half or more of Latin American exports.

U.S. hegemony in trade has faded, but because the United States is still so important its influence has not subsided entirely. It is a formidable trader in the Americas and will remain so, even if the trade patterns that have emerged in recent years become even more entrenched. After all, two thirds of Latin America trades more with the United States than it does with itself. What has happened is that (1) the United States now shares Latin America with others, (2) Latin American exports have diversified throughout the world, and (3) Latin America, as it has developed unevenly, has complementary rather than merely competitive goods to be traded within the Americas.

Between Openness and Closure

U.S. trade policy toward Latin America is another symptom of hegemonic decline. Although it has held to free and open trade, it has qualified this policy of openness. With some of the larger, more competitive states in Latin America, current U.S. trade policy recalls the old argument about reciprocity from the first half of the century.

TABLE 3.4 Share in World Exports of Latin American States, the United States, and Selected Other Countries 1950--1980 (in percentages)

Area	1950	1960	1970	1980
World	100.00	100.00	100.00	100.00
Argentina	1.92	.84	.56	.40
Bolivia	.12	.04	.06	.05
Brazil	2.22	.99	.87	1.01
Chile	.47	.38	.39	.24
Colombia	.65	.36	.23	.21
Costa Rica	.09	.07	.07	.05
Cuba	1.10	.48	.33	.20
Dominican Republic	.14	.14	.07	.05
Ecuador	.12	.11	.06	.13
El Salvador	.11	.09	.07	.05
Guatemala	.13	.09	.09	.08
Haiti	.06	.02	.01	.01

Honduras	.09	.05	.06	.04
Mexico	.86	.59	.40	.81
Nicaragua	.04	.04	.06	.03
Panama	.03	.02	.03	.02
Paraguay	.05	.02	.02	.02
Peru	.31	.34	.33	.19
Uruguay	.42	.10	.07	.05
Venezuela	1.91	1.90	1.00	.96
Latin America	10.91	6.70	4.85	4.60
ALADI	9.06	5.67	4.02	4.07
Andean Group	3.13	2.74	1.70	1.54
Central American Common Market	.48	.34	.36	.24
United States	16.91	15.91	13.60	10.87
Japan	1.37	3.16	6.17	6.48
West Germany	3.29	8.90	10.91	9.70

Source: Adapted from James W. Wilkie and Adam Perkal, eds., Statistical Abstract of Latin America, vol. 23 (Los Angeles: UCLA Latin American Center, 1984), table 2846, p. 602.

TABLE 3.5 Shares of Exports from Latin America and Selected Countries to the United States and Latin America, 1948--1983 (in percentages)

	Latin American Exports to U.S.	Latin Exports to Latin America	Mexico to the U.S.	Brazil to the U.S.	Argentina to the U.S.	Venezuela to the U.S.
1948	37.2	9.2	75.3	43.3	43.3	26.6
1952	49.7	8.6	---	---	---	---
1953	47.3	9.5	---	---	---	---
1954	43.7	9.0	73.1	37.0	11.3	37.0
1955	44.0	9.6	74.0	42.2	12.7	38.1
1956	44.6	7.7	72.6	49.5	12.4	39.1
1957	44.5	8.8	77.2	47.4	11.5	40.3
1958	44.7	9.3	74.7	43.0	12.9	42.1
1959	44.3	8.6	70.0	46.2	10.7	41.7
1960	42.0	7.9	62.5	44.4	8.5	43.9
1961	37.5	6.7	60.9	40.1	8.9	39.0
1962	36.0	7.3	59.6	39.9	7.3	34.5
1963	34.9	7.7	60.7	37.7	11.3	33.4
1964	32.2	9.2	57.9	33.2	6.7	33.9
1965	32.5	8.7	56.5	32.6	6.4	34.7

Year						
1966	34.0	16.4	54.3	33.4	7.9	36.8
1967	33.3	17.5	54.6	33.1	8.4	33.8
1968	34.6	18.4	65.3	33.3	11.8	32.6
1969	33.4	17.8	64.8	26.4	9.0	33.5
1970	33.2	16.7	70.3	24.7	8.9	35.4
1971	34.7	19.3	69.5	26.2	9.3	39.5
1972	34.9	18.6	20.3	23.3	9.9	39.5
1973	37.7	14.1	68.8	18.1	8.2	45.7
1974	38.5	19.7	58.8	21.8	8.5	44.0
1975	35.3	19.7	58.3	15.4	6.6	39.4
1976	35.8	19.7	55.7	18.2	7.3	38.4
1977	34.7	15.7	67.0	17.7	6.9	42.9
1978	34.0	15.3	65.6	22.7	8.6	36.5
1979	33.5	17.5	69.4	19.3	7.5	37.3
1980	34.2	17.3	64.7	17.4	8.9	27.7
1981	33.2	16.4	55.3	17.6	9.4	25.6
1982	34.4	14.4	52.0	20.5	14.1	26.3
1983	38.1	11.7	58.2	23.1	9.3	29.1

Source: Data calculated from United Nations, Year of International Trade Statistics for years 1957, 1958, 1962, 1964, 1968, 1972-1973, 1979; and International Monetary Fund, Direction of Trade Statistics 1984.

In other cases, especially in the Caribbean Basin, U.S. policy is that of a classic hegemonic state but with a new twist. The United States has hedged its bets, seeking openness and closure in trade with Latin America to help itself as much as Latin America.

A hegemonic state in robust health is committed to free and open trade, and a liberal trading order is held up as the desirable goal of hegemonic rule. As long as it is willing to pay for the stability of a free trade system, the hegemonic state allows relatively unrestricted access to its domestic markets by one and all. How open and liberal the trade policy of the hegemonic state is may be an indicator of its vitality. But openness to imports has a price that, at some point, must be paid. Subsidizing free trade risks the hegemonic state's place in the world economy. Conversely, restricting access (and therefore doing what the "free riders" do) means protecting the domestic market, even at the price of slower growth.

The United States is no longer willing to be as open to Latin American imports as it once was, and it has long since disapproved of Latin America's protectionism called for in development strategies. The trade policy of the United States toward the Western Hemisphere over the last decade or so reflects a flagging commitment to openness. By the late 1960s and early 1970s, U.S. policy even veered more toward protectionism and qualified openness in its economic relations with Latin America. The traditional "special relationship" which granted special privileges to Latin America was abandoned, and it was made clear that Latin America must turn more toward the global economy. By 1971, U.S. trade policy had turned "defensive."

However, the U.S. market was still open. The General Agreement on Tariffs and Trade (GATT) and the General System of Preferences (GSP) ensured that. In fact, free trade through GATT required some reciprocity and "fairness," not the unilateral benefits flowing from a dominant hegemonic state. The GSP, adopted by other countries as well, and renewed in 1984, carried forward a commitment to free trade from the Western Hemisphere by granting duty free access for 2,800 products.

But the GSP seeks a balance between reciprocity and nonreciprocity. It limits the U.S. commitment to openness and allows important "safeguards" to be used in the potential search for "negotiability" with the larger, more competitive exporters, such as Brazil and Mexico. U.S. reluctance in recent years to use statutory provisions to exempt such exporters from ceilings reflects its growing ambivalence to openness. U.S. trade policy toward Latin America in effect differentiates the bigger, more competitive states from the smaller, less competitive ones. In 1989, the United States charged Brazil (along with Japan and India) of unfair trading practices. It has also sought to offset Brazilian restrictions on the importation of U.S. computers. Such qualified support of openness suggests only a selective commitment to hegemony in trade policy.

The Caribbean Basin is seen as a special region—so special, in fact, that it deserves preferential treatment in trade policy not accorded to other areas. By enticing Caribbean states to revitalize their exports to the United States, the policy aimed at the traditional goal of the hegemonic state. It bowed to the needs of the smaller states of the Caribbean Basin in 1983 via the Caribbean Basin Initiative (CBI). This policy did breathe life into free trade, although it was only a partial measure. It offered generous but still limited trade benefits to the twenty-eight eligible states and opened the U.S. market even more widely than did the GSP. It also afforded more extensive product coverage, greater security of eligibility for products, and more flexibility in the rules of origin of exports from the Caribbean Basin states to the United States.[17] Furthermore, it was nonreciprocal because it created a Free Trade Area (FTA) in which export products could enter the U.S. market without conceding something in return for this access. The CBI also complemented GSP foreign assembly provisions as well as the Lomé III Convention that allows eleven of the eligible CBI states to have duty free access to the EEC. Such inducements were intended to lure U.S. investors into promoting greater export-led development in the Caribbean Basin.[18]

But why was the CBI only a half-way measure? First, some exports important to the region were excluded from the provisions of the Caribbean Basin Economic Recovery Act. Second, the CBI was less an attempt to develop and stabilize the whole region within a renewed hegemonic system than it was an attempt to serve geopolitical and security goals of the United States within Central America and other selected areas. It was not a plan for the Caribbean Basin but rather a plan for the establishment of bilateral relations with particular individual nations within the Caribbean region. Third, the CBI was minimalist. The twelve-year Free Trade Area would affect only 5 percent of all exports from the region since 87 percent of the exports were already duty free. Nearly 30 per cent of the eligible states in the Basin did not embrace the CBI. Mexico and Venezuela—the two powers of the Basin—were cool to it; many of their traditional exports, especially oil, were excluded anyway.

Essentially then, the trade policy of the hegemonic state has been equivocal. Reluctant to allow the more competitive and larger states unbridled entry to its markets, the United States extends some free trade to the extent it can afford it to others, especially to small, poor countries in the Western Hemisphere. Making such distinctions is an interesting posture. It strongly implies that Latin America has changed significantly and that the United States no longer can or wants to support an unqualified, free trade policy.

No Farewells to Hegemony

It would be premature to say farewell to U.S. hegemony in the Americas. However, the uneven diffusion of economic growth, the shifting patterns of trade in the hemisphere, and the weakening of U.S. free trade policy all suggest that it will never be what it once was, either. Clearly, U.S. dominance is in decline, but it has yet to disappear. And if its preeminence has eroded, the disproportionate role the United States seems destined to play in the Americas has not.

The decline of hegemony has varied in time and place, and it has been uneven geographically. It has slowly ebbed with respect to trade, reflecting differences in policy toward small and large states in Latin America. It has also coincided with a growing instability in inter-American relations. Above all, it mirrors the inherent asymmetries of power within the Americas and within Latin America that uneven growth and change cannot entirely obliterate.

4

Participation Crisis in Central America

Hegemony in a pure sense did change in the Americas, but modest shifts in power resources over the third quarter of the twentieth century still left intact vast disparities between the United States and Latin America. To understand hegemonic decline in the Americas, we must therefore look to other aspects of U.S. power. Domestic convulsions within countries may have international effects. In other words, major crises in small countries may weaken or even sever the bonds of hegemony.

Central America during the 1980s showed that change within countries rather than the diffusion of power between countries can change hegemony. Although the diffusion of economic power has changed U.S. relations with Brazil, Mexico, and other more developed countries, it has had little effect on U.S. relations with the small, less developed countries of Central America. True, the shift of economic power has emboldened other states to play a larger role in Central America. But the shift in material resources between the United States and Central America was negligible. Thus, U.S. decline and regional instability must also be understood in terms of what has occurred *within* Central America itself.

Domestic instability and revolutionary defection have undercut U.S. control over states whose leaders were once more closely aligned with the hegemonic system. In the early twentieth century, U.S. policy fashioned systems of domestic control in Central America. Somoza in Nicaragua was the "last U.S. Marine." The U.S. alliance with domestic elites only worked as long as those elites could manage crisis and perpetuate the system of economic and political domination from which they and a few others reaped disproportionate benefits. But this alliance has fallen into disrepair. Central America has suffered from the failure of states to manage political order and to incorporate new, insistent groups into the political process. Today, the besieged regimes of Central America face a crisis of participation, and one of the effects of Central America's participation crisis is to curb U.S. hegemony.

Alternative Perspectives

The Central American crisis stems from a complex interaction of both international and domestic elements. Let us look first at three international perspectives that attempt to explain the crisis: (1) *the strategic, or East-West, perspective,* (2) *the interdependence perspective,* and (3) *the hegemony perspective.* These international perspectives share the view that Central America is a target of intruders, and that outside factors set the stage or even triggered the crisis in Central America.

The strategic perspective of the crisis is the U.S. security view of Soviet and Cuban involvement that regards Central America as the latest battlefield in the revived cold war of the early 1980s. The Sandinista Revolution is not seen as a homegrown, nationalistic Marxism but rather as the opening volley of the Soviet and Cuban attempt "to absorb the closest neighbors of the United States into what (President Reagan) has called the 'most aggressive empire' the modern world has seen."[1] In Central America, a southern part of the soft underbelly of the United States, U.S. adversaries are believed to be mischievously at work. The Kissinger Commission endorsed the strategic perspective in 1983 when it concluded that

> the crisis in Central America is of large and acute concern to the United States because Central America is our near neighbor and a strategic crossroad of global significance; because Cuba and the Soviet Union are investing heavily in efforts to expand their footholds there, so as to carry out designs for the hemisphere distinctly hostile to U.S. interests; and because the people of Central America are sorely beset and urgently need our help.[2]

According to the second international perspective, Central America is seen as a victim of imported economic problems. The interdependence perspective places Central America within the international political economy and also stresses the region's vulnerability to international sources of economic instability. The small, dependent, cash-crop exporting economies of the five Central American republics have always existed on the fringes of the world economy. Marginally situated within the international division of labor, this region was very susceptible to the economic and energy crises of the late 1970s. And with only weak defenses against these outside threats, the Central American economies had little choice but to import hard times, with growing unemployment, inflation, debt, and trade deficits. Therefore, interdependence in the 1970s and 1980s was destabilizing for Central America.

The third international perspective, the hegemony perspective, sees the crisis as arising from the inability or unwillingness of the United States to adjust to overdue changes in the domestic affairs of Central America. Maintaining a system of hegemony and resolving crises in the Caribbean Basin is a U.S. obsession. But though the United States could easily dominate the internal and external affairs of its nearby client states in years past, this is no longer true. From this perspective, Central America exemplifies the crisis of hegemony.

The decline of hegemony has been widely proclaimed. Despite its small size and entrenched poverty, Central America is affected by this decline, which has brought instability and the collapse of old means of domination. Today, instead of secure hegemony, a more fluid relationship is emerging. Where stability under the thumb of the hegemonic state once prevailed, a more uncertain and chaotic situation is moving toward multiple centers of international power. According to this perspective, Nicaragua is less a Soviet puppet than it is a weak state charting a course of national independence or "diversified dependence."[3] The international dimension of the crisis is less a strategic threat to the United States itself than it is a threat to its credibility as a hegemonic power.

These international perspectives on the tragedy unfolding in Central America were acknowledged even in the early 1980s. Yet they remain incomplete and may exaggerate outside factors. Pushed to the extreme, such perspectives make Central America superfluous to its own problems; it becomes just a stage for foreign intruders, impersonal structures, and theories of world or regional leadership.

The domestic (or regional) perspectives on the crisis are more sensitive to local factors; they address issues of order, change and development within Central America. Domestic perspectives assert that insurgencies, revolution, intervention, and civil war did not just happen, but that they emerged from structural flaws in the internal order of Central America. The indigenous conflict arises from outmoded systems for preserving order and for sustaining the self-aggrandizement of the cash-cropping oligarchy and its allies. We must therefore look within the region and individual countries to see the disorder and fighting more clearly. As an example, Baloyra believes that national history, rather than international factors, was responsible for El Salvador's crisis: The "historical roots of the crisis are Salvadoran."[4]

The three perspectives on the domestic nature of the crisis are *neoconservative, liberal,* and *radical.* The neoconservative perspective stresses the need to restore and impose order. The liberal perspective regards genuine reform and a political center as necessary for a new, legitimate order adept at accommodating new demands. The radical perspective sees the crisis as a revolutionary process in which the old order and such liberal reformism will both be swept aside.

For the neoconservatives, development and modernization pose dilemmas for maintaining order. For example, modernization frequently jeopardizes order. As industrialization takes place, urban and rural workers become more mobile and more aware of economic inequity. And as economic growth ripples unevenly across a society, political instability grows more pervasive. The credo of the neoconservatives is that political order must be imposed upon societies where force and power preempt a legitimate system. Steps must be taken to invigorate, rather than weaken, authoritarian rule. For these disciples of order, the crisis in Central America comes from modernization and change, and if instability is the unavoidable price of growth and development, then the price must be kept as low as possible.

The liberal perspective sees the crisis as a denial of justice, rather than the collapse of order. Although growth has occurred in Central America, the liberals believe poverty and injustice remain deeply imbedded in these societies. Thus, the crisis is caused by the miserable toll exacted by life itself on the majority of people in Central America. (Indeed, the Economic Commission for Latin America estimated that 42 percent of the people in the region subsist in extreme poverty.[5]) In the liberals' view, the crisis could well endure as long as poverty and injustice do.

> There will be neither peace nor stability in Latin America until the basic needs of the people are met . . . by a fundamental restructuring of privilege, so that the right of the minority of Latin Americans to spend their vacations at Disneyworld is made subordinate to the right of the peasants to eat.[6]

Some liberals are attracted to political, rather than structural, interpretations of the crisis. They are worried about viable coalitions, not just basic conditions. For example, they contend the demise of a political center in Central America makes reform a less likely solution. They claim that the center must be restored but believe that, by steadfastly opposing the center and the left-of-center parties, the military and the oligarchy have polarized the situation.

The radical perspective departs from that of the neoconservatives and liberals, predicting that sweeping and irrepressible revolution is the destiny of Central America. Thus, a Sandinista forecast that "there are undoubtedly going to be profound changes in the coming decade. That is something that neither we nor the United States can avoid. . . . The political models in this region are worn out."[7] Nineteenth-century liberalism and capitalism failed as viable models for dealing with the crisis but the stubborn and powerful proponents of the old order have made reformism almost impossible to achieve.

The growing power of the Left as a political and military movement cannot be repealed. A slogan painted on walls in Guatemala during the early 1980s proclaimed: "Ayer Nicaragua, hoy El Salvador, mañana Guatemala." New forms of participation have been used to organize the Left, the working class, and segments of the church against the oligarchy and the military. For their part, the rightist coalitions in El Salvador and Guatemala are just as determined to contest the future as they did the past. As the head of the Democratic Revolutionary Front (FDR) sees it, "The history of democracy in El Salvador has been written in blood."[8] The radicals see armed struggle as inevitable, even desirable.

Crisis and Participation

The roots of the crisis can be traced to the unresolved issue of the twentieth century in Central America: Who should have a *voice* and who should hold *power*? If participation is tied to power, then denial of genuine participation is the denial of power. Actually, the old order subverted its own power base. By changing and modernizing the economies of the region, the oligarchs and the military inadvertently created new groups who wanted to participate and to share power. Ralph Woodward accordingly sees the problem in historical perspective:

> The current crises all represent the inevitable collapse of political, economic, and cultural structures erected in the late nineteenth and early twentieth centuries to serve the interests of the elites who commanded the Liberal reforms or Revolutions of that era, but that fail to meet the demands of the societies they created.[9]

The oligarchy tolerated and then repressed participation in order to prop up the old political order in the face of changing realities. Denied access to national power, new groups nevertheless insisted on taking part in national life, but real political power remained concentrated in the hands of the privileged few. As a result, participation without democracy created tension and crisis. In recent years, broad-based participation has been hard to contain, and it has magnified the crisis (and vice versa) without meaningful power sharing.

People in the developing countries of Central America and Latin America as a whole now seek political participation in order to gain more control over their own destinies. Examining how this is done and what participation is defined is important to understanding the Central American crisis.

The first type of participation is "activity by private citizens designed to influence governmental decision-making."[10] Essentially, it is the making of demands on government. This may be done through voluntary associations and independently of ruling elites, resembling democratic pluralism. Or, in a more populist or corporatist system, individuals may be mobilized within a larger collective effort. But mobilized participation is manipulation by the elites. It is elicited by elites and by the government to justify what they would do anyway. The people do not rule but they are not entirely powerless either.

The second type of participation is broader, and it can and does happen almost anywhere, with or without government involvement. It may occur in a rural cooperative of poor peasants or in a Christian-based community. This participation, then, is really any behavior that influences or attempts to influence the distribution of values and goods. Thus, anything done to increáse the resources of a specific group would qualify as participation. The poor have their ways of participating, just as the elites have theirs, as John Booth explains:

> For example, marginal sectors such as the urban and rural poor engage more frequently in collective problem solving within the communal arena, while the urban middle and upper sectors, integrated into and served by the national political system, take a more active part in the national arena. Elites manipulate mass participation to serve elite goals . . . [and yet] a large proportion of Latin American citizens take part actively in politics.[11]

Participation in Central America mushroomed in the 1970s and 1980s. The only liberal and truly stable state in the region, Costa Rica, has genuine participation within a legitimate system. There, a competitive party structure, with group organizations and factions, has been able to accommodate both demand-making and stable institutional development. Class-based politics is less important in Costa Rica than in El Salvador and Guatemala.

Yet participation is not just something for the elites in Costa Rica. Indeed, poor peasants are often the most active at the local level. With few public services available to them, they organize at the communal level to build their resources and meet their own needs. The richness of this participation is impressive, but it is not so extreme that it makes violence as prevalent as it is elsewhere in Central America. Elections, lobbying, particularized contact with officials, and organizational involvement are signs of pluralist democracy in Costa Rica.

When it comes to participation, Honduras, unfortunately, is not Costa Rica. True, it has been able to accommodate limited participation and to experience some political stability. But until recently, the military was the ruling elite at the national level. During the 1980s, the Liberal party and the "rodista" majority within the Liberal Party were junior partners with the military. However, despite the fact that it is no liberal democracy, Honduras has been able to avoid the very worst ravages of illiberal politics. The poor and the peasants of Honduras have a stake in the land tenure system, which makes restrained participation at the local level more likely than the unrestrained violence of more class-based politics.

The participation crisis is most severe in El Salvador, Guatemala, and Nicaragua. The military and the oligarchy grudgingly have compromised with populism and reformism as a last resort, but both reform and repression have been used to perpetuate oligarchic rule. At the national level, they have denied a democratic path to those demanding a voice, thereby forcing the centrists and the leftists to fight fire with fire.

Demands for broad-based power sharing have been thwarted over many decades in these countries. Mario Vargas Llosa, the Peruvian writer and politician, believes this dynamic invites disaster because antidemocratic measures only make revolution more alluring.[12] Just as democracy may help immunize a country against revolution, the denial of democracy may hasten it. To paraphrase John F. Kennedy, those who make democratic change impossible make totalitarian revolution inevitable.

The subversion of meaningful participation spread frustration and extremism throughout El Salvador, Guatemala, and Nicaragua. By permitting ritualistic participation, the ruling elites quite unintentionally fostered even more participation. But this was participation without power sharing, and it could hardly contain a broadly and deeply felt sense of injustice. Thus, the denial of meaningful participation pushed these countries towards civil war. As time went on, participation leading to crisis grew even as the socioeconomic conditions of most people declined. And with the polarization of politics came the inevitable consequence: Power could not be shared, only seized. Participation in Central America during the 1980s was less the prerequisite of democracy in the 1980s than it was a prelude to revolution, civil war, and domestic deterioration.

Three Life Signs

Participation outstrips democracy in Central America. Where the crisis is most acute, participation is rampant and uncontrolled. This, in turn, makes democracy even harder to nurture because it becomes a casualty of civil war and generalized violence. Consequently, the denial of democracy ushers in domestic disorder that eventually diminishes the long-run prospects for meaningful democracy. The unfortunate reality is that participation and disorder overwhelmed democracy.

Although beleaguered, democracy does exist in Central America. It survives here and there and takes on different guises. Where once the military was the government, it became a partner with civilian leaders for governing the region during the 1980s. In El Salvador, a form of "reactionary despotism" did not fade away completely. A civilian president struggled to hold together an uneasy alliance with the military and business sector against the guerrillas between 1984 and 1989. In Guatemala, a virulent form of military repression was moderated in a similar alliance between a civilian president and the military. After years of war and sacrifice, Nicaraguans ousted the Sandinistas in the 1990 election called for in the Central American peace agreement. In Honduras, democracy is fragile and limited; the military and mounting economic and security problems threaten its future. Finally, Costa Rican democracy is well entrenched, but Costa Ricans are not complacent about its fate.

In much of Central America, democracy is more apparent than real. What too often passes for democracy is *form* rather than *substance*. Many of the elections are good examples of how this can happen. But democracy means more than holding elections, something that Central America has done frequently during the 1980s. It must also transcend the mobilized participation of formalistic democracy. Democracy in Central America must mean sharing power in a more or less inclusive, more or less legitimate regime that protects the integrity of popular will through elections, the individual rights of all, and the conditions under which Central Americans live.

Democracy is often an ideological weapon and a political resource rather a deeply rooted set of rules for resolving the crises infecting severely troubled societies. The term has been used by both the Left and the Right to advance causes or policies that are blatantly undemocratic. To assess the state of democracy in Central America is therefore a challenging and risky venture at best.

If democracy is a key to the crisis, what are the vital signs of democracy, and what is its prognosis? There are three major signs to consider: *elections, individual rights,* and *the human condition.* Progress must be made in all three areas before a stable, legitimate order can emerge in Central America.

The Riddle of Elections

If simply holding elections were the sole requirement of democracy, Central America would be substantially more democratic than it actually is. Voting in Central America became a rather common political act during the 1980s. When given the chance, voters there do go to the polls, and the turnout for national elections is fairly impressive. Head and shoulders above the rest, Costa Rica has held elections on a regular basis since 1949. In 1982, when voters elected a new president and national assembly, 87 percent of those eligible voted. Like clockwork, the Costa Ricans again went to the polls four years later; more than 80 percent of the voters turned out to elect President Oscar Arias Sanchez.

Voting is participation, of course. Yet is it really a "practical guide of democracy," as the U.S. State Department insists?[13] If the voting in El Salvador was more than a political circus, then it was a major improvement over the elections of 1972 and 1977. But the extent and meaning of democracy cannot be judged merely on voter turnout. In the midst of a bitter civil war, Salvadoran elections in the 1980s promised democratic change. The 1982 and the 1984 elections stirred hopes that voting was more than a ritual. Yet the 1982 election proved that form and substance did not always go together. Duarte, the centrist candidate, won the election (by getting more votes than anyone else) but lost the presidency in the national assembly to a coalition of right-wing parties who supported his opponent. The irony was that an election with a high turnout ultimately brought about a victory for those who abhor reform and democracy. It failed the test of inclusion and, for that matter, of legitimacy. Naturally, this compromised the meaning of the election itself. The voting did have a "demonstration effect," however.[14] It bestowed an aura of popular support on the government it might not otherwise have had. But by failing to address power-sharing, democracy was denied. Whatever else is done to bring peace to El Salvador, the exclusion of the democratic Left will only prolong the crisis.

Although more honest than those of the past, the 1984 Salvadoran election was no model of democratic rectitude. For one thing, there may have been a lower turnout than was officially reported. In fact, the actual turnout may have been about one half the turnout estimated by government sources.[15] For another, the election took place in a very inhospitable atmosphere. Voting is required by law in El Salvador, and both fear and compulsion no doubt induced many to vote. In essence, the voter was caught in the middle. "The government says if we don't vote, we're terrorists. The guerrillas say if we do, we're against them."[16]

In 1989, the Salvadoran national election returned the right-wing to the presidency. Alfredo Cristiani of the Republican National Alliance party (or ARENA) assumed office. Bringing an end to the Duarte years, this election confirmed that the political center had been discredited by corruption, drift, and interminable civil war.

Elections were part of the landscape in revolutionary Nicaragua, too. When they came to power, the Sandinistas had promised elections. In 1984, they delivered on their promise. Still, although these elections were fair by Nicaraguan standards, they were held to validate and to perpetuate the revolution rather than to share power with the growing opposition to the Sandinistas. A broad alliance of Sandinista opponents, called the Democratic Coordinadora, decided to pull out of the campaign. Without a level playing field, this coalition of centrist and right-wing parties was not going to play ball. The outcome was not in doubt. With the only serious opposition sitting on the sidelines, Daniel Ortega won the presidency easily and the Sandinistas had a secure majority in the assembly.[17] A leading Sandinista had predicted that anything less than an overwhelming victory would force the Sandinistas to "reconsider many things."[18]

It was not until the next election six years later that the Sandinistas had to do just that because, although they were still the single largest political force in the country, the political balancing act had shifted. This time, the opposition was broad-based and determined. The National Opposition Union (UNO) was made up of a hodgepodge of fourteen political parties. Led by Violeta Barrios de Chamorro, the widow of a martyred political figure in the Somoza years, UNO was well financed with millions of dollars from the United States. Aided by U.S. funds, national weariness, and Sandinista concessions to the peace process, UNO stunned Nicaragua and the world with a victory over the Sandinistas. Although the 1990 election was no panacea for Nicaragua's agony, it certainly showed how an extraordinary election can have sweeping implications for power sharing and even democracy.

Individual Rights

Individual rights are a sterner test of democracy than elections are, and, by this standard, Central America fares less well. Protection of political and human rights is very uneven in the region. Costa Rica once again is the beacon, but everywhere else, it is common to find gross violations of individual rights, even when judged by the constitutions of the countries in which these abuses take place. Where the crisis is most serious, even very basic human rights, such as the physical safety of the person and the right to a decent life free from persecution, are trampled by both governments and guerrillas. Civil wars, insurgencies, and counterguerrilla campaigns make things even worse; they only make casualties out of individuals *and* of these rights.

The trauma of the 1980s tested the staying power of the liberal democracy in Costa Rica. José Figueres, the father of modern democracy, once remarked that the Communists were the devils decades ago, but with the passage of time, "we have lost a little bit of our saintliness."[19] The signs of a wary democracy are not hard to spot. For example, the Nicaraguan threat next door led to modest militarization in Costa Rica. Military assistance from the United States to this "Switzerland of Central America" jumped substantially in the 1980s, although the 1987 peace plan briefly fueled hopes that regional threats to Costa Rican democracy would abate. Social programs and civil rights became political issues once again. But individual rights have not been sacrificed on the altar of national security.

Individual rights are less secure in Honduras. A relatively powerful military and the depressed economic conditions of the second poorest country in the Western Hemisphere put a cap on the expansion of individual rights. Still, this "Cinderella" of Central America has managed to avoid the abuses of rights found in neighboring countries. A "state of siege" mentality, nourished by the witches' brew of regional conflict, could puncture the fragile shield that imperfectly protects individual rights in this country.

Always the dominant partner during the interludes of civilian presidents, the Honduran military is more interested in curbing dissent from the Left, such as it is, than in defending individual rights. Given its general poverty but low level of class polarization, Honduras has been spared ferocious campaigns by the military against individual rights. Even so, the government was accused of killing or "disappearing" perhaps 200 or more Leftists and arms traffickers between 1981 and 1984. Meanwhile, weak democratic institutions offer little guarantee that individual rights will easily flourish in an uncertain future.

Costa Rica and Honduras may have avoided the more egregious violations of individual rights, but El Salvador, Guatemala, and Nicaragua unfortunately have not. The rights to speak out, to organize, to assemble, to vote, and to make demands on public officials are hardly taken for granted in these highly charged, war-torn countries of Central America. Where the right to participate is at risk, other individual rights are often trampled. In the Caribbean Basin, only Haiti and Suriname have poorer records than these countries for respecting political and civil rights.

Since 1980, more than 30,000 people have died at the hands of the paramilitary death squads in El Salvador. Death threats were even made against the U.S. ambassador to El Salvador for his alleged support of Duarte's bid for the presidency in 1984. During the second half of the 1980s, gross violations of human rights abated somewhat. Death squad activity became more intermittent, but the death of six Jesuits at the hands of security forces in late 1989 revived a tragic sense of the past. Meanwhile, the civil war goes on, turning the country into a refugee camp.

Until the mid-1980s, the Guatemalan government had probably the worst record on individual rights in Central America. The military's crusade against various guerrilla movements in the countryside made the military itself a death squad. But it did not stop there. State terrorism victimized democratic, centrist, and reformist elements in the cities, too. In 1970, President Araña virtually made the wholesale violation of individual rights official policy: "If it is necessary to turn the country into a cemetery in order to pacify it, I will not hesitate to do so."[20] Between 1966 and 1976, perhaps as many as 20,000 were killed by the army or paramilitary death squads. A policy of repression led to the butchery of individual rights, and between 1978 and 1982, at least 12,000 unarmed civilians were killed. The political center dissolved in a country where the going rate to hire an assassin was a mere $50 (US) during the early 1980s.

The picture on human rights brightened somewhat with the advent of a civilian president in the mid-1980s. However, the army still ruled in the countryside, and President Vinicio Cerezo carefully refrained from abolishing the rural civilian defense patrols of the army that were the backbone of military control over the peasants. The civilian-military alliance in the late 1980s relented on abuses of individual rights, but it has by no means ended them entirely.

The record of the Sandinistas raised issues over basic human rights and the political rights of Nicaraguans to peacefully oppose the government or its policies. The critics of the Sandinista human rights policy find little to applaud about their treatment of citizens. Although the Sandinistas had not been extremely brutal, abuses of human rights were systematic and widespread. For example, Nicaragua's Permanent Commission on Human Rights claimed that terrorizing the population was a policy, not merely an exception to policy. The International League for Human Rights, based in New York, believes the Sandinistas violated major international agreements on human rights, and practiced arbitrary arrest and detention, torture, cruel and inhumane and degrading treatment, and imprisonment. The government was also accused of abusing prisoners during interrogation.

Apologists for Nicaragua's record on human rights disagree. They minimize both the scale and the meaning of human rights abuses, which are portrayed as exceptions and contrary to general policy. The average citizen had nothing to fear, they contend; only the enemies of the revolution did. Amnesty International believed that torture was not widely practiced, at least in the early 1980s. Americas Watch agreed, adding that, during the later years of the civil war, the government did not practice wholesale violations of the laws of war or carry out violations of the physical integrity of the person. Soldiers and death squads, they said, did not burst into homes and massacre everyone inside. By and large, citizens loyal to Nicaragua and the regime had no fear of torture or abuse, according to the apologists. Nonetheless, the Sandinistas themselves confess to minor violations of human rights but justify them on the grounds that their country was at war. They adopted a plan to grant some autonomy to and redress grievances of the Miskito Indians on the east coast.

Sandinista policy toward political and civil rights was just as controversial as its policy towards basic human rights. In the 1984 election, the opposition parties were harassed, and their rallies were disrupted by *turbas* or mobs—actions that Daniel Ortega defended. The opposition parties were denied access to the media, which were in large part under the thumb of the Sandinistas. Still, the election did grant a degree of freedom to organize and participate. Most observers (but not the U.S. government) believed it to be one of the fairest in Nicaraguan history, which may not, of course, be saying a great deal.

The government became more sensitive about its policy toward the opposition as criticism mounted. The state of emergency, in place for several years, permitted government controls over the media, press, and other modes of potential antigovernment expression. Toward the end of the Sandinista era, the government remained thin-skinned but more tolerant. Complying with the Central American peace treaty and conducting the campaign for the 1990 election loosened the control from above even more. However, intimidation was still felt in some quarters, as indicated by the inaccuracy of opinion polls taken prior to the election.

The Human Condition

The third life sign of democracy is the human condition. The enduring challenge for Central America is to elevate the social, economic, demographic, and cultural conditions of most people and thereby create more democratic and egalitarian societies. Without an improvement in the human condition, the long-term prospects for democracy and for resolving the crisis are quite bleak.

Unfortunately, the human condition in Central America went from bad to worse during the 1980s. In Guatemala, for example, plummeting incomes for people working for subsistence in the countryside was symptomatic of the decline in the export economy. The human condition in El Salvador is also inhospitable. Since 1980, the economy has been a casualty of the fighting. The investment climate is chilly; guerrilla attacks on the economy have disrupted productivity and infrastructure; and U.S. foreign aid and leftist insurgency inundate the small country. The business community remains suspicious of moderate reformism. Economic growth and persistent poverty may be underlying causes for the civil war, but the civil war itself erodes even further the human condition of most Salvadorans.

Taken at their word, the Sandinistas were very interested in the human condition. Early on, they expressed a commitment to upgrade the quality of life for the poor and the peasants. From most accounts, their early campaigns to improve literacy, health, and other social conditions confirmed their rhetoric. These policies of redistribution, though not always well managed, helped the great bulk of Nicaraguans. For the Sandinistas, social rights are given greater weight than political and civil ones, and democracy is equated with literacy, land reform, education, and public health.

But the early gains in social policy have succumbed to harsh reality in Nicaragua. Whether despite or beause of Sandinista policy, the human condition has worsened. Economic malaise, policy mistakes, and years of war have impoverished nearly everyone. Nicaraguans are more dis-illusioned than ever about declining standards of living, shortages, rationing, and mismanagement. The Sandinistas blame the war as well as the U.S. diplomatic and economic pressure that bled the economy. Meanwhile, the private sector is hesitant and sullen, lacking the confidence to make long-term commitments for new investment. In fact, per capita income of Nicaraguans as a whole has slipped since 1980. Thus, the Sandinista policy of redistribution had a paradoxical effect on democracy: It upgraded the human condition of the many, but it also sacrificed political and civil rights of others.

Neighboring Honduras has a long way to go to improve the human condition. Before the civil wars next door in El Salvador and Nicaragua, it was the poorest republic in Central America. It is resource-poor, with many demands straining those scarce resources. This long-standing problem was greatly aggravated by the economic recession which descended upon Honduras and its neighbors in 1979. Since then, the situation has gone from bad to worse. Neither God nor the United States has indicated a willingness to become the savior of Honduras.

Costa Rican democracy rests on economic viability and on the legitimacy of a truce between the oligarchy, labor, and the middle class. However, that truce could disintegrate if the human condition ever becomes a hotly contested issue in Costa Rican politics. Living standards have declined in that country during the 1980s, but the human condition has not sunk so far that it has been fatal for liberal democracy.

Crisis, Democracy, and the United States

The participation crisis in Central America has become a struggle for power, rather than a search for democracy. The broadening of conflict has introduced more players, but the crisis has also victimized democracy, as indicated by uneven and sometimes faltering life signs. With fractured political arenas in Guatemala, Nicaragua, and El Salvador, the evolution of a stable, legitimate order is stunted by the apparently irreconcilable aims of power contenders. Each contender uses its unique advantages to punish or outmanuever the adversary, and compromise is rare in this harsh reality. Meanwhile, the Right and the military still retain the advantages of wealth, power, government, and arms. In all but Nicaragua, the Right controls or has a dominant position in the national government, a potent weapon in the struggle for power. And even though the state may be used to promote sectarian interests, it is too weak to build a legitimate, viable, and inclusive political system. Genuine power sharing remains illusive. The Left and a good part of the center Left will be denied power as long as the military and the Right can manage it. But in spite of its impotence in government, the Left has forever broken the Right's monopoly of force.

The crisis of participation shattered the domestic political order in much of Central America. Unable to gain a foothold in the government, the opposition has invented an alternative political order—a recipe for endless civil war. The central challenge is to construct *one* legitimate, national order in every country of Central America. Failing that, Central America must face the prospect of fragmented societies ruled by opposing "governments." One thing is clear: Order cannot be imposed across whole societies under current conditions. Instead, order must be reinvented.

What has been and should be the role of the United States in inventing a legitimate order? To date, it has done very little to move Central America toward such a condition. U.S. support for elections may have moderated the Right, but waging proxy wars has not brought peace. Rather, its hegemonic interests have been to impose an artificial stability on illegitimate domestic orders and use force, reform, intervention, and preponderant resources to stifle important realignments among domestic groups.

The ordeal of hegemony facing the United States is that it may be unable to hold to this strategy—a fact it has apparently failed to realize. Instead, it insists upon pursuing recycled policies to repeal what cannot be repealed. The ordeal for Central America is that it is responsible for its own fate, though it does not have the power to determine it.

The United States has at times confused long-term stability with the short-term status quo. The participation crisis is an example. This crisis in Central America centers on the failure to legitimately govern and to effectively reform unequal but changing societies. The crisis is more homegrown than imported. Yet the inflow of aid, arms, and moral support to governments and insurgents, coming from the United States and others, threatens to perpetuate it indefinitely. Long-term stability requires a policy that looks at the domestic needs of a legitimate political order in Central America.

Sweeping changes in small countries can weaken if not destroy the hegemonic system. They nibble on the edges of hegemony, without necessarily bringing it to its knees. And throughout the region, participation has transformed but not yet transcended the hegemonic system or the domestic order upon which it relied for so long. The crisis has also forced the hegemonic power to go on the defensive. But ultimately, the United States has no viable strategy for restoring its power because it has no strategy (except for formalistic elections) for dealing with the crisis of participation.

The frailty of Central America is ominous for the future of U.S. hegemony. The crisis weakened the domestic order that made U.S. influence in the region possible. In fact, the upheaval has been so severe that it has diluted the bonds of hegemonic control but has not severed them.

5

The Containment of Central America

The crisis in Central America has withered hegemonic bonds between the United States and local ruling elites who are no longer in secure control of their countries. Added to this, U.S. allies and adversaries have intruded in the region, transforming and offsetting U.S. control over Central America in the process.

Although the foreign policy of the United States remains vital to friends and foes alike in Central America, what others want and do there has become increasingly important, and competing powers have broken the near monopoly of U.S. relations with the five small republics. Certainly, Central America has never been in complete control of its affairs, but the international dimensions of the crisis today have vastly complicated its prospects for designing its own future. Never before has the region been the battleground for such a diversity of international players.

Strategies of Containment

At the fulcrum of clashing interests, Central America is both a participant and a spectator to three types of *containment strategies* designed to enhance interests of different players.

In the 1980s, the United States adopted a strategy of *containment of the Left*. The goal was actually "containment plus." That is, the United States sought to contain *and* to overturn what it saw as the "source" of the problem in Central America—a Sandinista Nicaragua—believing this would restore its influence. However, even passive containment could end if not reverse the decline by hemming in the Left and preventing it from gaining influence beyond its current domain.

The second strategy of foreign policy sought *the containment of the conflict.* Major states in Western Europe and Latin America took this approach to bring reconciliation to Central America, rather than attempt to rollback the Left. For them, then, containing the conflict superceded containing the Left. For example, during the mid-1980s, the Contadora group (Mexico, Venezuela, Colombia, and Panama) and its "support group" sought a multilateral and comprehensive negotiated settlement of the conflict in all of Central America.

A third strategy, the *containment of counterrevolution,* hoped to repel or hold at bay U.S. hegemony. The radical regimes that sought to contain and reverse hegemony wanted to hold on to the Sandinista revolution in its consolidated form and deny any victories to counter-revolution.

The clash of these strategies is far from resolved, even with changes in leadership in the United States and in the region. But analyzing the strategies themselves reveals the extent to which the United States pursues its own interests, often alone or nearly so, against the growing independence of those who insist on the second and third approaches to the crisis. These divergent interests and strategies also show how far Central America has moved away from the quiet subservience of the past. Meanwhile, the intrusion of others has diluted the U.S. presence and added one more element to hegemonic decline in a region that presents no direct threat to the economic preeminence of the United States.

Containment of the Left

Containing the Left is a policy of a declining hegemonic state. In fact, the very *existence* of the Left in power raises doubts about hegemonic vitality. The current situations in Cuba and Nicaragua would have been unthinkable in the distant era of ascendant hegemony.

What interests, vital or otherwise, does the United States really have in Central America? Actually, they are much the same as they once were; only the times have changed. Historically, of course, the United States sought a sphere of influence. At the outset, U.S. hegemony imposed stability on a region of friendly governments in the Caribbean area, and foreign interests were restrained in the "American Mediterranean." But the Caribbean Basin and Central America are no longer isolated. As a result, the United States currently seeks what seems more and more remote as time goes by: a region that it can control, that is compliant, and that is a secure asset.

The United States has a wide array of political, military, and economic interests in Central America. The threats to these interests are often portrayed as objective (e.g., preventing Soviet bases) and subjective (e.g., suffering a loss of face in being unable to control the Sandinistas).

Central America has few resources, and is of little direct economic importance to the United States—indeed only 2 percent of U.S. foreign investment and trade is with Central America. Consequently, the region is more important for its proximity to the Panama Canal, shipping routes, supply routes, strategic minerals, and oil. For some U.S. strategists, large countries and stakes are just a domino or two away. The western Caribbean Basin is close to key listening posts and military installations, and geographically, Central America is a bridge over which refugees and guerrillas could move. The importance of Central America is less a matter of what is there than how the region is perceived in relation to other interests.

Other U.S. interests are subjective. Power and credibility are at stake here, because they are allowed to be. And if certain premises are accepted about U.S. power, Central America becomes more vital as a testing ground for U.S. capabilities to impose hegemony.

Containment of the Left is a counterrevolutionary strategy that asserts that radical Third World governments must be confronted, not accommodated. Therefore, denying the Soviet Union its allies in the Third World is a vital strategic goal for a United States that seeks "stable, friendly, prosperous countries that are not allied, formally or informally, with the Soviet bloc and that do not promote revolution in the region."[1] U.S. policy in Central America was designed to deny Cuba and the Soviet Union bases, allies, communication lines, and access. However, strategists must realize that the threat exists at two levels. That is, radical states are a threat by what they *do* beyond their borders and by what they *are* within their borders.

The maximum objective of the United States is to reestablish its control. The minimum to be tolerated is a halt in the erosion of hegemony. A hegemonic imperative comes into play: "the United States has to exercise dominant power and influence in its 'backyard' (hegemony, albeit benign, however rationalized or euphemistically labeled)."[2] Indeed, security interests may justify a resurrection of hegemony, and modernizing the Monroe Doctrine may require updating the primacy of U.S. power in the Caribbean Basin. Still, the central issue is how to accomplish this. As a U.S. legislator remarked, "the debate over U.S. policy in Central America is not, as the (Reagan) administration so often claims, a debate over whether or not to assert U.S. power and influence in the region. It is a debate over how best to use U.S. power and influence to ensure that developments are more, rather than less, favorable to U.S. interests. It is a debate over how to use U.S. leverage, in what proportion, and for what purposes."[3]

Containing the Left confronts impressive hazards for traditional means of containment are costly and risky. Since old-style imperialism "would be an unwise, infeasible objective for U.S. strategy,"[4] new bottles must be found for old wine. U.S. influence might be restored in other ways, such as shared objectives, greater cooperation, and interdependence within the Caribbean Basin. However, these alternatives were not part of the containment policy of the Reagan administration.

Containment of the Left also tempts the hegemonic state to recycle interventionism. During the 1980s, the United States mobilized Nicaraguan factions and some governments against the Sandinistas. The contra war, a kind of Bay of Pigs in slow motion, raised the costs to the Sandinistas, eroding their popular support.

Containing the Left can be hazardous in other ways. For example, it can drive a wedge into domestic support. In a 1985 Gallup poll, only 27 per cent of the U.S. public expressed approval of the Reagan administration's Central American policy. Even later in the 1980s, the support was never widespread. Furthermore, containing the Left may be counterproductive because counterrevolution may actually harden the Sandinista regime and make it difficult for the Soviets and Cubans to gracefully withdraw their limited support. Pressuring, confronting, and badgering the Sandinistas may have at times moderated their behavior. But it may have portrayed the United States as a determined bully as well. Finally, containing the Left in Central America is part of a global strategy to restore the U.S. credibility as a hegemonic state. Wisely or not, the United States staked its reputation in Central America.

The United States had three containment options: It could moderate the Left; it could bleed the Sandinistas, weakening if not toppling them from power, or it could try to remove them from power. These options share an underlying assumption—the United States as the hegemonic state cannot accept the existence of any regime that it does not control. The radical regime, or the radicalism of a regime, must go. During the 1980s, the United States supposedly sought rollback, but appeared at times to be practicing the other options as well. The CIA war, the trade embargo, and resistance to negotiated settlement were all weapons that were used in the containment strategy. In fact, if the purpose was to topple the Sandinista government, then these weapons misfired. But if the purpose was to raise the cost of political heresy in a fading hegemonic system, then they were more successful.

The United States initially found some regional support for its strategy in Nicaragua, but its allies gradually had second thoughts about the strategy and eventually abandoned it in 1987. In fact, Honduras and Costa Rica at one point considered bilateral accords with Nicaragua to stabilize borders and to control the contra war even before they independently adopted the Central American peace plan.

To stave off a regional détente, the Reagan administration resorted to both carrots and sticks. Economic support and military assistance were extended to El Salvador, and coupled with Duarte's election in 1984, they were major tools to implement the containment policy. Honduras, the stepchild of U.S. policy, has received a smaller bounty, yet five military bases and greater assistance have anchored U.S. support for the Honduran government.

Containing the Left and restoring hegemony led the Reagan administration to a covert search for a new hegemonic alliance. Frustrated by congressional skepticism and intermittent support for its policy, as well as by constraints on its ability to wield policy with a free hand, the administration believed its troubles were rooted in domestic and international opposition. In response, it sought to circumvent such opposition via a covert alliance of domestic and international allies designed to support its goals in Central America. It persuaded Brunei, Saudi Arabia, and others to contribute secret funds to the contra cause; it "privatized" counterrevolutionary activities to thwart Congressional constraints; it turned the National Security Council into an operational center under Colonel Oliver North; and it diverted funds from the sale of arms to Iran to support contra activities. But the tactics of this peculiar alliance belied a fundamental problem: The Reagan administration did not have a unified domestic political base from which to carry out its policy. Unable to prevail through normal channels, it sought by stealth to shore up its war by proxy against the Sandinistas.

Clearly, the United States has the power to redefine and transform the conflict. But it does not have the power to achieve its ambitious goals of hegemonic restoration. Central America is not what it once was. And for the United States, behaving like a hegemonic state in a situation that is no longer hegemonic may be harmful if "continued adherence to this hegemonic presumption serves only to diminish [U.S.] influence further and to exacerbate . . . [the] . . . conflict and instability in the area."[5] The United States has tremendous power to reward and to punish, but it has not been able to impose its own solution. The containment of the Left as a strategy has proven that the United States can be very influential—but only that and nothing more. It may not be possible for the United States to wave a hegemonic wand and make things right once again.

Containment of Conflict

The second strategy is the *containment of conflict.* Unlike the first, it promotes a modified status quo with the Sandinistas, rather than going to war to get rid of them. Containing the conflict is a regional version of détente in which those in power, on the Left or on the Right, are granted a kind of legitimacy. Containing conflict does not mean necessarily accepting the Left as a desirable state of affairs, but it does assume that everyone has a stake in stability and that the Left will eventually be less of a threat if it is not bombarded from all sides.

During the 1980s, containing conflict was a strategy preferred by three groups of states. The regional powers of Mexico, Venezuela, Colombia, and Panama (the Contadora group) were leaders in promoting a negotiated settlement in Central America as a way of ensuring their own interests during the early 1980s. A second group, including France, the Federal Republic of Germany, Spain, and other OECD countries, saw the crisis in Central America as a product of developmental problems rather than of strategic gamesmanship. They believed that peace was a prerequisite for solving these long-term problems. Mexico was more inclined to agree with France and Spain's percepton of the crisis, but Venezuela and Great Britain were closer to the U.S. perspective. (Just as the United States is divided over the policy of containment, Europe and Latin America are prone to accept some U.S. premises and disinclined to accept others.) The third group, the Central American allies of the United States, adopted a peace plan in the late 1980s and therefore sided with the strategy of containing conflict. They did, however, agree that the Sandinistas had to democratize before peace was possible— containing the Left and containing conflict had to be done together.

Yet the interests and the power of those countries preferring the strategy of containing conflict differ from those of the United States. Mexico, Venezuela, France, the Federal Republic of Germany, and the United Kingdom have few vital and concrete interests of any substance in Central America. Of these countries, the Federal Republic of Germany has the broadest range of interests in Latin America as a whole, but the region accounts for only 13 percent of all German foreign investment and about one-half of all its development assistance. Unlike the United States, the Federal Republic is, by and large, indifferent about security issues in the Americas, but it is the most significant European presence in Central America.

Other "outsiders" have commercial, ideological, and cultural interests in the region, but none of them are vital. Great Britain, for example, is deferential to the United States in the region (except on Grenada). France and Spain have ideological and cultural interests but do little to advance them. Japan is a commercial power but is politically low-key. And Canada's relations are negligible.

However, European interest in Central America is greater than these objective issues. This is because the European interest in Central America is, in reality, an interest in *U.S. policy* toward the region.

Europeans would not be so concerned about Central America if the United States had not insisted on treating the area as a vital issue in the East-West rivalry. But by placing Central America in an East-West context, the United States has almost compelled Europe to become involved in the region's crisis. In other words, Central America has become a European issue because the United States has, quite unintentionally, made it one. As unlikely as it seems, it became one more test of the political cohesion within the Atlantic alliance during the 1980s. The credibility of the United States—as well as that of the West—has been put on the line in Central America.

Although European powers empathize with the United States, they have their own views about the origins of and solutions for the crisis. The United States staked its credibility on expelling the Left and denying the Soviet Union a client state in Central America. Europe, however, is more inclined to regard the problem as a matter of how the West should adapt to unavoidable change in the Third World.

European powers tend to believe that the Left should not be isolated or contained but integrated and moderated within the Western economic and trading system.[6] It is best for all concerned to remove the Central American conflict from the East-West rivalry. Otherwise, some believe, the United States is unwisely raising the stakes in a risky adventure. As Wolf Grabendorff argues, "the inability of the United States to stabilize a region so close to home . . . will very likely contribute to the further erosion of the U.S. global position, and this is contrary to Western European interests."[7]

Whatever their reservations about U.S. policy, Europeans are far from united on Central American issues. Some are more willing to accept the U.S. perspective on the conflict, but others believe that the United States made a strategic mistake. Futhermore, they differ over the appropriate level of activity and degree of support for the U.S. policy. Interestingly, some of the most involved Europeans are not even the leaders of European states, and it is the European political parties, unions, and churches that have most often questioned the U.S. policy of containment and intervention. The United Kingdom has been silent and supportive, and West Germany has been cautious, sidestepping direct confrontation with the United States. But France and Spain have been more vocal and critical. At the same time, Latin American states have focused their interests and funneled their resources into Central America. Their interests were great, but their resources were modest, and, with the oil bust of the early 1980s, an important source of leverage dwindled further. What is more, their relations with the hegemonic state remained vital to their own national interests, and they could not act without regard for what the United States might do.

To complicate things even more, these states did not always agree among themselves. For example, Mexico's revolutionary tradition as well as its domestic constraints dictated a more independent and nationalistic role in Central America, at least in the beginning. It was openly sympathetic with the Sandinistas even as it sought to mediate the conflict. But, Venezuela, lacking a revolutionary tradition, was more attuned to U.S. perceptions. It advocated the containment of the Left but with a nod toward regional sensibilities and a concern for negotiating a settlement. Colombia and Panama, with fewer interests and resources to protect, stood more on the sidelines of the movement to bring about a negotiated settlement.

However, these differences did not obscure the essential thrust of the strategy to contain conflict. A fragile consensus on what was and was not desirable held together through the long and eventually unsuccessful attempts by the Contadora states to devise an agreement. First, the regional powers favored a new stability but not one based upon restored hegemony. They learned to fear an active, interventionist United States, rather than the more distant Soviet Union. They believed that a stable region should be exempted from "hegemonic appetites," as the president of Venezuela once claimed.[8] Second, they agreed that a new stability was compatible with regional diversity in Central America, an unspoken premise behind the strategy for containing the conflict. The way to achieve stability, they implied, was to integrate and moderate the Left, which given a stake in peace would lay down its arms. Third, they believed that the Sandinistas could be contained through negotiated settlement and a judicious blend of carrots and sticks rather than by using intimidation and quasimilitary instruments like the contras. Fourth, the regional powers acknowledged the great powers' interests in the crisis, but they were not disposed to regard the situation as a great power conflict. Indeed, they saw great power rivalry in the region, unless strictly circumscribed, as contrary to their own interests.

Mexico had the most to lose if the containment of conflict eventually failed. The view from Mexico City was that, one way or another, the crisis in the region threatened to ripple northward, which is why Mexican leaders stressed the containment of conflict. Basically, they felt they could live with the Left in Central America (if not in Mexico), but they could not live comfortably with turmoil next door.[9]

Mexico's interests in containing conflict in Central America exceeded their reach. It sought regional stability by embracing leftist reformism and the containment of U.S. hegemony, yet its position eroded during the 1980s. With oil revenues in decline, it lacked the funds and even the prestige it once had to affect the balance of power in the region. Also bedeviling its policy was the tension arising from its dual role as a partisan for the Left and as an arbiter for a negotiated peace.[10] Neither the United States nor Central America fully accepted this balancing act.

Venezuela was also committed to a policy of containing conflict in Central America during the 1980s. But given its own history, interests, and resources, it did not subscribe whole-heartedly to Mexico's perspective on Central America. Although the Malvinas/Falklands War tempered its enthusiasm for U.S. foreign policy in the region, Venezuela's perspective on Central America was at times closer to the United States than to Mexico. The containment of conflict required the containment of the Left. But it was divided over the implications of revolutionary regimes in Central America for the security of the region and especially for Venezuela itself.

Unlike Mexico, Venezuela was cool toward the Sandinistas. In fact, it supported their foe in El Salvador, the Christian Democrat José Napoleon Duarte. Although it opposed U.S. intervention in Central America, it sent its own military advisers to the Salvadoran government. Fundamentally, then, Venezuela opposed the revolutionary Left but did not want to be engulfed in an East-West conflict in the region. It championed elections and democracy in Central America, while keeping its distance from the Left. For a time, both Venezuela and Mexico, via the San Jose (Costa Rica) agreement, extended oil credits to Central America, although the cost later became too burdensome for both.

The Contadora group (Mexico, Venezuela, Colombia, and Panama) first exemplified the strategy for containing conflict in Central America. The formation of the group in 1983 was clearly a step toward broadening the legitimacy of a multilateral, negotiated settlement. This became the most ambitious alternative to U.S. containment policy and represented a regional effort to minimize the East-West character of the conflict, to restrain unilateral U.S. actions, and to stabilize the region.[11] The Contadora process implicitly rejected hegemonic restoration.

From 1983 until 1986, the Contadora group vainly sought to contain conflict by developing a multilateral treaty, but, after a number of drafts, the group was unable to arrive at or to impose a settlement. For their part, the Central Americans detected a bias in favor of the Sandinistas in the treaty drafts and tended to resent this as another form of outside intervention. The United States attitude wavered between ambivalence and hostility. Although the Contadora process filled a vacuum and deflected some criticism away from U.S. containment policy, it was also an irritant. Meanwhile, the United States paid lip service to multilateral negotiation at the same time that it pursued its policy to depose or cripple the Sandinistas. Although Contadora's plans for peace contained attractive provisions, such as democratization, the United States believed that, on balance, the document favored the Sandinistas and that U.S. preferences in a settlement were only vaguely endorsed or unenforceable in the Contadora proposal.

Honduras, El Salvador, and Costa Rica issued a rebuttal to Contadora with their own plan. Nevertheless, their efforts were stimulated by the Contadora process and demanded guarantees of democratization, "simultaneity," verification, enforcement and balanced demilitarization of the region. Endorsed by Nicaragua and Guatemala, the Central American initiative took up where the Contadora process left off. The peace plan of 1987 affirmed the containment of conflict not by regional powers or by extrahemispheric allies but by the very Central American allies the United States had enlisted a few years before in its campaign of confrontation and containment against Nicaragua. Stalemate and fatigue had overwhelmed the Contadora process, but out of its dissolution came the home-grown attempt of the Central American states themselves to end the conflict.

Containment of Counterrevolution

Containing the United States in its efforts to depose revolutionary governments and thwart revolutionary movements is the antihegemonic strategy of radical states. The containment of counterrevolution seeks to defend, consolidate, and promote revolutions in the face of U.S. desires to restore hegemony and repeal revolution in the Third World.

The survival of the Nicaraguan revolution is the centerpiece of this strategy. Nicaragua realigned its foreign relations, for without sympathetic Western states and the assistance of Cuba and the Soviet Union, it would be hard-pressed to persevere. Given harsh geopolitical realities for revolution in the Americas, such radical states must chart a course of containing counterrevolution through a hostile sea. To date, Nicaragua has been able to find few safe harbors.

The containment of counterrevolution takes place both inside and outside the radical state. First, the radical state tries to erode the willingness of the hegemonic power to allocate resources for counterrevolution. In other words, a new radical state must engage in a battle of wills in which divisions within the hegemonic state are exploited to the point of provoking hegemonic weariness with counterrevolution. Since there is little a revolutionary regime can do to erode the economic power of the hegemonic state, it must sow doubt within that state itself about its government's policy.

Second, the revolutionary regime must consolidate its own power at the very time that its resources are being depleted due by the cost of defending itself. Immediately after coming to power, a revolutionary government must mobilize what power there is. This "hardening" of the revolution may lead to greater domestic opposition, and it will certainly do little to calm the worst fears of the leaders of the hegemonic state. Yet the radical regime must do even more. It must generate new resources if it hopes to discourage the counterrevolutionaries. It must create power, not just mobilize, it. And the leaders must rely upon subjective as well as objective power resources. One such resource is ideology, which is used to confer legitimacy and can help defend the revolution. Additionally, tangible resources such as military equipment and personnel must be mobilized within the radical state, and advisers, equipment, and training must also be imported.

Third, because the containment of counterrevolution is a power struggle on a global level, a new foreign policy must be adopted by the revolutionary regime. No longer a client of the hegemonic state, the radical regime must restructure its foreign relations. In the Cuban case, this involved a rather clear-cut strategic defection for its counterrevolutionary plans required that it accept Soviet hegemony and defending the Cuban revolution required Soviet protection.

Nicaragua under the Sandinistas diversified its foreign relations without mimicking the Cuban model. Early on, the premises of Nicaraguan foreign policy were that the new government must rally European and Latin American support, diversify its markets, stake out its presence in world forums, maintain relations with all Latin American governments, seek cordial ties with regional powers like Mexico and Venezuela, and keep the support of socialist international elements. But as the price of containment mushroomed, Nicaragua gradually drifted toward the Soviet-Cuban bloc, without becoming a full-fledged member of it. Its strategy did lead to an irrevocable alliance with the Soviet bloc.

The containment of counterrevolution is the initial, defensive phase of a broader foreign policy by which radical regimes seek to keep U.S. hegemony at bay. Later, with an offensive foreign policy, they may even aspire to roll back hegemony. But the extent to which radical states pursue radical foreign policies is a matter of heated conjecture. Clearly, the Sandinista government was unable to avoid conflict with the hegemonic state or with its own neighbors; this imperiled its tenuous position. And yet the Sandinistas gave the rebels in El Salvador moral, military, and logistical support. While ensuring their own survival, revolutionary governments also seek to divert hegemonic attention and resources elsewhere.

The containment strategy of Nicaragua was heavily military in the beginning but turned to diplomacy later. The government used military force to resist the contra insurgents of the Nicaraguan Democratic Force (FDN), headed by Adolfo Calero and by others, as well as the insurgents of the Democratic Revolutionary Alliance (ARDE) led by Alfonso Robelo and others. These Nicaraguan government forces are several times greater in numbers than their armed opposition. The Nicaraguan armed forces probably exceed 60,000 men; contra forces never were more than 13,000, and have dwindled since 1987. Approximately half of the country's GNP was dedicated to defending the revolution.

The Sandinista arsenal was also stronger than that of the insurgents. The Soviet Union and its bloc supplied economic assistance, credits, and military equipment to fight counterinsurgency, and the arrival of several Mi-24 helicopters in 1985 was heralded as a major improvement in Nicaragua's antiguerrilla capabilities. But, from most accounts, the contras were no serious military threat to the army. What is more, they are politically unsavory to many Nicaraguans because their counter-revolutionary tactics included attacks on the people and the economy of Nicaragua. They succeeded in making life harder for many Nicaraguans.

The military containment of counterrevolution has been costly, but the Sandinistas endured the cost given the fact that there was no acceptable alternative—until the Central American peace plan of 1987. Their government was open to other strategies of containing the counterrevolution of the United States. And over time, diplomacy and negotiation have actually served Nicaragua's goals. A negotiated settlement of the conflict would, under certain conditions, be agreeable to Nicaragua. In fact, the Sandinistas explored diplomatic avenues with the Contadora group, the Central American republics, and the United States.

The Sandinistas at first preferred to negotiate bilateral security agreements with their neighbors. Such agreements would have done what their military strategy could not do: They would have driven a wedge in the counterrevolutionary alliance. Failing that, the Sandinistas sought a diplomatic avenue to deflect the hegemonic insurgency of the United States. Nicaragua was more receptive to Contadora than the United States was, and it seemed willing to consider a comprehensive, regional settlement through the Contadora process or, failing that, through direct negotiation with its Central American neighbors. The 1987 Central American peace plan reflected this shift in tactics.

Negotiation served Sandinista goals if it guaranteed the survival and the hegemony of the FSLN within Nicaragua. But negotiations in the 1980s did not always promise this. For example, the Reagan peace plan of April 4, 1985, failed to provide this multilateral framework because it insisted upon continued aid to the contras *and* democratic guarantees within Nicaragua. This would have imperiled the Sandinistas' hegemony over their country, and they were only willing to consider a settlement that would keep them in power. The Sapóa truce of 1988 between the Sandinistas and the contras may have served this goal.

Although managed conflict or even wary détente may advance Sandinista interests in Central America, the conflict between a revolutionary government and a counterrevolutionary alliance actually led to the intrusion of other radical states. This means that the Nicaraguan revolution and the U.S. response to it eroded a principal goal of classic hegemony in the Americas: to keep strategic adversaries out of its sphere of influence. The leftist leanings of the Sandinistas no doubt encouraged the Soviets and Cubans to aid Nicaragua, and U.S. insurgency against the revolution in their view no doubt justified the assistance they provided. In fact, the Soviets and Cubans were invited to help Nicaragua consolidate and defend its revolution. They did not cause the revolution, but they have been participants in it since 1980.

The Soviets were initially reluctant to make a major commitment to the Sandinista revolution due to its doctrine of "geographical fatalism."[12] Central America was far away and unimportant to the Soviets. But nestled under the belly of the hegemonic state, it was both very close and very important to the United States. Nonetheless, neither superpower wanted "another Cuba," albeit for very different reasons.

Meanwhile, from the Soviet perspective, Cuba, which is active and intrusive in the Americas, can continue to serve "anti-imperialist" objectives in the region. It is also a major factor in the counterrevolutionary strategy. The role of both Cuba and the Soviet Union in Nicaragua's plans to contain counterrevolution was shaped both by the goals of a radical state in a declining hegemonic system and by the relationship between Cuba and the Soviet Union itself. In general, these two countries share the goal of advancing "anti-imperialist" aims. Yet, Cuba has its own interests in the Caribbean Basin which it pursues for its own purposes.[13] In addition, Cuban and Soviet leaders agree with U.S. leaders that what happened in Central America was part of a larger struggle. To the Cubans, the Nicaraguan struggle was a regional one that has some global side effects, and they wanted the Soviets to help more than they had. For their part, the Soviets are more prone to see the struggle in a global perspective. Though they believe Nicaragua should be helped, they have broader concerns that also deserve resources and promise more important gains. And they believe that, with or without Soviet and Cuban aid, revolution would still occur in places like Central America.

Specific Cuban and Soviet goals in Latin America are to weaken U.S. hegemony, to isolate the United States from its more independent-minded neighbors, and to fragment its regional security system. In pursuing these goals, Cuba is hardly a passive tool of the Soviet Union.

Without assistance and weapons from the Soviet Union, Cuba would, of course, be less effective in Nicaragua; in advancing its own interests, it lends aid and comfort to the counterrevolutionary strategy of the Sandinistas.

Cuba and the Soviet Union were important to Nicaragua. Cuba's counterrevolutionary strategy was to fortify the regime and to counter U.S. containment policy. Cuban advisers, both civilian and military, peaked in numbers in late 1983, stabilized at somewhere between 5,000 and 10,000 by the mid-1980s, and seem likely to remain at lower levels. Military aid from the Soviet bloc likewise reached its peak a year later and then levelled off.[14] Assistance to Nicaragua ebbed during the late 1980s.

The essential premise of Cuban and Soviet policy is that containing counterrevolution in Central America must be achieved with limited means and limited conflict. This means that Sandinista Nicaragua was to be helped within a broad-based radical front without being fully admitted as a client state within the Soviet-Cuban alliance. Yet, by the early 1990s, it was apparent that the policies of containing the Left and containing the conflict were more influential than the policy of containing counterrevolution. The limited commitments and resources the Soviets made to the Sandinistas were not enough to stop counter-revolution. Furthermore, in the late 1980s and early 1990s, the Soviets under Gorbachev began to trim their support for Third World allies and for their client states within their own sphere of influence, Eastern Europe. For the Sandinistas, containing counterrevolution for a decade was debilitating. They find themselves in a position of trying to redefine their role in a government they do not control.

The End of Exclusivity

Crisis and instability within Central America have transformed foreign policies toward the region, and as the crisis has been internationalized, U.S. control has diminished. The three strategies of containment are as much attempt to deal with powers outside Central America as they are approaches to the region's internal problems. Furthermore, the very fact that the other countries pursued strategies apart from the United States plainly points to the decline of U.S. hegemony and exclusivity in Central America. Even more telling, the U.S. strategy itself had moderated by the late 1980s.

Containment strategies in Central America indicate how the strategic intrusion of others, with their own perceptions and policies for dealing with change and conflict, undermines U.S. influence. Certainly, not all containment strategies are equal, and U.S. influence still outweighs that of its rivals. But the strategies do represent alternatives to U.S. policy, and, directly or indirectly, they imply that the strategy of containing the Left has not restored U.S. dominance.

The intrusion thesis on U.S. decline argues that the mere presence of adversaries and allies with their own agendas, interests, and policies is enough to erode the subjective belief in U.S. omnipotence—the high standard by which the United States judged its own prowess in the region. The diverse foreign policies swirling around Central America in the late twentieth century suggest that both the power *and* the legitimacy of the United States for dealing with the crisis are on the wane. Central America is no longer the exclusive domain of the United States.

6

Security

The partial erosion of U.S. influence does not mean that the United States is powerless to get what it wants in the world. But it does mean that two issue areas vital to the management of inter-American relations—*security* and *economics*—are more prone to change, uncertainty, confusion, and instability.

Security embodies interests, threats, capabilities, and issues that increasingly test U.S. hegemony in inter-American relations. In the hemisphere, the ordeal of hegemony means working for U.S. security even as such interests collide and military capabilities change. But is restoring hegemony the way to ensure security? There is some reason to think not. In this era of regional change, as insecurity pervades both the north and south, the irony is that U.S. military power in relative terms has not diminished as much as has its economic power has.

Although insecurity is growing in the Americas, it should be recalled that the hemisphere has enjoyed stability for most of its history, and armed conflict between states in the Americas is still relatively rare. Indeed, Latin America still resembles Europe in this respect. And though the military is important to the defense and politics of the Americas, it has never reached profoundly into the societies of these states. As Table 6.1 indicates, only Cuba, the United States, Uruguay, and Chile (in that order) have moderate or high levels of armed forces as a percent of population.

Although Central America is less pacified than South America, Latin America has been spared the large-scale conflicts endemic to most of the Third World. During the twentieth century, Latin America experienced 1,159,000 war and war-related deaths, more than half of them civilian.[1] That may seem like a great deal of killing, but comparatively it is not. Only the Middle East, with a population about one-third the size of Latin America's, had fewer war deaths. In relative terms, Latin America is fortunate.

TABLE 6.1   Force Levels in the Americas

Country	Armed forces as % of population
Cuba	1.31%
United States	0.95
Uruguay	0.95
Chile	0.82
Haiti	0.80
Argentina	0.67
Nicaragua	0.62
Peru	0.57
Paraguay	0.53
Bolivia	0.50
El Salvador	0.48
Ecuador	0.47
Dominican Republic	0.38
Belize	0.34
Guatemala	0.26
Colombia	0.26
Venezuela	0.24
Costa Rica	0.23
Brazil	0.21
Mexico	0.17
Honduras	0.16

Sources: Adapted from Adrian J. English, Armed Forces in Latin America (New York: Jane's, 1984), appendix 1; Ruth L. Sivard, World Military and Social Expenditures 1985 (Washington, D.C.: World Priorities, 1985), p. 35.

However, a stable peace may no longer be taken for granted. Armed conflict and insecurity are not as "foreign" to the Americas as they once were, and military conflict is more thinkable because there is more to quarrel over. The region is being militarized as governments, insurgents, and drug lords resort to force in an atmosphere of hatred and vigilance. Furthermore, insecurity and instability have grown as U.S. preeminence has declined. The Americas are more turbulent in the 1980s than they were in the 1940s when the hegemony of the United States was at its peak. For whatever reasons, from the security perspective, the Americas are becoming more like other Third World regions and less like Europe.

Interests and Threats

The conventional concept of security is the defense of one state against a direct, armed attack from another. Although attack can and sometimes does happen in the Americas, a more likely scenario might involve domestic fighting that spills over borders. So national security in the Americas is more than simple defense against aggression. States also must seek to remain free from internal and external threats to national interests, defined not only in military terms but in political and economic terms. To survive and flourish, they must protect the homeland, advance "vital interests," defend their credibility, and promote national values. Depending on their power and disposition, states may also try to shape, not just adapt to, the international scene.

On the face of it, the United States and Latin America have everything to gain and nothing to lose from pursuing these interests in the Western Hemisphere. Regional wars, both contained and contagious, could imperil everyone's security. Even if fought on someone else's turf, war in the Americas would be a nightmare come true for U.S. security. It would threaten U.S. efforts to control domestic and international events in Latin America and offer an invitation to unwanted intruders. It would divert security resources from other critical areas and jeopardize "vital interests" and even territorial inviolability. And it would make the defense of the United States itself a central issue in the hemisphere for the first time since the Cuban Missile Crisis.

The demise of a stable peace is no less ominous to Latin America. War could topple ruling elites, decimate already marginal economies, threaten the stability of neighbors, attract the involvement of powerful outsiders with their own agendas, and cause untold human deprivation in terms of direct casualties and social disruption. In sum, war in Latin America would exact an enormous price from those least able to afford it. So it comes as no surprise that, even in this era of declining hegemony, the United States and Latin America share basic values and see some fundamental security issues in the same light.

But beyond these basics, the consensus begins to dissolve. National security interests, and threats to them, rarely converge; and as time goes by, they actually seem to diverge even more. At only a few turning points in the past was a consensus reached, such as during the Axis threat during the 1940s and the guerrilla threat in the 1960s.[2] When national security interests are refracted through specific issues and events, interests and perspectives may splinter rather sharply, and consensus exists only on a dwindling set of shared values. Thus, the agreement on security in the Americas does exist, but it is limited and decreasing, as disagreement on how to ensure security is growing. It seems the states of the Americas can concur on what no one wants, but they find it far more difficult to define what all *do* want.

There are three primary dimensions to this emerging divergence over security in the Americas: (1) global vs. regional perspectives; (2) strategic-military vs. political-economic concepts; and (3) hegemony and paternalism vs. autonomy and self-reliance.

First, the national security interests of the United States in Latin America are global and strategic; those of Latin America are regional, but, if they are global, they are economic rather than strategic. Second, the United States pursues security and political stability with minimal change, believing that these can be "enforced" through the application of military and other power resources. Latin America, on the other hand, seeks security through economic development (which may even run the risk of political instability) and believes that security must evolve over the long term through a more equally developed hemisphere. Third, the United States clings to a venerable vision: A hegemonic region is a secure one. For its part, Latin America glorifies autonomy from the hegemonic state.

Security of the Hegemonic State

Securing the Americas, from the U.S. perspective, means making the region a congenial stage for exercising U.S. power to achieve its hegemonic aims. This view of security has less to do with the direct defense of the United States itself, although this is usually invoked to justify the exercise of power. More problematic are specific, "objective" U.S. *interests.* For example, the United States wants an open and secure Panama Canal and open sea-lanes in the Caribbean. However, such interests cannot fully explain the inordinate attention the United States pays to Latin America from time to time.

The tacit security interest that consumes so much U.S. energy is hegemonic restoration. To secure Latin America and U.S. interests there is to make the Americas safe for U.S. power and while maintaining a regional system of control. Ultimately, this entails defending against internal and external threats, promoting "vital interests," promoting national values, and making as well enforcing rules of conduct in the Americas and within the countries of Latin America.

Strategic Interests

The United States is a great power with grand strategies for coping with its great rival—the Soviet Union. Global, strategic interests rivet U.S. attention not on Latin America itself but on the Soviet Union and what it may be doing in Latin America. Strategic concerns are directed at the perceived Soviet headway made by the Soviet Union and its allies in Latin America, and they are used to explain and justify intervention to protect U.S. interests in that region. Thus, the principal security interests of the United States do not lie *in* Latin America as much as they are mediated *through* Latin America. It is the real or imagined Soviet presence (or that of its minions) that ties U.S. global strategy to Latin America and calls for intervention by the United States in the Americas.[3]

U.S. interventionism and Soviet opportunism meet in Latin America. As one analyst has stated,

> Washington's view that outside meddling in Central America constitutes a challenge to U.S. hegemony has changed little from the early decades of the century, and the Soviet Union's readiness to try to take advantage of political instability there has not changed much either.[4]

U.S. intervention can and has occurred without Soviet intrusion, of course. Yet Soviet interest in Latin America usually precipitates U.S. intervention of some sort.

The United States assumes several tasks as defender of the Americas. First, the Soviet Union must be kept out. Failing that, it and its client states must be contained. Second, U.S. interests cannot abide hostile (or leftist) states for they could become Soviet pawns. In addition, strategic interests intrude upon domestic affairs. If the United States "allows" a revolution to succeed, it has conceded another potential ally to the Soviet Union. Preventing or dislodging radical states from power is therefore both a hegemonic and a strategic imperative. Third, the United States must discourage Soviet assistance to client states. This means that no corner of the Western Hemisphere can be turned over to the military use of the Soviet Union. Although the United States is unable to banish the Soviet presence in Cuba, the Soviet military there was restrained by the U.S.-Soviet negotiations over the Cuban Missile Crisis. The dilemma currently facing the United States is that, although taking tough measures against Cuba or Nicaragua may weaken these countries, it may also expand the Soviet commitment to defend them.

Stability

The stability of the international and regional order has a high place in the hierarchy of U.S. security interests. The United States seeks friendly, stable allies who will not upset the hegemonic system in the Americas with radical domestic experiments, support the Left in neighboring countries, realign with global adversaries, or rebuke the old rules governing foreign relations within the hemisphere.

Yet a stable, liberal world order, of which Latin America is a part, requires a hegemonic state that is ready and willing to sustain such an order, just as it needs cooperative, even pliant states to accept it. Therefore, not just any type of stability will do. This helps us understand why the United States has sought destabilization of some states in the Americas while seeking long-term stability of the entire hegemonic system. When the United States acts as an insurgent, it is seeking to paper over the cracks in the stability of the system. All leftist regimes are likely targets of such a strategy: Arbenz of Guatemala, Castro of Cuba, and the Sandinistas in Nicaragua. Even nonleftist regimes sometimes go too far or mishandle matters, and the United States, later rather than sooner, has forsaken them when they could no longer control the situation or when they became a liability for U.S. strategic interests. Somoza in Nicaragua, Marcos in the Philippines, Batista in Cuba, Trujillo in the Dominican Republic, the Shah of Iran, and Noriega of Panama were all "abandoned" by the United States at some point. The underlying standard is that the United States will use destabilization against those who defy the rules, values, and vital interests as it defines them. Hegemonic intervention, then, is the use of force in search of a restored, preferred status quo.

Stability also calls for crisis management. Woven among the years of benign neglect are intense periods of panic in U.S. security circles when the decline of internal political order in a regional ally has threatened the stability that U.S. power craves. Though the security interest of stable, friendly, and prosperous countries may be served in the long run, the yearning for stability in the short term and the declining ability of the United States to guarantee such a state of affairs often produces an ephemeral air of crisis.

Crises and instability in U.S.–Latin American relations can, of course, arise from revolution, which evokes a defensive response from the United States that is fed by perceived Soviet involvement. Cuba, Guatemala, Grenada, the Dominican Republic, El Salvador, and Nicaragua have all, at one time or another, tested U.S. tolerance. Although the U.S. grip over Latin America is looser than the Soviet hold over Eastern Europe in the pre-Gorbachev era, the U.S. threshold of tolerance for revolution has always been low for, as seen from Washington, D.C., stability and revolution are irreconcilable.

The goals of checking Soviet influence and maintaining regional stability are tied to one another. In the U.S. view, instability is exported to Latin America by expansionistic opportunists who have no interest in letting things proceed as they have in the past. The search for stability is, therefore, the search for ways to deny a Soviet presence.[5] The problem is that the conditions leading to instability come from many sources, including from Latin America itself and from the world at large. However, the United States believes that, if forced to choose, stability not only takes precedence over but is a precondition for solving these problems of development.

Control

Hegemony requires control over Latin America even if the Soviet Union were effectively kept out of the hemisphere. It is the underlying concern of a hegemonic state, and it is necessary to protect strategic interests. Even now, in the twilight of its preeminence, the United States seeks to dominate key parts of the hemisphere, although it denies this interest or rationalizes it in terms of national security. Management of the region from Washington, as difficult as that has become, is considered indispensible, and the critical issue facing the hegemonic state today is how to mix force and consensus to accomplish this. The issue of control in the Caribbean Basin is justified with strategic and security rationales that are political as much as they are military. The control imperative arises from a deeply rooted belief among U.S. policymakers that instability compromises U.S. security.[6] Expansionistic communism, Latin American vulnerability, and relentless subversion are the primal fears of a security mentality. But concern over the consequences of losing geopolitical control of the Basin also play a part. As a result, the United States imposes (or reasserts) its dominance over the region to guarantee control of the far southwestern perimeter of NATO in the unlikely event of a major strategic crisis in Europe. Sea-lanes, communications, bases, and access to strategic raw materials in the Basin could be at stake. The Panama Canal would be even more vital in wartime; one half of NATO's supplies are shipped from gulf ports in the United States, and 45 percent of all oil imports to the United States come through the Caribbean Sea. Thus Central America becomes a symbol of the virility of U.S. power, and the presence of Soviet bases, as unnecessary as they might be, would symbolize a fading giant. For every real or imagined threat, there is a nightmare that feeds the security rationales, which make the most of the Basin as a vital interest and spin out worst-case scenarios that are both remote and possible.

True, this area is a transit route for raw materials, but the United States does not depend on Latin America for more than the majority of its strategic minerals. Furthermore, the U.S. advantage in controlling the Caribbean would be overwhelming even if the Soviets were to commit more of their navy to Caribbean operations. The Basin is also less vital in economic terms, and direct foreign investment there and in Latin America is not large.[7] Clearly then, control of the Caribbean Basin is a security issue. But it would be vital to the United States only in times of severe crisis, and by that time, many other regions in the world would also become vital.

Control is tested most strenuously by revolutions which challenge U.S. control. Revolutions are perceived as jeopardizing concrete, parochial, and economic interests, but they also convey a broader message of defiance: The system itself is being challenged. To keep a hostile element such as the radical Left from coming to power in a political system, the United States has resorted to a venerable option—intervention. It intervened in Nicaraguan politics in the 1920s and 1930s to install Somoza; in the 1980s, it intervened indirectly to expel the enemies of Somoza dynasty. To control the foreign relations of its hegemonic system, the United States also seeks to control the domestic politics of those states in that system.

U.S. security interests are affected and even defined by the *threats* made to those interests. In Latin America, these interests have been defined broadly; consequently, threats lurk almost everywhere. Besides the obvious—the threat to the territorial integrity of the United States itself—there are four basic threats to the interests of the hegemonic power in the Americas: (1) Soviet/Cuban intrusion into U.S.-controlled areas of the Americas; (2) intraregional subversion by the Left; (3) challenges to U.S. power and credibility; and (4) challenges to hegemonic control over internal and international rules, norms, and behavior.

If the United States seeks to exclude the Soviets from the Western Hemisphere, actual Soviet involvement is clearly a threat to this goal. Today, the Sovietization of Cuba is a regional reality, and the Soviet Navy regularly plies the south Atlantic. Still, changes in the Soviet Union may ripple across the Atlantic to Cuba and Latin America, perhaps serving this interest of the United States and lowering the threat to U.S. influence.

The threat of intraregional subversion rests on the assumption that radical regimes in Latin America are inherently expansionistic: Once they have consolidated their power, they turn their eyes towards vulnerable neighbors. Carried to its logical conclusion, this view of subversion as an external contaminant targets not just Nicaragua's neighbors but also Mexico and, in a more alarmist view, even the United States. Revolution leads to external aggression.

The third threat, the credibility trap, poses a subjective challenge to U.S. power because it projects the image and to some extent the reality of the United States as an inept or ineffectual giant. If the United States stakes its credibility as a great power on its ability to control a domestic situation in its own backyard and then fails to do so, this could raise doubts about its power and its will to lead non-Communist states elsewhere in the world. How great can a great power be if it cannot expel the Sandinistas from power?

The fourth threat concerns the erosion of the values and norms of hegemony. If the hegemonic power cannot or will not enforce the accepted rules of behavior among states and if Latin America no longer sees these rules as fair or legitimate, then military power cannot obliterate the threat. Panama under Noriega defied the rules by dealing with Libya and the Soviet Union. Nicaragua received much of its military aid and a good deal of its economic assistance from the Eastern bloc. And Brazil suspended payment on the principal of its foreign debt for about one year. This is not "acceptable" behavior, according to the United States, but it is not always able to make others abide by its rules. A weakened sense of subjective hegemony can make a more troublesome region even more difficult to govern.

The rule that most essentially defines the U.S. interest and the threat to the United States from Latin America is exclusivity. Above all, the United States seeks to preserve its exclusivity in Latin America. In other words, the myth governing U.S. security thinking in the hemisphere is that Latin America is the unofficial empire of the United States.

Security of Latin America

Basic security values are shared widely throughout the Americas. Among these core values are national viability, sovereign integrity, progress, democracy, stability, human rights, expanded international economic activity, a "place in the sun," independence, and multiple paths of development.[8]

However, an abstract consensus on these values is one thing; defining security interests in terms of the concrete realities of power and threats is quite another. There is no doubt that U.S. power weighs heavily on Latin America, and this cannot help but affect perceptions about interests and threats to those interests. But interests evolve over time and with changes in power. As power has shifted throughout the hemisphere, perspectives on security interests and threats became more, rather than less, splintered.

Regional Interests

The security interests of Latin American countries are regional, rather than strategic. Despite their rise in the world power structure, these states of Latin America have national, regional, or Third World interests to protect, and they become absorbed by broader strategic concerns only when they imperil such interests. Furthermore, the area's security interests and the threats to them come from within or, are rooted in other regional concerns. Unlike the United States, Latin American countries see extrahemispheric threats to their security as remote. And when they do occur, they may take on the guise of a North-South conflict (such as the Malvinas/Falklands war) rather than that of an East-West conflict.

Threats often shape the security interests in Latin America. First of all, though direct threats to U.S. territory from Latin America are virtually absent, the reverse is not the case. And the imprint of history on the security views of Latin Americans is indelible: When aroused to action, the hegemonic power does intervene in Latin America. The threats can also come from next door. Thus, regional military threats, border disputes, and U.S. intervention may all risk the security of Latin America.

Internal security, even in more developed states, remains the predominant obsession. Drug traffickers in Colombia are essentially an alternative government unto themselves. Insurgents roaming the countryside in Guatemala, Nicaragua, and El Salvador imperil domestic order. And the use of terror by the Shining Path (*Sendero Luminoso*) in Peru forces the government to redouble its efforts to gain domestic control.

Latin American states worry about threats from both the United States and the Soviet Union, not just from one of them. The United States warns of Soviet adventurism, but Latin Americans vividly recall the history of U.S. interventionism. And just as revolution is the most severe threat to the internal security of Latin American states, revolutionary governments have the most to fear from U.S. intervention.

Economic Security

In the Latin American perspective, security and economic development go hand in hand, and the economic dimensions of security are constantly on the front burner in Latin America because the region cannot be secure unless it is economically developed. But, for the United States, the economic dimensions of security are more incidental, although, at times, economics is used as a strategic weapon to thwart a revolution or calm a crisis. The debt problem of the 1980s is illustrative. Latin America saw this as a critical security issue, but the United States ignored it in these terms.[9] Therefore, for Latin America, security can be a North-South issue as well as an East-West one.

Economic security has long been reflected in Latin American priorities. After World War II, the United States and Latin America found it hard to view the world in the same terms or from the same perspective. For the United States, the central issue in U.S.–Latin American relations was anticommunism. The stability of the region was guaranteed by U.S. containment of Soviet power. As much sense as this might have made to most North Americans at the time, it was not the most pressing security interest for Latin America itself.

What most preyed on the security thinking of the Latin American states was their sense of economic weakness and underdevelopment. What they most sought from the United States was a plan to elevate their place in the world, not a shield to protect them from Soviet expansionism. Latin Americans believed their security as viable states in the postwar world required economic growth and development. Anticommunism was seen as strategic rather than an economic goal, and it was peripheral, if not totally irrelevant, to the security of Latin America.

Autonomy

The widespread conviction in Latin American states is that security is best served if they have a degree of autonomy from the United States. This is not to say that autonomy is possible or even desirable all the time. But it does rest on assumptions about who can best defend the security of Latin America and and what constitute the most formidable threats to that security. The smothering embrace of hegemony may be in the security interests of the United States, but it is not perceived to be in the best interests of Latin America.

If a global threat to the region were imminent and real, then the protective wing of the U.S. eagle would make sense for Latin America. But if the very act of U.S. intervention strips Latin America of its own security, then putting more distance between U.S. and Latin American security interests is vital to Latin America.

U.S. hegemony and Latin American autonomy are divergent, perhaps irreconcilable, issues of the hemispheric security. For the United States, its power is equated with its security; for Latin America, U.S. power is often seen as the main security threat. Therefore, security becomes a fault line between the powerful and the not-so-powerful and between the haves and the have-nots.

Security issues embody basic cleavages in U.S.–Latin American relations that reflect the diversity of national power in the Americas. Faced with an interdependent existence of unequal states, security interests and threats to those interests are naturally seen in different terms.

Security and Military Power

In terms of security, the central paradox of hegemonic decline is that the United States has vast military capabilities but cannot, on many occasions, use them to achieve its aims in the Americas. What exactly are the military capabilities of the United States and Latin America and what role do they play in managing security issues in the Americas?

Although military power is often seen as vital for the defense of the state, it does not guarantee security. For example, the military might of Israel dwarfs that of its Arab neighbors; it has ensured for now the defense and survival of the Israeli state. Yet Israel exists in a constant state of insecurity. Military power may deter attack, but it alone cannot foster a sense of security.

The United States is still militarily preponderant, even preeminent, in military capabilities in the Western hemisphere. On virtually every important measure, the United States is ahead—often far ahead—of Latin America. In fact, the disparities in military power are so great they almost defy meaningful comparisons. Consider the following:

1. U.S. defense spending is about *twenty* times greater than that of *all* of Latin America.[10] (See Table 6.2.) As years go by, Latin America spends more on defense, but so does the United States. For example, Latin America spent 31 percent more on defense in 1983 than it did in 1973. But, with the Reagan buildup, the United States increased military spending, both in absolute terms and in terms of the U.S. GNP. Military spending per capita in the United States is about twenty-seven times greater than in Latin America, and the it spends almost ten times more per soldier than does Latin America.
2. The United States also has far more people in uniform than does all of Latin America. During the 1980s, there were about one million more U.S. soldiers than there were Latin American soldiers. In a country of 232 million, the U.S. military makes up 0.95 percent of the population. In Latin America, only two countries— Cuba and Uruguay—equal or surpass this percentage.

3. Defense spending in the mid-1980s accounted for 6.4 percent of the GNP of the United States, whose economy was three times the size of Latin America's. Only Cuba and Nicaragua committed as much or more of their economies toward defense in relative terms.
4. The U.S. military has a *global* reach with the vast strategic and conventional forces of a superpower. By contrast, the military forces of Latin America are *local*. Modest and conventional, they are shaped around the more limited goals of internal security and border defense.
5. Self-sufficiency is another difference. The United States is far more self-reliant for its own defense than Latin America is. However, it is less self-sufficient than it once was. The United States imports some strategic minerals from Latin America and elsewhere, but it is virtually self-sufficient in technology and weaponry. In addition, it is a large net exporter of military equipment and expertise. Latin America, in contrast, is very dependent upon outside sources of military power. Despite the arms export industry in Brazil and Argentina, the region as a whole remains a net importer of military resources.

The gap between U.S. and Latin American military power is cavernous. The United States is a military superpower in the Americas to an even greater extent than it is in the world. And by these and other measures, its strength appears overwhelming. Yet what does this predominance in military might really mean for securing the Americas? There is less to this military predominance than first meets the eye.

There are several compelling reasons for deflating the U.S. advantage in Latin America.

1. Military power in and of itself falls short of securing hegemonic interests in the Americas. More tanks, artillery, helicopters, and troops do not guarantee security and sometimes may even induce greater insecurity. Military power is most effective when it deters aggression, and it must have a specific mission, with a good match of goals to resources, as well as the support of important groups. This is often not the case in the Americas.
2. The use of force is a peculiar issue in the post-Vietnam United States. Its citizens and Congress are willing to acquire military might, up to a point, but it is quite something else again for them to approve its use in Central America or elsewhere. There are no blank checks on the use of force, although a shrewd president knows just how far he can go. Having the military

TABLE 6.2   Comparative Military Spending, 1982

	Public Expenditures per Capita		Public Expenditures per Soldier		Public Expenditures per Sq. Km.		Economic-Social Standing
	Rank	US $	Rank	US $	Rank	US $	
WORLD		147		26,373		5,074	
Developed		487		52,141		9,665	
Developing		43		9,808		1,934	
AMERICA							
North America		788		88,742		10,476	
United States	9	845	7	89,228	23	20,975	4
Canada	27	252	9	75,707	87	622	7
Latin America		31		9,054		576	
Argentina	58	72	57	11,783	85	766	44
Barbados	74	32	80	8,000	25	20,000	30
Bolivia	92	18	120	3,741	125	92	89
Brazil	86	20	70	9,436	107	303	56

Country						
Chile	48	100	59	11,186	74	1,433	50
Colombia	92	18	86	7,441	93	444	68
Costa Rica	--	--		---		---	64
Cuba	45	111	74	8,516	37	9,478	39
Dominican Republic	95	17	112	4,417	65	2,163	80
Ecuador	79	28	98	5,795	84	796	61
El Salvador	75	31	97	5,800	45	6,905	91
Guatemala	108	12	108	4,895	82	853	93
Guyana	79	28	122	3,143	123	102	72
Haiti	120	5	123	3,125	80	893	119
Honduras	99	15	106	5,000	89	536	96
Jamaica	86	20	44	15,000	53	4,091	51
Mexico	102	14	76	8,317	91	506	58
Nicaragua	58	72	71	9,091	71	1,538	69
Panama	99	15	127	2,900	97	377	45
Paraguay	85	21	111	4,500	115	177	74
Peru	78	29	119	3,882	94	411	73
Trinidad & Tobago	72	41	36	23,000	38	9,200	32
Uruguay	37	140	47	13,600	63	2,318	37
Venezuela	58	72	30	28,342	75	1,274	48

Source: Adapted from Ruth L. Sivard, World Military and Social Expenditures, 1985 (Washington, D.C.: World Priorities, 1985), p. 30.

capabilities to reach out across the region is preferred to actually using them.

3. The use of force to achieve complex political goals is at times counterproductive. In a turbulent domestic situation in which rival factions vie for power, U.S. military action may do more harm than good, and the political fallout from the the use of force may override any military advantage. In Grenada, U.S. might was successful, and even welcomed by most of the population, but in a more complex and mobilized society, it could add fuel to the fire, leading to less control over an eventual outcome.

4. An overwhelming military advantage can be inappropriate because it is not geared to low-intensity conflict. For example, the high-tech weaponry for which the United States is well known has its limits in the jungles and mountains of Central America. Every one remembers the loss of high-tech strategy to low-tech strategy in Vietnam. Thus, military preeminence is devalued somewhat where political and ideological factors are more important. The kinds of military resources in which the United States is so impressive are not as useful for waging a limited, proxy war in Latin America.

5. Priorities are mismatched. Most often, this is to Latin America's advantage. For the United States, Latin America is usually on the back burner, with Nicaragua and Cuba being possible exceptions. But for Latin America, the United States is always on the front burner. With higher priorities elsewhere, the United States devotes a small fraction of its attention to the Americas. In contrast, Latin America devotes *most* of its attention there.

6. The military balance in the Americas is hardly etched in marble. It is shifting, ever so slowly and has changed enough to give Latin America limited capabilities to do limited things. A small change in military capability must be taken seriously because conflict in the Americas is often waged on a low budget and with relatively unsophisticated arms. Though still weak in armament, Latin America does have some military powers, including Cuba and Brazil, and the region is part of a world-wide balance of power. The world comes to Latin America bearing arms. The arms of Latin America once were stamped "Made in the U.S.A"; today they are also made in Europe, Israel, the Communist bloc, and in Latin America itself.

The quest for military power propels change. First, building military power is everyone's priority. This is equally true for those who can afford it and for those who cannot. Second, the militarization of the

Americas reflects the shift of power in the hemisphere. At the top, of course, is the United States. Next come the regional military powers: Cuba, Argentina, Mexico, and Brazil. Third, the transfer of military capabilities reflects this shift of power and the less preeminent place the United States now holds in the arming of Latin America; it keeps its hand in the game but there are many players around the table.

Militarization has a high price tag—rarely does it come cheaply. In economically troubled countries, this is a harsh lesson. The "Big Five" in regional defense spending in 1982 were Argentina, Cuba, Brazil, Mexico, and Peru which each spent almost one billion dollars on defense that year. With its war against Britain fast approaching, Argentina outspent all the rest by a ratio of 10 to 1 and more than that in some cases. Not all of the "Big Five" were really big spenders, however. Only Peru and Argentina allocated sizeable portions of their federal budgets to the military. Still, the "Big Five" also had big problems to which revenue was not applied. Averaged together, Argentina, Cuba, Brazil, Mexico, and Peru only rank fifty-fourth among the world's nations in terms of economic and social well-being.[11]

Military Endowments

The "Big Five" command the greatest armed forces in Latin America. In descending order, Brazil, Cuba, Argentina, Peru, and Mexico are the largest in terms of personnel. In the mid-1980s, Brazil had about 277,000 in uniform; Mexico had about 120,500. Elsewhere in Latin America, the national armed forces are smaller and more like national constabularies than defense forces. (Table 6.3)

Latin America relies on the four branches of the army, navy, air force, and paramilitary forces. The armies of the region have more manpower than do the navies and other branches of the military establishment, which is, of course, to be expected because they are used for internal security, border defense, and territorial integrity. However, the navies and air forces of Argentina, Brazil, and Peru are substantial by Third World standards. What is more, El Salvador, Guatemala, Paraguay, and Peru rely on fairly large paramilitary forces to quell domestic upheaval. However, the armed forces of Latin America have only a modest reach beyond their own borders.

The region lags behind much of the world in military equipment and technology, due to need, circumstance, and affordability. Though many Latin American militaries are museums for equipment that is two or more decades old, some have upgraded lethal and nonlethal equipment and communications networks during the last decade. Brazil, Argentina, and Chile even manufacture their own military hardware

TABLE 6.3 Comparative Military Capabilities*

Country	Manpower**	Manpower Quality	Weapon Effective- ness	Infrastruc- ture and Logistics	Organiza- tional Quality	Coeffi- cient Average	Equiv- lent Units of Combat Capa- bility
United States	2068	1.0	1.0	0.9	0.8	0.9	1861
Brazil	274	0.4	0.4	0.4	0.3	0.4	110
Cuba	159	0.4	0.5	0.3	0.4	0.4	64
Argentina	133	0.4	0.4	0.4	0.3	0.4	53
Mexico	97	0.4	0.3	0.5	0.3	0.4	39

*Coefficients show quality of strength.
**In thousands.

Source: Adapted from Ray S. Cline, World Power Trends and U.S. Foreign Policy in the 1980s (Boulder, Col.: Westview Press, 1980), table 29, pp. 126--127.

for export to the Middle East, Africa, Belgium, Canada, and Latin America.[12] However, Latin America is not nuclear in military terms, although a nuclear future is not entirely out of the question. The Treaty of Tlatelolco, which prohibits nuclear weapons in Latin America, is in force for all but five countries (Argentina, Brazil, Chile, Cuba, and Guyana).

Like economic power, military might is unevenly distributed throughout the Americas. Just as there is an enormous gap between the United States and Latin America in military capabilities, so, too, is there is a less impressive but still significant gap between regional big powers, on the one hand, and all the rest of the countries in Latin America, on the other. The well-endowed countries are either allies of the United States, or industrializing states, such as Brazil and Argentina, or small radical states such as Cuba and Nicaragua armed for strategic or defensive reasons. (See Table 6.4.)

Military Transfers

Military transfers from one country to another have a role to play, too. The infusion of military aid may tip or level out the domestic balance of power *within* a small country, but the transfer of military capabilities does not usually entail a wholesale redistribution of military power within the Americas. However, arms transfers *do* tell us about how power and hegemony are changing at a more general level. Arms sales and grants, treaties, technology transfers, military training and education programs reflect the interests of states and the distribution of power; when these change, so do the patterns of transfers.

Since 1946, the United States has made use of both military and economic assistance to serve its security interests in the Americas. It has extended more than $16 billion in economic and military assistance to Latin America since the end of World War II. (This does not include private or multilateral financing.) Just over $2 billion was allocated for military purposes; the balance was technically classified as economic aid, regardless of its real intent or effect.

U.S. military assistance to Latin America mirrors the asymmetry of threat to U.S. security interests and it has been disbursed unevenly. A pro-U.S. government will get aid if imperiled by a domestic or foreign threat. A large country that has large needs for equipment to control the domestic population may receive a hefty allotment. Aid may be used to retain U.S. influence in Latin American politics and to lubricate inter-American relations. Insurgency against a regional ally can also bring aid, as happened in El Salvador during the 1980s. In fact, that country with five million inhabitants was the foremost recipient of U.S.

TABLE 6.4 Latin American Defense

	Defense Spending (1985)		Military Personnel**				
	Total Spending*	As % of GDP	Total in Active Armed Forces	Army	Navy	Air Force	Para-Military
Argentina	4,685	3.1	78.0	45.0	20.0	13.0	27.0
Bolivia	129	2.1	27.6	20.0	3.6	4.0	19.0
Brazil	2,108	0.8	295.7	197.0	48.0	50.7	243.0
Chile	1,955	7.8	97.5	57.0	25.5	15.0	27.0
Colombia	301	0.8	66.2	57.0	9.0	4.2	55.0
Cuba	1,660	N.A.	175.5	145.0	12.0	18.5	1370.0
Dominican Republic	90	1.3	21.4	13.0	4.6	3.8	1.0
Ecuador	203	2.1	37.0	29.0	4.0	4.0	0.2
El Salvador	127	4.5	47.0	43.0	1.5	2.5	24.0
Guatemala	266	N.A.	40.2	38.0	1.5	0.7	736.6
Honduras	20	1.6	17.0	14.6	0.9	1.5	5.0
Mexico	1,221	0.7	254.5	105.0	23.0	6.5	120.0
Nicaragua	193	11.1	77.0	74.0	0.1	3.4	59.0
Paraguay	70	1.3	17.1	12.5	0.1	1.4	6.0
Peru	722	4.4	113.0	75.0	23.0	15.0	51.6
Uruguay	224	2.5	27.1	18.8	4.4	3.0	2.7
Venezuela	851	1.7	69.0	34.0	10.0	5.0	N.A.

*in millions of 1980 U.S. $
**in thousands

Source: Adapted from International Institute for Strategic Studies, The Military Balance 1987--1988 (London: I.I.S.S., 1987), pp. 221--222; 179--200 passim.

military assistance in the Americas; due to U.S. concern for "drawing the line" against the Left, its government received about 25 percent of *all* U.S. military assistance intended for Latin America.

Brazil was the only major military power in Latin America to receive a substantial infusion of military aid from the United States. Honduras, a small bulwark in U.S. security policy, that is sometimes referred to as the "U.S.S. Honduras," received some $234 million in aid, meant to sustain this thin reed upon which the Reagan administration depended in its war against Nicaragua. Chile received $177 million. Peru and Colombia received modest allotments of $151 million and $143 million, respectively. But most of Latin America gets little or nothing.

Arms transfers are an extension of U.S. security interests. By arming its allies, the United States protects itself against domestic and, to a lesser extent, foreign threats. This, at least, is the intent. The United States has been a major supplier of arms to Latin America for years, but it has refrained from showering an endless cornucopia of arms and military goods on the region. For domestic and regional reasons, it has even been tightfisted in both the quality and quantity of arms it hands out to Latin America. From 1979 until 1983, the United States disbursed land armaments (mostly field artillery). Most of the aircraft supplied were subsonic planes and helicopters; no missiles were dispatched. Such transfers were modest by world standards but reasonably generous by regional ones.

This policy trimmed the relative influence of the United States. Though the value of its arms transfers was by no means negligible, it was far from the main supplier. The most free-handed exporter of arms to Latin America was actually the prime adversary of the United States. Between 1979 and 1983, the Soviet Union sent $3.6 billion worth of arms to Latin America, 85 percent of which went to Cuba. In fact, during the same period, the United States was only the fifth largest supplier, trailing three European suppliers—Italy, Federal Republic of Germany, and France—that sent $715 million in arms to Latin America. But unlike the Soviet Union, which used its arms to keep Cuba afloat militarily, the United States dispersed its arms transfers more widely throughout the hemisphere, with Mexico, Venezuela, El Salvador, Argentina, and Brazil as the leading recipients of American largess.[13] Except in El Salvador, the U.S. policy was to give relatively little to several countries, rather than to give more to many or, as in the Soviet case, to give a lot to a few or even to only one.

Training programs for Latin America probably give an edge to the United States. Although the United States is not dominant in arms transfers, it is better situated to influence the officer corps of Latin America and U.S. education and training have been helpful for keeping communication channels open and sharing security views. From 1950 until 1982, 90,297 Latin Americans were trained under the U.S. international military education and training program (IMET).[14] Military leaders from the region have undergone counterinsurgency training in Panama and in the United States. And Hondurans and Salvadorans learn English at Lackland Air Force Base in Texas so that "they can deal with the weapons or military training their countries buy."[15] The United States has also assiduously cultivated good relations with the Latin American military establishments over decades. Nonetheless, nationalism in these organizations may diminish influence of U.S. training programs in the future.

Military treaties are another indication of the U.S. security presence in Latin America. Mutually binding legal agreements on subjects like military assistance, procedure, and missions reflect the prominent place in Latin America the United States occupies in Latin American military security. Such treaties used to be more common than they are now, as shown in Table 6.5. In the 1940s and 1950s, Latin America concluded 135 bilateral treaties with other countries on military and security issues. In the 1960s and the early 1970s, the total dropped to 82. The participation of the United States made a difference. In the earlier, more prolific years, it was a partner with Latin American countries in 78.5 percent of these treaties. Later, its role declined to 63 percent of all military treaties in the region. Clearly, U.S. military treaties with Latin America are not as important as they were during the apogee of hegemony.

Military power has changed in the Americas, but not drastically. Today, everyone has greater military stores, if not greater security. The really significant change is that Latin America now has more resources and more transfers of military resources, rather than the fact that the United States is still far and away the truly muscle-bound colossus of the north. Military power in the Americas equates more with prestige and the redistribution of power than with resolving national security issues which are an ordeal for both the United States and Latin America. Bringing security to the hemisphere involves more than applying military power to a problem. Indeed, such military power may imperil as well as safeguard the security interests of the Americas.

Security Issues

There is something almost immutable about U.S.–Latin American security issues. Names, faces, and places change, but the bedrock issues seem forever etched in the context of the hegemonic system. For example, U.S. irritation in the 1940s and 1950s with Juan Perón of Argentina

TABLE 6.5   Latin American Military Treaties,* 1946--1975

Country	1946--1960		1961--1975	
	U.S.	Total	U.S.	Total
Argentina	8	21	8	25
Bolivia	5	5	4	8
Brazil	12	19	4	5
Chile	6	10	2	4
Colombia	5	7	3	4
Costa Rica	1	1	1	2
Dominican Republic	5	6	3	3
Ecuador	9	9	1	1
El Salvador	4	4	3	3
Guatemala	6	6	3	3
Haiti	8	8	0	0
Honduras	6	7	3	3
Mexico	1	1	1	1
Nicaragua	6	6	3	3
Panama	1	2	3	3
Paraguay	3	7	5	6
Peru	13	13	2	3
Uruguay	2	2	2	3
Venezuela	5	5	1	2

*Military treaties cover the following topics: alliances,
armistice, arms control, military aid, military procedure,
military missions, occupation, and status of forces.

Source: Adapted from a special compilation by Peter H.
Rohn, Treaty Research Center, University of Washington,
Seattle, September 9, 1986.

was replaced by U.S. irritation with Antonio Manuel Noriega in the late 1980s. While Castro remains high on a list of U.S. nemeses dating from the 1960s, Daniel Ortega was added to the ranks, as well. An eerie sense of *déjà vu* pervades U.S.–Latin American relations.

What has changed is the ability of the United States to define and resolve security issues. Very gradually, the tide is running against the United States on some of these matters. This does not mean that the United States can no longer defend itself against direct and immediate threats, but it is having a difficult time of defining and defending its historical concept of security interests based upon a traditional hegemonic role.

Several enduring security issues are now surfacing in new ways in the Americas, including: (1) *U.S. intervention,* (2) *defense of the hemisphere,* (3) *adaptation to pluralism in the region,* and (4) *multilateral resolution of conflict.*

Intervention

Intervention is the "central unresolved issue in U.S.–Latin American relations."[16] It is also one of the most durable. As recycled during the 1980s, it is a policy of hegemonic restoration that is very much alive today. And, as events in Grenada and Panama proved, even U.S. *military* intervention is not dead. Interventionism still permeates the hemisphere.

Intervention is troublesome in several ways. First, it provokes negative reactions. The secrecy behind the Iran-contra affair was meant to support interventionism in the face of domestic and foreign opposition. But an interventionist alliance may well be countered by an antiinterventionist alliance, both inside and outside of the United States. Second, intervention may fail. The success of Guatemala in 1954 and of Grenada in 1983 lends little comfort to those who might have high hopes for it working in Central America. The Guatemala of 1954 is not the Guatemala of the 1980s; Grenada and Panama are not Nicaragua. While intervention may get rid of an irritant or a rascal, it hardly solves the problems of the country. Third, intervention erodes what little consensus may still exist in the Americas over security issues. The norm of nonintervention has been a part of the legal and ethical superstructure of the inter-American system for decades. However ineffectual that system may be for resolving conflict, it is one of the few remaining threads of agreement in Latin America about what should *not* be done by the United States to cope with security problems. The message imbedded in U.S. interventionism is: If a regional consensus fails to underwrite U.S. hegemony, then the sword will be taken from the scabbard and used *without* Latin American approval. If intervention by the United States unites Latin America, intervention by Latin America promises to divide it. As hegemony declines, the region itself has fallen prey to a mild virus of interventionism. Costa Rica intervened politically in Nicaragua during the twilight of Somoza during the late 1970s; the Contadora intervened in the Central American crisis during the mid-1980s. Curiously then, Latin America opposes U.S.intervention, but finds itself practicing it in a milder form to serve its own goals.

Hemispheric Defense

Just as Latin America dreads U.S. intervention, the United States abhors a strategic threat from outside the region. The two possibilities have been historically bound together ever since the Monroe Doctrine and its corollaries warned outsiders about intruding into Latin America, then reserved unto itself the right of the hegemonic state to do exactly what it cautioned not to do.

Defense of the hemisphere and U.S. hegemony in the area are actually two sides of the same coin; the coin is the power of the United States to dictate Latin America's foreign and domestic affairs. Coleman argues that a primary myth has been nurtured that "we rule you because it is in your own best interest to be ruled by us." What is more,

> The Monroe Doctrine has survived in the political mythology of the United States because it applies the primary myths to the circumstances of U.S. hegemony in the Americas [and] the Monroe Doctrine is the secondary myth required by the fact of U.S. hegemony in the hemisphere. The idea of protecting the hemisphere from the alleged malevolence of extrahemispheric forces is central to the themes of the primary myths.[17]

Historically, defending the hemisphere meant ruling it. Likewise, any outside presence which called this rule into question became a threat to the hemisphere. But this concept of defending the hemisphere is greeted less warmly in Latin America in recent decades because it has so often been invoked to justify interventionism. To be sure, most Latin American states are wary of superpower motives and actions, be they U.S. or Soviet, and two superpowers, let alone one, complicates the destinies of these states. Yet there is a resistance in the region to the idea of thinking about the Soviet-Cuban presence as a defense issue in the same way the United States does.

The Soviet military presence is modest, but, in Latin America, that may be enough to make political waves. Take troop strength, for example. The Soviets have 2,800 combat troops in Cuba. There are virtually none anywhere else in Latin America, although Soviet and East bloc advisers are assigned to Cuba and have been sent to Nicaragua. Total Soviet military personnel in Latin America may be about 8,000; most of them stationed in Cuba and perhaps as many as 40 or 50 are in Nicaragua.[18]

Cuba is the staging area for Soviet strategy in Latin America. The Soviet Union uses the island for both naval and naval air deployments; it conducts joint training operations with Cuban forces; it has established extensive signal intelligence facilities in Cuba. The island outpost has also become the Soviet's Nicaraguan connection, through which Soviet equipment was sent to Nicaragua: tanks, armored personnel carriers, reconnaisance vehicles, trucks, other vehicles, and mortars, not to mention the several Mi-24 helicopters used for counterinsurgency.[19] On the other hand, the Soviets have shown restraint. There are no surface-to-air missiles or sophisticated jet combat aircraft in Nicaragua.

The Malvinas/Falklands War in 1982 tested inter-American cohesion on hemispheric defense, and it was found wanting. The challenge came not from U.S. adversaries but from its closest ally—Great Britain. The U.S.–Latin American consensus on defending hemispheric interests against the West dissolved when the United States helped the British in their war against the Argentines. And just as the United States perceives Soviet-Cuban influence as a threat to hemispheric defense, Latin America sided with Argentina in asserting that the British had to give up their colonial anachronism, one way or the other. When the United States failed to take the same view, collective security and hemispheric defense were critically, perhaps mortally, wounded. Further, the 1982 war laid to rest the Monroe Doctrine for Latin Americans. However, the post-Malvinas era was much like that just preceding it. On the defense of hemisphere, the United States and Latin America would agree to disagree.

Pluralism

Security concerns in the Americas are political as much as military, and their political character is perhaps best exemplified in the issue of pluralism. Can and will different regimes in Latin America live next door to each other in relative peace, or is there something about different regimes that compels them to oppose (and even to engage in armed conflict with) one another? That is a critical challenge to security.

Latin America is a breeding ground for all kinds of regimes, whether they be authoritarian, quasi-authoritarian, quasi-democratic, democratic, and even totalitarian political experiments. And the future holds out the prospect for more, rather than less, pluralism. This is particularly evident in the Caribbean Basin and Central America, two subregions that have experienced the most severe bouts of insecurity.

Pluralism is a threat to security, according to the U.S. view during the 1980s, if it means radical states sharing borders with democratic ones. The United States believes that such radical states have expansionistic designs on their neighbors and that, when once they consolidate their own power at home, they will export help to insurgents. But some analysts view political and ideological pluralism as a challenge, not a threat. They contend that, as Latin America changes, we should expect more pluralism, and we must devise ways to live with this, not try to eradicate it. Whatever its type, they say, no regime in Latin America is inherently or necessarily expansionistic. On the pluralism stemming from the rise of revolutionary regimes, this view would offer this advice: "Accept it, befriend it, integrate it, and moderate it."

Even when stripped of its strategic overtones, pluralism challenges regional security in other ways. First, pluralism makes it harder to devise a regional consensus on security issues. It may raise the stakes for conflict and complicate the resolution of conflict as well. Second, pluralism may evoke animosity such as existed between Costa Rica and Nicaragua. In the longer term, it may force states to work harder at resolving disputes. Third, pluralism once again raises the temptation of intervention. A revolutionary state may lend support to guerrillas fighting a regime of another type. A democratic state in the region or even another type of state outside the region may funnel support to counterrevolutionaries, as became evident in the revelations of the Iran-contra affair. Fourth, pluralism challenges the Americas to come to terms with diversity. The cherished myth that all Latin America must march to the same beat dies hard. The region will change and as it does it will become more pluralistic. Some way must be devised to ensure that pluralism does not aggravate mounting tensions in an era of hegemonic decline.

Conflict Resolution

During the 1980s, the use of conflict to accomplish national goals eclipsed the multilateral resolution of disputes. Indeed, the unilateral pursuit of security interests through the limited use of force was the hallmark of hegemonic restoration. Latin America advocated multilateral settlements on Central American and foreign debt issues, but the United States only paid lip service to, avoided, or even subverted these independent attempts to devise alternative mechanisms to resolve conflict. Of course, the United States can ultimately veto any multilateral plan to bring peace to Central America, but it might eventually be possible for a group of Latin American states to prevail upon the United States not to execise that veto.

For the multilateral resolution of conflict to succeed, a negotiated settlement must accomplish several things:

1. It must halt the flow of arms into the region and hold out the prospect of demilitarization. The great powers need to curb their regional involvement.
2. It must foster tolerance of the political and ideological pluralism in Central America at the same time that it tries to minimize its divisiveness. A *modus vivendi* between governments and opposition must be worked out.
3. It must guarantee the security interests of both radical and hegemonic states. Those caught in the middle must be convinced that they, too, will be secure. If the interests of the United States are narrowly defined, this may be possible. Or the security interests of states may change if their governments do. Nicaragua in the

1990s may not have the same security problems of Nicaragua in the 1980s.
4. It must enshrine a "live and let live" policy among the states. In other words, aggression across borders would invalidate a settlement and make a mockery of the belief that pluralism can be tolerated in close quarters.

Conflict resolution must work elsewhere in Latin America, too, and efforts must be reinvigorated to prevent, control, and deal with tensions *throughout* the Americas. New multilateral efforts to resolve Latin American conflicts could be constructed around specific subregions or issue areas, including arms control and proliferation, the containment of domestic conflict, and confidence building measures. To erect mechanisms for conflict resolution would take into account how complex international relations have become in the Americas. For now, it is challenging enough just to contemplate, let alone devise, a consensus between the north and the south on the principle that multilateral conflict resolution is worth resurrecting and pursuing as a security issue.

Securing the Americas or Securing Hegemony?

Are security and hegemony compatible in the Americas? Diversity in interests, threats, military capabilities, and bedrock issues suggest that they may not always be. The search for security seems quite illusive in an era of declining hegemony.

As mentioned earlier, the United States and Latin America share an abstract consensus on *values* about security. However, contention arises over specific challenges. For example, the United States and Latin America can agree on defending the Western Hemisphere from outside attack. But what if Soviet involvement comes via an invitation from within the Americas rather than from a military offensive? What if British colonialism in the South Atlantic is the target of an assault by Argentina?

The consensus on security is feeble; worse, the divergence on security is growing. In the United States, hegemonic policy is still often seen as a path to greater U.S. security. Yet this has not really proven to be true, and the attempt to restore hegemony in reality engenders even more insecurity in Latin America. Meanwhile, security goals in the hemisphere exceed military capacity. Despite its clear edge, the United States does not use its military power effectively to achieve political ends. And despite changes in *its* military prowess, Latin America cannot devise a pax Latina built on regional consensus and multilateral cooperation.

The ordeal of securing the Americas, too often, collides with the ordeal of restoring hegemony, as U.S. security interests remain tied to U.S. control. The United States can make the region tremble, but it cannot make it quiescent. The United States can attempt to impose its own security interests on all of Latin America and the weight of this is still keenly felt in some quarters of the region. But by unilaterally pursuing its own interests in this way, it may also sacrifice U.S.–Latin American relations in the name of national security.

Neither the United States nor Latin America can be secure under the view that hegemony can bring security to the Americas. The ordeal for Latin America is that it must live with a hegemonic state that has not yet adapted its security interests to changing times.

7

Economics and Debt

The ways in which economic growth and debt burdens affect Latin America will have a monumental influence on U.S. power in the future. The 1980s, a "lost decade" for Latin America, proved how vital economics can be. According to a former Mexican finance minister, "The 1980's have been called the 'lost decade,' because income and well-being levels [in Latin America] are no better, and in some cases are lower, in real terms than they were ten years ago."[1] This decade of economic travail and crushing debt was also a turning point in U.S.–Latin American relations, interrupting the gradual diffusion of economic power from the United States to Latin America. It halted, at least for a time, hegemonic decline in economic terms.

Debt casts a long shadow over the fate of hegemony. During the 1980s, the debt crisis not only proved that the decline of hegemony can be arrested if not reversed, it also confirmed the essential asymmetry of power in the Americas: The United States came out of the debt crisis far better situated than much of Latin America. Even more significant is the fact that failing to deal with the debt problem may make it all but impossible for Latin America to rekindle the growth it once experienced, the burden of debt may preempt the kind of economic growth that originally made the diffusion of economic power toward Latin America possible.

The third quarter of the twentieth century was a period of economic growth, signaling a modest shift in regional economic power. Latin American growth outpaced that of the United States for some three decades as population increases, growth in national product, rising per capita incomes, and Latin America's plunge into world export markets cut into the U.S. advantage in the hemisphere. The region was ready to be taken more seriously, and, by the mid-1970s, U.S.–Latin American relations were thought to be "maturing." The third quarter also prompted a modest decline in the U.S. relative advantage. But in the fourth quarter of the twentieth century, many of the earlier gains of Latin

America were lost, with recession and debt in the 1980s doing more damage to that region than to the United States. Clearly, issuing a death notice for hegemony based on the economic growth of the third quarter was premature. Furthermore, the fourth quarter has proven that the diffusion of economic power can be checked. In this unfortunate period, Latin American economies, large and small, reeled under the most severe recession since the 1930s. Across the board, they were wounded, even devastated, by the economic and debt crisis of 1982. And not only did the recession halt the limited progress of the third quarter for Latin America, but it also raised questions about the supposedly inevitable and irreversible decline of U.S. economic power *vis-à-vis* Latin America. If nothing else, the crisis recalled the vast power still residing in the north. As Paul Krugman stated, "the time [had] not yet arrived when the United States lost its ability to strike out on an economic course of its own and to shape the economic environment of others."[2]

Hegemony and Debt

Before the recession of the early eighties, U.S. growth rates were lower than those of Latin America; during the recession, they were higher. The U.S. economy also recovered more quickly. Latin America generally fell farther and harder than did the United States, especially those countries that had most challenged U.S. economic preeminence during the third quarter of the twentieth century. And they may not recoup the high growth rates of the past until the next century.

An essential goal of the hegemonic power is to stabilize the international financial system, by avoiding widespread default and by seeking to keep debtors liquid. Ultimately, stability is tied to the development and solvency of the debtors. But the 1980's debt crisis transcended international finance, and, according to Fishlow, "In the last analysis, the debt problem is a development problem."[3]

The debt crisis has profoundly affected U.S.–Latin American relations in three ways. First, it led to a reversal of the net transfer of financial and other economic resources; it began to flow northwards in the 1980s rather than towards Latin America. Coping with recession and debt in Latin America depleted the financial resources needed for future growth. Second, the debt crisis eroded subjective hegemony. It shredded regional confidence in the United States as a hegemonic giant able and willing to dictate a solution that would transcend its own national interests. Democratic leaders of the 1980s, Peru's Alan Garcia and Argentina's Raul Alfonsín, called for U.S. understanding because democracies must balance popular demands against debt repayment. And as the post-election economic riots in 1989 proved, the Argentines had had enough. Third, the debt crisis reinforced interdependence. The immense jump in the prices of staples for the Mexican working class may have meant little to North Americans, but the inability of Mexico to meet its financial obligations shook the financial boardrooms, not just in New York but throughout the U.S. heartland. This interdependence of debtor nations and creditors in the OECD countries had curbed the unilateral exercise of hegemonic power. In the end, preserving international financial stability, the main goal of the hegemonic state, may not entirely be up to the United States government alone. In fact, the United States has asked Japan and other countries to come to the rescue.

The Roots of Crisis

What happened in the third quarter of the twentieth century to set the stage for the economic setbacks suffered by Latin America during the 1980s? What brought about the debt crisis and the relative decline of Latin America's position in the hegemonic system?

Home-grown structural failures in the region's economies and the evolution of its dependency on the international economy in the 1970s, coupled with convulsive shocks imported from beyond its borders, interacted eventually to produce the worst recession experienced in Latin America since the 1930s. The roots of the crisis can be traced to both *external* and *internal* factors. They are tied to changes in advanced (OECD) countries and to Latin American responses to these changes. The crisis in Latin America also emerges from long-standing problems in economic structure and from the failure of developmental policy to overcome these problems.

External Causes

The crisis spread to virtually every nation, a persuasive reason to suspect that some causes precipitating and deepening the crisis were imported into Latin America. Dependency did not ebb during the era of general economic growth in the 1980s. Rather, Latin America's growth was still conditioned on outside forces.

> Although Latin America increased its relative economic strength . . . [before the crisis], the asymmetrical and unfavorable basis of its foreign relations, particularly with the U.S., has not changed substantially in the last two decades.[4]

Latin America's historical vulnerability to developments outside the region continued into the 1980s. A slowdown in the developed nations was felt globally but even more drastically in the developing world. And Latin America's growth was closely linked with that in OECD countries.

Economic interdependence affects this region differently than it does the developed OECD countries. Here, it is more vital, intense, and potentially harmful. The differences between the developing countries in Latin America and the developed nations of the world are exemplified in matters of trade. First, Latin America depends more upon trade than the OECD countries do and certainly far more than the United States does; it must trade profitably or it will falter. Second, developing countries in Latin America trade a great deal with the industrialized world but not always very effectively. Their trade is heavily vertical and asymmetric, rather than horizontal and symmetric. In other words, they endure unbalanced trade with rich nations. And during the 1980s, this structure was reinforced with the collapse of intraregional trade in the Americas. Third, trade in developing countries, especially in Latin America, is concentrated on just a few important partners. This pattern was reinforced for a brief time in the 1980s after decades in which Latin America had gradually moved away from the United States as a trading partner.

However, the debt crisis and economic recession in Latin America were triggered by more specific causes. For example,

1. *Terms of trade* for Latin America declined from the more favorable position of the 1970s.
2. High, floating *interest rates* in OECD countries critically affected many countries in Latin America that had resorted to massive foreign borrowing during the 1970s.
3. A sharp drop in the *net inflow of capital* brought new investment virtually to a halt, forcing Latin American governments to adopt brutal measures with very high price tags.[5]

A perennial issue for most Latin American countries are terms of trade, that is, how much a country can sell its exports for and how much it has to pay for its imports. Commodities, still a major component of Latin American exports, are subject to price volatility. Coffee, oil, and other raw material exports consequently provide an uncertain income. Nonetheless, Latin America on the whole did tolerably well during the 1970s. Thanks to oil and other commodity exports, some countries enjoyed favorable terms of trade for a while, although others, of course, were less well situated to benefit as generously from the economic growth of the 1970s.

There was a dramatic reversal, however, in the terms of trade after 1981, as Table 7.1 reveals. The oil crisis which had helped the region's

TABLE 7.1 Changes in Terms of Trade and in Current Accounts for the Western Hemisphere, 1967--1986 (in percentages)

	Terms of Trade	Current Account
1967--1976	3.2	----
1980	7.4	-29.3
1981	-5.7	-43.1
1982	-5.2	-42.1
1983	-1.5	-11.7
1984	-1.2	-5.5
1985	-1.0	-7.5
1986	-0.9	-6.8

Source: Adapted from IMF data in Chris C. Carvounis, The Foreign Debt/National Development Conflict (New York: Quorum Books, 1986), Tables 1, 3.

oil exporters for a time pushed the rest of the region into a severe current accounts deficit. As commodity exports prices began to weaken, rising prices for imports forced the deficits even higher. Soon, oil, once the black savior of Mexico, became a black demon in the mid-1980s; the international price of its oil dropped from about $25 a barrel to less than $10 a barrel within just a few months. Thus, unfavorable terms of trade cut into growth and made the debt crisis more acute.

Once the recession hit, terms of trade did not rebound in favor of the developing countries. In fact, just the opposite happened, and only spasmodic upward movements in prices brightened an otherwise depressed picture. In 1983–1984, non-oil developing countries posted a 1 per cent improvement in their collective terms of trade. In late 1984, a brief recovery in prices soon evaporated, leaving behind a 6.5 percent decline in non-oil commodity prices. Terms of trade did not return to 1980 levels, and most estimates, including those of the International Monetary Fund, predict they will remain depressed in the near future.[6] In sum, the "haves" held a clear advantage over the "have-nots" in the terms of trade during the 1980s.

The second economic blow came from interest rates. Monetary policy and particularly the high interest rates in the United States were devastating for Latin America for several reasons.

First, Latin America had resorted to heavy borrowing during the 1970s. The very high growth rates of Mexico and Brazil, for eample, were propped up, to some extent, by external borrowing at a brisk pace. This led Albert Fishlow to conclude that Latin America was practicing a development strategy of *debt-led* growth.[7]

Second, changes in financial flows during the years prior to the crisis brought forth harsh consequences. Latin America had turned more toward borrowing than toward investment for raising capital abroad. But public external financing could no longer meet this new demand. Rather, it became increasingly focused more on the specific problem of balance of payments. What most transformed the financial picture was the entry in a major way of foreign private lending into the Latin American capital markets. Petrodollars soon supplemented Eurocurrency as a major source of capital. And with an abundance of petrodollars and Eurocurrency, as well as a willingness of private banks to funnel them to Latin America, debt became a tempting addiction. The volatility of this highly concentrated source of capital became all too apparent in the financial downturn of the early 1980s. By using debt to gain outside financing, Latin America had set a course fraught with financial dangers.

Further complicating matters, privately funded debt had short-term maturities with high real interest rates, pushing Latin America to the wall just as servicing the debt or paying the interest on it became more difficult. This short-term, "floating rate" debt for the developing countries created a new and direct dependence on international financial markets. And the tight money policies of the United States in the early 1980s may have brought on an even deeper recession in the developing world than they did in the United States itself.[8]

High interest rates in the United States, coupled with other macroeconomic policies, further impoverished Latin America. The U.S. government ran up unprecedented fiscal deficits, more than doubling the federal debt during the first half of the 1980s. Whatever it might have done to the U.S. economy, the federal deficit was even more harmful to Latin America .because it had a "strongly negative impact on every external variable affecting LDC foreign debt repayment."[9]

Foreign demands for adjustment and austerity called for great sacrifice in Latin America, "not in the national accounts, but in the streets, the barrios, and the villages of the Third World where the very fabric of civil life has been rent by austerity cuts."[10]

Internal Causes

The economic recession and debt crisis in Latin America were home-grown, too, not just imported from outside the region. Latin America played a supporting role—perhaps even a featured role—in its own economic tragedy.

The internal causes of the crisis and recession stemmed from domestic structures, strategies, and policies.

1. *Development strategies* helped to bring on the crisis. Import substitution, export-led growth, dependency, and international monetarism are four models of development thinking. A consensus on which of these to pursue, and to what extent, has eluded Latin America. When translated into development strategies, they failed to head off or deal with the development problems of the 1980s.

2. Latin American governments in the 1970s followed development strategies addicted to *borrowing*. As we have seen, raising capital from private international borrowing was a fateful choice for Latin American policymakers.

3. Latin America adopted *monetary policies* that, taken together, eventually made matters worse. Liberalization of financing, high real interest rates, overvalued exchange rates, and short-term borrowing all contributed to the crisis.

4. *Fiscal policy* was out of control in much of Latin America. By spending more than they could afford, many governments were undercutting their economic situation. This boosted both prices and debt, making it more likely that a debt crisis and economic recession would materialize sooner or later.

5. The *policy response* to the crisis in Latin America was disappointing and even counterproductive, at least in the short term. Slow to respond with austerity measures, governments put on the brakes rather late. Tight monetary and fiscal policies during the 1980s may have been necessary at one point, but when and how they were applied deepened the recession throughout the region. The bitter medicine worsened the patient's condition for a time.

6. Foreign exchange and foreign capital were hard to come by due to domestic shortcomings such as *corruption, inefficiency, price distortions,* and *protectionistic subsidies.*

Debate on the internal and external causes of the crisis comes full circle on the issue of economic recovery. Those who hold to the view that the crisis was largely imported harbor a skepticism about the magic of the international marketplace as a solution. Those on the other side of the issue see recovery of the industrial countries as not only crucial for growth and recovery in Latin America but as the only hope for stimulating regional exports enough to make payments on the massive foreign debt.

Aftermath

The economic downturn in the 1980s jolted U.S.–Latin American relations, and it may take years, even decades, before all of the ramifications of the crisis surface. From the incomplete record of the 1980s, however, there is little room to doubt that Latin America has lost a great deal in relative terms and may not regain this lost ground for quite a while. The aftermath of the crisis affected growth, incomes, trade, investment, and aid in Latin America, and it put the region further behind the United States.

Economic recession and the debt crisis cut a wide swath through Latin America, affecting nearly every type of economic issue and every economic sector. Nearly every country was impoverished, although some were hit harder than others. And virtually every man, woman, and child felt the brunt of recession, directly or indirectly.

The economic distress of the 1980s cut across many issues. Debt curtailed growth, and dwindling trade made debt repayment harder. Foreign exchange had to be accumulated to retire some of the debt or pay the interest on it. Debt repayment depressed incomes, drying up domestic demand and economic growth. And lethargic growth subsidized debt repayment. As a result, Latin America's depressed position relative to the economic power of the United States may be perpetuated, making the "lost" decade of the 1980s the "long" decade as well.

Economic growth in Latin America had been buoyant until the 1980s. From 1950 until 1980, its GNP rose at average annual rate of 5.5 percent, and the volume of its economic activity was five times greater in 1980 than it had been thirty years earlier.[11] For its part, the United States managed growth rates of less than 3 percent during most of this time.

When growth slowed and then declined in the 1980s, the debt crisis became a growth crisis. Not only had growth rates of national economies shriveled and even turned downward, as in the cases of Argentina, Bolivia, and Costa Rica during 1981–1982, but growth rates in personal (or per capita) income were even more depressed throughout Latin America. In 1984, the Latin American economy was about the size it was in 1980 but there were thirty-three million more people to support by that time.[12] Economies *and* people suffered. The debt crisis was no distant abstraction.

The year 1983 was disastrous. Latin America as a whole experienced a −3.2 change in its growth rate. Yet many countries showed negative growth rates from 1981 until 1985. Even the regional Big Four—Argentina, Brazil, Mexico, and Venezuela—did not escape this assault on growth. Argentina was able to muster positive growth rates for only two years (1983 and 1984). Brazil suffered two years of negative growth. Mexico's recession bottomed out in 1983. After riding high on oil revenues as late as 1981, Venezuela did not fare as well, having virtually no positive growth from 1981 to 1985.

Elsewhere in Latin America, the record of the previous decades was tarnished in the 1980s. In fact, no country was able to sustain positive growth rates in each of the years between 1981 and 1985. At the depths of the recession, the big losers were Chile, Guyana, Haiti, Peru, Costa Rica, Bolivia, El Salvador, Uruguay, and Trinidad and Tobago.

Where growth was positive, it was still anemic, never reaching the rate that occurred during the third quarter of the twentieth century. Though Brazil, Chile, and Paraguay bounced back better than most, growth for Latin America as a whole in the mid-1980s was still only about half of what it was during the third quarter.

The recession changed the winners and losers in the Americas. During the 1970s, growth in U.S. GDP was 2.8 per cent; that of the Western Hemisphere was 5.8 percent. But the first half of the 1980s changed all that. (See Table 7.2.) For the first time in fifty years, the United States had higher growth rates than Latin America. The recovery in the United States also came quicker and was more robust.

Per capita income fell further and more broadly than did economic growth—the personal tragedy of the debt crisis. For the region, per capita income fell 12.5 percent between 1981 and 1983. Some countries were able to salvage positive economic growth from the recession between 1981 and 1985, but virtually no country had higher per capita incomes in 1985 than in 1980, with the possible exception of Panama. In 1984, per capita income in Mexico was at its 1978 level; Brazil's was at its 1976 level and, worst of all, Argentina's had dropped to its 1970 level.[13] Furthermore, the decline in per capita income in Latin American countries was steeper than in the United States and most other developed countries. For example, the region's per capita income was equal to 15.8 percent of that in OECD countries in 1980; four years later, it fell to 13.7 percent.

TABLE 7.2 Net Change in Real GDP and in GDP per Capita for Latin America, 1980--1984 (in percentages)

	GDP	GDP per capita
Argentina	+5.0	-13.2
Bahamas	+6.7	-3.3
Barbados	-5.0	-8.0
Bolivia	-19.0	-32.6
Brazil	+5.4	-8.8
Chile	-4.6	-10.8
Colombia	+7.4	-1.3
Costa Rica	-1.1	-10.9
Dominican Republic	-10.6	-0.8
Ecuador	+2.2	-7.0
El Salvador	-12.8	-17.3
Guatemala	-5.4	-15.4
Guyana	-17.7	-18.0
Haiti	-5.7	-10.2
Honduras	-1.1	-11.0
Jamaica	+5.9	-2.1
Mexico	+5.2	-5.4
Nicaragua	+8.9	-7.2
Panama	+9.0	-3.3
Paraguay	+7.4	-1.8
Peru	-5.1	-14.4
Suriname	-1.6	-0.1
Trinidad & Tabago	-3.5	-9.6
Uruguay	-12.3	-16.6
Venezuela	-6.9	-17.1
LATIN AMERICA	+0.2	-9.2

Source: Calculated from InterAmerican Development Bank, Economic and Social Progress in Latin America (Washington: IDB, 1985), Table 3, p. 388.

Trade

Latin American trade took two steps backward and one step forward during the worst of the recession in the early 1980s. Several trends at the height of the crisis were clear and mostly adverse for Latin America. First, the region earned less from its exports than before, as terms of trade deteriorated overall. Second, several countries expanded the volume of their exports to offset the declining terms of trade and to rectify as much as possible their beleaguered current accounts. Third, imports were trimmed drastically in an attempt to cope with the debt by imposing austerity on domestic consumption and investment. Fourth, trade among Latin American countries all but plummeted during the depths of the crisis, especially for the primary goods exporters of the region.[14] This was a setback to the gradual trend toward greater intraregional trade. And fifth, the trend away from trade dependence on the United States was actually reversed in 1983–1984. This important, if temporary, reversal came at the expense of trade with other OECD countries and with Latin America itself.

The economic recession and the debt crisis bludgeoned imports. They declined an average of 12.3 percent a year between 1982 and 1984,[15] and as a percent of GDP they returned to the levels of the early and mid-1970s. Obviously, putting imports through the ringer was a function of recession. U.S. exports to Latin America and the Third World slowed, Latin America importing $12 billion less in 1985 than in 1981.[16] In the early 1980s, Mexico slashed its imports by two-thirds in a two-year period; Argentina and Brazil cut theirs in half. As a result, the U.S. trade balance with Latin America and the Caribbean went from a $1.3 billion surplus in 1981 to a $17.9 billion deficit in 1983.[17] But U.S. trade value with Latin America did not change significantly between 1980 and 1984.[18]

To compensate, Latin America stepped up its exports. Its primary markets were the OECD countries and the United States, where affluents were able to absorb more exports at lower prices during their faster paced recovery. For some, the results were dramatic. Between 1980 and 1984, Brazil turned its trade balance around, turning a $7.8 billion deficit in 1980 to a $13 billion surplus four years later. Another member of the regional Big Four, Mexico, was even more impressive. Mexico went from a trade deficit of $4 billion in 1981 to a trade surplus of $14 billion in 1985.[19] In 1983–1984, although seven countries suffered negative growth in exports, eighteen others registered gains, with Brazil being the leading exporter by far that year. However, impressive as this might be, it pales in comparison to the need to earn even greater surpluses in lieu of massive foreign debt.

With the economic downturn, trade dependency on the United States grew at the same time that Latin American economic growth shrunk. Until the early 1980s, most Latin American countries had gradually drifted away from U.S. markets for their exports. Other OECD countries and Latin America itself were able to compete with the United States for certain markets in Latin American economies.

Meanwhile, the United States not only held its own in inter-American trade, but it actually gained ground on its competitors. This was not a full-blown return to the early days of U.S. trade dominance in the Americas, but it did evoke a faint memory of those times. At the depths of the 1980s' recession, one observer concluded that "increasingly, it is the markets of the United States that absorb the export flows emanating from debt-troubled Latin economies."[20] For example, between 1982 and 1983, Latin American exports to the rest of the world declined. On

TABLE 7.3   Distribution of Latin American Trade (in percentages)

	Exports			Imports		
	1981	1982	1983	1981	1982	1983
United States	35.8	39.3	43.3	39.8	37.6	40.0
Japan	6.9	7.0	7.3	10.2	10.7	13.5
European Community	19.8	20.8	21.2	17.4	16.8	18.5
All other trade	32.9	28.6	23.6	30.3	32.3	25.7

Source: Adapted from "The European Community and Latin America,"
Europe Information: External Relations, no. 82/85 (November 1985),
p. 14.

the other hand, deliveries to the United States rose by $4 billion a year, and in 1984, the United States received about 45 percent of all exports. To be sure, Latin America still traded with the European Community. The EC was Latin America's second biggest customer and its second biggest supplier after the United States; 23 percent of all Latin American trade was carried on with the EC.[21] (See Table 7.3.) But almost all of the increase in Latin American exports between early 1983 and early 1985 went to the United States.[22] Fundamentally then, in terms of Latin America's trade, the 1980s reset the hands of the clock back at least a decade on trade. It will take time and good fortune to undo what has been done.

Investment and Aid

What happened to other kinds of external financing for Latin America? Did they fit into or diverge from the existing pattern of debt?

The debt crisis narrowed the options for the region on the question of financing economic growth. But as the weight of debt pressed down on Latin America, foreign investment began to look more promising by comparison.

As Table 7.4 demonstrates, U.S. foreign investment in Latin America gradually subsided during the 1980s. In 1980, it represented 18 percent of all U.S. investment abroad; five years later, it had fallen to 12.7 per cent. Similarly, U.S. investment in Latin America absorbed 72 percent of its total investment in the developing world in 1980. But by 1985, that share had declined to 54 percent.

The distribution of U.S. foreign investment within the Americas also shifted during the first half of the 1980s, as shown in Table 7.5. In 1980, most of this investment—58 percent of all U.S. regional invest-

TABLE 7.4 Latin America's Share of U.S. Direct Investment Abroad, 1979--1985

	U.S. direct investment in Latin America as a percent of all U.S. direct investment abroad	U.S. direct investment in Latin America as a percent of all U.S. direct investment in developing countries
1979	18.7	78.7
1980	17.9	72.6
1981	17.0	69.2
1982	14.7	62.0
1983	11.6	52.8
1984	11.8	50.3
1985	12.7	54.1

Source: Data calculated from Survey of Current Business, 62 (August 1982), pp. 21--22; 64 (August 1984), pp. 46--47; 66 (August 1986), pp. 48--49.

ment—went to the Caribbean Basin. Five years later, this pattern was reversed. South America had become the principal beneficiary by the mid-1980s, and Brazil and Mexico, in that order, were the leading recipients for U.S. foreign investment in 1980 and in 1985. Argentina (but not Venezuela) was also among the favored states.

Three trends marked the 1980s: (1) total U.S. investment stagnated and even declined in Latin America; (2) U.S. investment was no longer as important in Latin America relative to the rest of the world as it once was; and (3) U.S. investment that did remain in Latin America found its way into the larger, more developed and more stable states of South America.

Foreign aid from U.S. coffers continued to be a minor source of foreign financing. This public source of funds, given over a thirty-year period (1954-1984), was channeled to very few countries in Latin America. Of the Big Four, only Brazil received any truly sizeable amount of aid during these three decades.

Along with some of the more developed countries in the Third World, Latin America is not seen by Washington as particularly deserving of certain kinds of economic assistance. Paradoxically, though it is too poor not to need it, it is too rich to be given much aid within the larger framework of U.S. global priorities. However, Latin America *is*

TABLE 7.5 U.S. Direct Investment Position Abroad in Latin America, 1980--1985*
(in billions of dollars)

	1980	1981	1982	1983	1984	1985
All Countries	215.5	227.3	207.7	207.2	213.0	232.7
Developed Countries	158.3	167.1	154.4	155.7	157.5	172.7
Developing Countries	53.3	56.1	48.1	45.7	50.1	54.5
Latin America	38.8	38.9	28.2	24.1	25.2	29.5
South America	16.3	18.1	19.8	18.7	19.0	18.6
Argentina	2.5	2.7	2.9	2.7	2.7	2.8
Brazil	7.7	8.2	9.3	9.1	9.4	9.5
Chile	0.5	0.8	0.3	0.1	0.0	0.0
Colombia	1.0	1.2	1.8	2.1	2.3	2.1
Ecuador	0.3	0.3	0.4	0.4	0.4	0.4
Peru	1.7	1.9	2.0	2.0	1.9	1.7
Venezuela	1.9	2.2	2.6	1.7	1.8	1.5
Other	0.7	0.7	0.5	0.5	0.5	0.5
Caribbean Basin	22.5	20.7	8.4	5.4	6.2	10.9
Mexico	6.0	7.0	5.0	4.4	4.6	5.1
Panama	3.2	3.7	4.4	4.8	4.5	4.6
Bahamas	12.4	3.0	3.1	3.8	3.4	3.4
Bermuda	2.7	10.4	11.5	11.1	13.0	14.1
Netherlands Antilles	11.0	-6.7	-19.8	-23.0	-24.6	-21.6
Trinidad & Tobago	-4.2	0.9	0.9	0.9	0.9	0.5
Other	2.9	2.5	3.1	3.4	4.5	4.8

*Discrepancies due to rounding

Source: Adapted from Survey of Current Business 62 (August 1982), pp. 21, and 22 and Survey of Current Business 66 (August 1986), pp. 46, 47, 48, and 49.

TABLE 7.6   U.S. and Soviet Economic Aid to Latin
America 1954--1984 (in millions of dollars)

	United States	Soviet Union
Latin America	16,129	1,804
Argentina	199	295
Bolivia	923	188
Brazil	2,428	158
Chile	1,181	238
Cuba	N.A.	33,320*
Colombia	1,383	---
Dominican Republic	929	---
Ecuador	493	---
Guatemala	530	---
Mexico	362	---
Panama	466	---
Peru	1,060	---
Venezuela	202	---

*Preliminary data for 1984; not included in Latin
American total.

Source: CIA, Handbook of Economic Statistics 1985
(Washington D.C.: Directorate of Intelligence,
September 1985), tables 77, 80, and 84.

on the list for aid from *other* donors. European donors have gradually
increased their aid commitments, although they still remain very modest
in relative terms. And the Soviet Union, which is tightfisted about
economic aid in general and with respect to Latin America in particular,
nevertheless, extended aid to Latin America from 1954 to 1984, sending
most of it to Cuba. U.S. and Soviet commitments are summarized in
Table 7.6.

The "Lost" Decade of Debt

Foreign debt was *the* issue in U.S.–Latin American economic relations
during the 1980s. In the 1990s, massive debt remains perhaps the
principal obstacle to Latin American economic recovery, and it may be
the most pressing issue in inter-American relations for years to come.
Debt and the means of coping with it will affect the diffusion of
economic power and hegemonic decline in the Americas well into the
next century.

Three questions capture the significance of debt for U.S.–Latin
American relations. First, what is the extent and the nature of foreign

indebtedness? Second, how have debt and debt adjustment policies affected Latin America and its relations with the United States? Third, what, if anything, do creditors and debtors think can be done about debt relief, and what would this do to U.S.–Latin American relations?

Debt and the measures adopted to deal with it may have widened, rather than closed, the gap between the United States and Latin America in terms of material (and financial) resources. In other words, foreign debt has slowed, perhaps halted, hegemonic decline for a time. Second, the debt problem has deepened the interdependence between the United States and Latin America. This has made it all but impossible for the United States to act unilaterally as an old-style hegemonic state on the debt issue. Without doubt, the hegemonic state and the private banks holding Latin American debt are indeed formidable in this dance of billions, but they, just like their Latin American debtors, are held hostage to financial interdependence.

Dimensions of Debt

The cornerstone of the debt crisis was laid during the 1970s. Between 1973 and 1976, Mexico and Brazil accounted for one quarter of the increase in all debt for developing countries. In a five-year period during the mid-1970s, the total Latin American debt grew at the rate of 22 percent a year, and debt for all developing countries went up almost as fast, 20 percent annually.[23]

Mexico's announcement in 1982 that it could not meet its obligations to foreign creditors was the warning shot signaling the official arrival of the debt crisis. The dire straits of others in the same boat became well known soon afterwards. Interest payments more than tripled between 1978 and 1981, and most debtors were very hard pressed to meet these obligations. At the same time, the banks were dangerously overexposed; in 1982, the nine largest U.S. banks had outstanding loans in Latin America that amounted to an average of 172 percent of their capital.[24]

By the end of 1983, one estimate pegged the total Latin American debt at approximately $332 billion.[25] The region had made use of the Eurocurrency market in 1982 to a greater extent than any other developing area, when matters turned grim, some countries in Latin America found their debt service ratios to be alarming; others were in less critical condition. (The debt service ratio is interest payments as a percent of total export earnings.) In 1982, this ratio for Latin America was at a very high 47 percent; by 1986, it had gone down to 34 per cent.[26]

At first, the debt crisis was seen as a liquidity or cash flow crisis—Mexico and the other debtors had simply run up against the exigency of trying to meet debt obligations with too little foreign exchange in the current account. The crisis was a cash flow problem. However, this view was not widely endorsed in the debtor countries, especially as time went on. To them, it began to look more like a solvency issue. Not only did the debtor countries have too little in their reserves to meet the short-term maturities coming due but they seemed to be unable to pull themselves out of the hole and might never be able to repay the loans.

As debt threatened to overwhelm the debtor countries, it seemed hard to envision any realistic plan for the repayment of the principal or interest, given the deadening impact repayment had on capital accumulation and economic growth. The debt crisis soon took on a monstrous appearance, raising serious issues for the debtor countries and questions about creditor-debtor relations on the international level. Thus, international economic conditions and domestic policies combined to bring on a debt crisis that vacillated between being a liquidity problem and a solvency one.

Just as the regional Big Four (Brazil, Argentina, Mexico, and Venezuela) accounted for most of the rise in economic power of Latin America during the third quarter of the twentieth century, they also accounted for most of the region's debt. (See Table 7.7.) For example, estimates for 1984 put Latin American foreign debt at about $360 billion. (A year later, the debt reached $375 billion and was still climbing, primarily due to loans to meet interest payments.) Approximately three-fourths (77 percent) of that debt was owed by the regional Big Four, with Brazil and Mexico once again leading the way, just as they did with respect to their share of economic growth in Latin America during the glory years. The large, high-growth countries were the big losers in the debt crisis.

The change in the structure of external public debt also compromised the independence of the Latin American state. The thrust of this change was toward privatization of international lending, a trend that had been underway for more than twenty years. In 1961, foreign loans from public sources to Latin American states accounted for a little more than half of all foreign credits. But in 1984, well into the debt crisis, the majority of Latin America's public debt—72 percent—came from private rather, than public, sources.

Even as Latin American indebtedness began to signal severe economic distress, a shift in the financial status of the hegemonic state was occurring in the north. Before its ascendance to its hegemonic position,

TABLE 7.7 Foreign Debt of the Regional Big Four and of Other
Latin America Countries (in billions of dollars)

	1981	1983	1983	1984*
Latin America	275.4	315.6	340.9	360.2
Argentina	35.7	43.6	45.5	48.0
Brazil	78.7	87.6	96.5	101.8
Mexico	72.0	85.0	90.0	95.9
Venezuela	29.0	31.0	31.5	34.0
Bolivia	2.5	2.4	3.1	3.2
Dominican Republic	1.8	1.9	2.6	2.9
Colombia	7.9	9.4	10.4	10.8
Costa Rica	3.3	3.5	3.8	4.1
Chile	15.5	17.2	17.4	18.4
Ecuador	5.9	6.2	6.7	6.9
El Salvador	1.5	1.7	2.0	2.3
Guatemala	1.4	1.5	1.8	1.9
Haiti	0.3	0.4	0.4	0.6
Honduras	1.7	1.8	2.1	2.3
Nicaragua	2.2	2.8	3.3	3.6
Panama	2.3	2.8	3.3	3.6
Paraguay	0.9	1.2	1.5	1.6
Peru	9.6	11.1	12.4	13.5
Uruguay	3.1	4.3	4.6	4.7

*Estimated

Source: Data from Economic Commission of Latin America,
reprinted in "The European Community and Latin America,"
Europe Information: External Relations, no. 82/85 (November
1985), p. 17.

the United States had been a debtor nation. By 1984, after its ascendance,
it had become a net creditor to the world.

Ravages of Debt and Debt Adjustment

What massive debt and debt adjustment policies have wrought is hard
to gauge precisely. However, there is little doubt that the impact has
been toxic, widespread, and perhaps long lasting. Governments, macroeconomic policies, imports and exports, consumption and investment,
income distribution, economic growth, and even political stability have
all either been affected already or may be in the future. Just as war
is too important to be left to the generals, foreign debt is too important
to be left to the bankers.

Debt unquestionably threatens economic growth in Latin America,
most directly that of the largest debtors such as Mexico. Yet world

economic growth is also at risk. And by posing a worldwide threat, debt becomes part of a "broader global economic disequilibrium."[27] Unless foreign debt is reduced or better managed, long-term economic growth for almost everyone could be imperiled. Of course, debt servicing may drain capital away from domestic investment, a key requisite for future growth. But this is not the only reason for sluggish growth. Another is the reality that foreign capital is hard to come by. After growing at a rate of 6 to 7 percent for two decades, investment capital in Latin America declined by 19 percent in 1982 and 14 per cent in 1983.[28]

Economic growth and debt repayment are hard to reconcile in Latin America. Servicing debt eats into foreign exchange earnings from the sale of exports. This has even led to a "beggar thy debtor" effect: the transfer of financial resources from debtors to creditors has depressed consumption and investment in the developing countries. Some analysts have argued that repayment of debt makes the rich even richer in the international hierarchy if the developing countries must transfer more of their national output to OECD markets at reduced prices in order to meet some of their interest obligations on the debt principal.[29]

Debt and debt adjustment policies can also be corrosive for the social peace of the countries themselves. First, they exact a heavy price from the people through the decline in income and living conditions. Second, they have a potential impact on the political and social fabric of the region.

Latin Americans were forced to reduce their standards of living to pay back some of their foreign debt. IMF-sponsored austerity measures, which included reduced imports and spending, and higher taxes, fell heavily on those least able to afford it. Per capita income declined for virtually every country in Latin America. Furthermore, the burden of debt adjustment was put on the backs of wage earners in Mexico and Brazil who were forced to live with depressed real wages, higher inflation, higher unemployment, and job insecurity.[30] The working people in Chile, Peru, and Venezuela were less adversely affected. However, there and elsewhere, the losses in income were borne disproportionately by the poor. Clearly, then, economic development, not just economic growth, was severely and perhaps permanently harmed. The distribution of wealth and income in Latin America worsened as a result of the debt crisis, although austerity measures eased somewhat after the mid-1980s.

The impact on politics is harder to decipher. The rise of democracy in Latin America roughly coincided with the onset of the debt crisis, and one may have had something to do with the other. Recession and debt so impoverished most people that popular demands for government responsiveness became all but irresistible in some countries. Debt, therefore, may have hastened democracy. But debt may be the undoing of democracy, too. The debt crisis could erode the fragile democratic experiments of the 1980s from one end of the hemisphere to the other because debt repayment can depress individual incomes and gut social programs designed for the voting constitutents of democratic regimes.

Take Peru, for example. When President Alan Garcia, a democratically elected civilian on the moderate left, came to office in the mid-1980s, he was faced with the spectre of debt. One of the first heads of state to define debt as a political, not just financial, problem, Garcia also regarded debt as part of a larger struggle. At the UN, he argued that "the debt has become a conflict between the poor South of our American continent and the industrial, imperialist and financial North."[31]

Other civilian presidents have voiced similar views. In 1987, President Alfonsín, halfway through his six-year term as president of Argentina, made essentially the same point. Latin American debt to the industrialized nations, he said, "conspires against the consolidation of democracy."[32] Alfonsin would leave the presidency a few months early under a cloud of economic gloom. Today, democratic leaders in Latin America are caught between popular demands for growth and financial demands for debt repayment.

The debt crisis demands that tough choices be made—choices that will have direct and substantial consequences. Naturally then, debt adjustment policies reflect different national and financial interests as well as the relative strength of creditors, debtors, and the hegemonic state. The fundamental issue concerns who will pay for (and suffer from) debt adjustment. And the way in which this issue is resolved will affect the international financial system, the development of Latin America, and the diffusion of economic power from the United States to Latin America.

The initial response to "who pays" was that the debtors should. Thus during the liquidity crisis of the early 1980s, the debtors absorbed the losses, carried out austerity measures, and made most of the sacrifices bearing the burden virtually by themselves. But as the liquidity crisis passed, austerity on the part of debtors was no longer enough. And from their point of view, the burdens of adjustment had fallen too onerously on their own shoulders. If they were to have any chance at a viable future, the debtors would have to find other policies that would more evenly allocate the burdens between north and south. The call for debt adjustment soon became a call for more equal burden sharing between debtors and creditors.

Debtors offered a number of options for sharing the burden of debt adjustment, none of which were enthusiastically received in the United

States. This is because the debtor's hopes for debt relief implied a net transfer of resources *back to* Latin America. U.S. private banks and Latin American debtor states could agree on a number of debt reschedulings during the 1980s, but the debt reform packages suggested from Latin America remained out-and-out attempts to change the flow of financial power in the hemisphere.

Debtor Options

Early on, the main options proposed by Latin America for debt relief were conciliatory default, debt repudiation, and a debtor cartel. All of these rested on the premise that debt adjustment should not impoverish the debtors any more than it had already. Equalizing the distribution of burden was seen as necessary to put the hemisphere on a more even keel and to bring recovery to Latin America. But even in their desperation for relief, the debtors recognized the interdependence of debt: The creditors in the United States and elsewhere had to rely on the debtors to repay some of the debt, and the debtors had to rely on the willingness of creditors to play ball, too. The debtor's power *not* to repay was, of course, the counterpoint to the creditor's power to withhold new loans.

The option of conciliatory default was first pursued by Brazil, Bolivia and Peru, and Brazil even refused to make payments on its debt in 1987. Of course, such default could chill and even destabilize the international financial system, something that the hegemonic state is implicitly pledged to defend. Yet default need not be massive and across-the-board; if it were, it would be a direct assault on the legitimacy of the whole system. Creditors and debtors would both stand to lose.

Conciliatory default stands somewhere between outright repudiation and efforts to meet debts on schedule. It is more modest and less threatening than the former because the debtor acknowledges the debt as legitimate and binding. Even so, it implies that the north and south realize that there is no way the debt can be fully repaid, at least not under the original terms. Conciliatory default gives the debtor a chance to repay *part* of the debt owed on easier terms. Conciliatory default is also unilateral. Debtors simply look at their own situation and decide whether they can adopt such a strategy. This power of the debtor is partial but very real. For example, when conciliatory default of Brazil rippled across the financial world, Citibank set aside billions in loan reserves to cover the short-term consequences of the Third World inability to repay interest or principal.[33] Such a preemptive write-down of debt by the creditors serves virtually the same purpose as conciliatory default. But unilateral conciliatory default has a downside as well. With such a policy, Latin America would enjoy only very limited access in the future to international capital markets.

The Brazilian case proved that there was both a bark and bite to conciliatory default. It was first seen as a veiled threat that would jeopardize the international financial system and that of the United States only if other debtors in large numbers decided to take the same course of action. Such widespread conciliatory default would push international capital stability to the brink, even as the debtors paid lip service to the legitimacy of their original obligations. Brazil's abandonment of the policy about one year later sent a sigh of relief throughout financial circles.

The second option, debt repudiation, is more radical and less compromising. A few countries like Cuba advocated it, but its implications were generally forbidding to debtors and creditors alike. Repudiation by one creditor would be bearable, but repudiation by any number of them would be ominous for both the international system and for U.S. leadership of that system. In fact, wholesale rejection of all debt obligations would bring the system to its knees. It would call into question the legitimacy of the liberal international financial structure itself. And the debtors themselves would hardly be immune from the consequences because the instability and uncertainty surrounding such a drastic measure would affect everyone.

What makes debt repudiation different from conciliatory default is magnitude and ideological overtones. Those who lean toward conciliatory default are not inclined to endorse the overt rejection of the international financial system. Consequently, conciliatory default is the more likely option for debtor countries.

A cartel of debtors is somewhat different than the other options. It is a means to an end, rather than an end in itself. The theory behind such a cartel is that by forming a coalition debtor countries could enhance their collective bargaining power to achieve some debt relief. The Cartagena group of eleven Latin American states was a forum to coordinate debt policies and seek lower and fixed rates; it never was a cartel. No other formidable effort to germinate a cartel of this sort has taken root.

The United States did what it could to discourage such a cartel. In fact, the Baker Plan of 1985 was intended to deflate the prospects of just such a movement gaining headway among debtor countries by calling for a debt containment strategy, more cooperation, more loans from private banks, more growth in the Third World, and an enlarged role for the World Bank.

Underpinning these options for debtors is the premise that significant debt relief will come from what the debtor nations do, and not from what the creditors or the United States may be willing to concede in the face of critical challenges.

Creditor Options

The United States favors options that would avoid massive forgiveness of debt and therefore a massive net transfer of resources to Latin America in the future. The adjustment policies preferred in the United States and in the OECD countries would minimize but not prohibit the sharing of debt burdens. After all, the aim is to preserve the international financial system, and some relief is necessary to accomplish that. But both creditors and debtors will lose if massive debt relief is endorsed. And both will gain something by preventing debt relief from eroding the financial system.

So far, private banks have adopted several tactics on the debt issue. One of them is the *rescheduling and restructuring* of the debt. Chile, Mexico, and other Latin American countries have pursued such measures with their creditors. Yet these merely postpone, rather than resolve, the debt problem. Other incremental steps acceptable to creditors are *write-downs, discounting,* and *debt for equity swapping.* These measures concede Latin America's inability to repay its debts according to the original terms, but they stop short of admitting that the debt cannot be repaid at all. If insolvency is accepted as the key to debt relief, the gap between conciliatory default and partial repayment can be narrowed.

Debt-for-equity swaps have been attempted here and there. To reduce their exposure and loss, banks have traded Latin American debts among themselves at steep discounts. For example, in 1987, Mexican debt was sold at 59 cents on the dollar, Argentina's for 63 cents, and Venezuela's for 74 cents. The foreign creditor will sell the loan of a Latin American government to another investor at its (new) face value. The debt is then converted into local currency by the debtor government at not quite face value, and these funds are used to buy up approved local businesses. Unfortunately, debt-for-equity swaps are done for banks, who make some money of them, not for debtors. According to traders in Third World loans, this is like rearranging the deck chairs on the Titanic. Some debtors, including Mexico, have tried to limit such swaps. Furthermore, because foreign debt far exceeds the equity to be traded in direct foreign investment, this strategy limits the financing provided by banks while handicapping government intervention and debtor cartels.

Private banks have also built up their loan reserves in anticipation of more conciliatory default or the suspension of interest payments.

This is not such much debt relief as it is protection against unilateral debtor policies, and it acknowledges what is happening but falls short of a more multilateral, cooperative arrangement for dealing with the problem. Basically, then, private banks and OECD governments seem willing to muddle along on a case-by-case basis. This kind of patchwork debt relief is greeted with some skepticism.

In the first years of the debt crisis, debt adjustment hurt the debtors far more than the creditors. This exacerbated the relative decline of Latin America brought on by the economic recession of the 1980s. In the years to come, debt adjustment may not be so one-sided. Forced to the wall, Latin American debtors may have no choice but to default unilaterally and partially on debt repayment.

Crisis and Hegemonic Decline

The debt crisis and the economic recession of the eighties battered and bloodied Latin America more than any other region, and they changed the course of inter-American relations on economic issues.

The United States both won and lost from the tumult of economic instability in the Americas. It more than doubled its own federal debt during the first half of the 1980s and lost its claim to being a net creditor nation at the same time that many of its private banks were critically overextended. The United States responded to the crisis by doing what any hegemonic state would do—it sought to stabilize the existing financial and economic order even as it pursued policies for its own benefit that made it difficult to do so. Ultimately, it was able to avoid the collapse of the international financial order without making significant concessions to debtors. For its part, Latin America experienced oppressive debt and economic downturn, with little if any immediate chance of financial salvation from debt.

The Bottom Line for Hegemony

The economics of the crisis proved how incomplete, uneven, and fickle the diffusion of economic power could be. Trends that had gradually moved Latin America toward a prominent position within the hegemonic system were interrupted. (See Table 7.8.) The choices Latin America made were grave ones. The dilemma was that the region suffered and paid most for the predicament of negative growth and unimaginable debt burdens. In contrast, the United States improved its relative position at the expense of Latin America during the 1980s and largely achieved what it wanted to from the debt crisis. Although its stature on financial issues was fading, it nevertheless preserved the stability of the liberal,

TABLE 7.8   Growth in Real GNP 1970--1985 (in percentages)

	1970--1980	1980--1985	1982--1985
United States	2.8	2.4	4.2
Japan	4.7	3.9	4.3
France	2.7	1.2	1.2
Federal Republic of Germany	2.7	1.3	2.4
Great Britain	1.9	1.9	3.1
Western Hemisphere	5.8	1.0*	3.2**
Canada	4.6	2.5	4.2

*Preliminary estimates, includes 1986 data.
**Preliminary estimates, from 1983--1986.

Source: Economic Report of the President 1987 (Washington, D.C.: Government Printing Office, January 1987), pp. 104--105.

financial system at a very low cost to its own government. The burden was carried by the U.S. economy and particularly by Latin Americans. Those who had the least to gain from the system paid the most to keep it afloat.

Latin America has yet to the reap the benefits of its immense sacrifice. True, it was able to avoid some of the more dire calamities which stalked the hemisphere in the early 1980s, and it has been able to restore some growth. Yet it has not renewed the robust growth that earlier helped narrow the gap separating it from the hegemonic state. In the last decade of the twentieth century, unemployment is high; capital formation from abroad is stagnant; and trade is dormant and may be dependent upon external conditions beyond the control of Latin America.

Economic distress did for U.S. hegemony what economic growth could not. Although recession and crisis did not put Latin American self-reliance and diversified relations back to square one, they certainly put a major crimp in this trend. The United States became more, rather than less dominant, economically during the crisis. In effect, "the debt crisis and slow European recovery from recession have brought many Latin American nations back into the orbit of the United States, after they had diversified successfully in the late 1970s."[34]

This did not result from any deliberate plan by public and private leaders within the hegemonic state. And in the future, different responses to the economic crisis and different macroeconomic policies among the

OECD countries may perpetuate what has already happened. "[U]nless Europe shows sustained economic recovery and a new generosity toward imports from outside the EC [European Community], most Latin American nations will continue to orbit the U. S. trade system."[35] The irony is that the United States was more dominant in the 1980s even though the hegemonic system was unable to sustain growth throughout the world and the Americas.

The "Lost" Decade and Hegemony

What do the debt crisis and economic recession reveal about the fate of hegemonic decline in the Americas? Though it may be too soon to tell with certainty, some tentative judgments can be offered about hegemony during the economic distress of the 1980s:

1. The diffusion of economic power from the United States to Latin America was arrested due to the economic crisis of the 1980s. This halted the hegemonic decline in terms of material economic resources even if it did not fully restore hegemony.
2. Diffusion of power in the Americas will be affected by the way in which the burden of debt is shared in years to come.
3. Unilateral steps to deal with the debt are inadequate—they do not go far enough in deciding who pays what amount. Unilateral measures also may inspire countermeasures between the hegemonic state, creditors, and debtors. Given the interdependence of debt, measures that recognize the multilateral management of burden-sharing should be developed eventually.
4. As the hegemonic state, the United States still retains impressive influence over the net transfer of resources in the Americas. On the debt issue, it gained its ends in the short term and at low cost even as Latin America failed to achieve massive debt relief and has had to pay for much of the debt readjustment.
5. The debt crisis and economic recession proved that diffusion of power and resources is not to be taken for granted, at least in the short or medium term. The transfer of financial resources to the north proved that to be the case during the 1980s. The weakened hegemony of the United States was still vigorous enough to protect the private financial interests of major banks as well as the liberal economic order itself.

The ordeal of hegemony has been indelibly shaped by the the "lost" decade of the 1980s. Although the position of the United States with respect to the economic power of the Americas was improved by the recession, this glitch in hegemonic decline may be only transitory. The present-day ordeal for the United States is that it can take no comfort in its relative advantage because a debt-ridden, stagnating Latin America may present a serious, long-term threat to the hegemonic system.

For Latin America, the ordeal is harsh and immediate. Although the hegemony of the north was not fully restored in the 1980s, the crisis sent Latin America reeling, turning gains into losses and offering only a very clouded future for the major debtors in the 1990s.

8

Hegemony and Intervention

Intervention is the primal expression of U.S. power in Latin America, and, as mentioned in Chapter 6, it is the leading security issue facing that region. It is also a stern test of U.S. will. Direct military intervention requires, at a minimum, international acquiescence and a durable domestic consensus. The right or the need to intervene in Latin America has never been widely doubted in the United States, but the consensus over what to do and how to do it has eroded since Vietnam. Intervention in the defense of U.S. hegemony has also prompted Latin American states to offer a response, making this issue critical to U.S. power and its decline in Latin America.

The United States seems irresistably drawn to intervention to control the foreign and domestic affairs of its hemispheric realm. Most of its targets have been regimes whose very existence challenged the credibility of its hegemony in the hemisphere. For example, in 1954, it relied on CIA-sponsored insurgents in Guatemala to topple the leftist government of Jacobo Arbenz. In 1961, it tried but failed to oust Castro with a CIA-sponsored invasion of Cuban exiles. Four years later, it sent thousands of U.S. troops to the Dominican Republic to protect U.S. citizens, stabilize the country, and prevent another Cuba. And in 1973, it used the CIA and economic pressures to force the first elected Marxist in the Americas from power in Chile. Thus, intervention has been used to arrest hegemonic decline in the face of revolutionary defection and strategic intrusion. Intervention has been used to bolster the image of the United States as a great power.

The Reagan administration reacted to the decline of U.S. power by trying to contain the Left and dictate events. Therefore, the Reagan Doctrine, which was intended to reassert U.S. power and restore its hegemony, was a policy of intervention. U.S. actions in three Latin American "hot spots" of the eighties—Nicaragua, Grenada, and Panama—demonstrated the limits and dilemmas of military solutions for political problems in the hemisphere. They also revealed that intervention, in an era of hegemonic change, may produce a mixed harvest. Although intervention may remove a government from power, as happened in Panama, Grenada, and perhaps Nicaragua, it does not address the reasons for long-term changes that affect the fate of hegemony in the hemisphere as a whole.

The strategic perspective excused hegemonic intervention even as it relaxed U.S. thinking about the Soviet Union in the Gorbachev era. And the Reagan Doctrine, a classic example of reviving past policy, was also an example of regional hegemony: As the United States embraced Gorbachev and looked forward to the end of the cold war, it prolonged this war against Soviet allies in Latin America.

The Latin American response to the interventionism of the Reagan Doctrine pointed to an alternative for conflict resolution—multilateral negotiation. However, a pax Latina base is ultimately impossible without the acquiescence or support of the United States. Another regional approach, the Central American peace plan of the late 1980s (Esquipulas II), illustrates both the opportunities and limits of Latin American activism in regard to U.S. intervention.

Sharing Losses, Dividing Gains

Living with the ordeal of hegemonic decline is painful indeed. To date, neither the United States nor Latin America has entirely adapted to this difficult reality or fully adjusted to the ebbing influence of the North and the greater turmoil in the South. And until they do, they will only reap greater mutual losses, rather than share significant gains. Haunted by its past preeminence, the United States seems unable to let go of a hegemonic vision that has seized its imagination for decades. The challenge it must now wrestle with is that what it *wants* to do and what it *is able* to do as a hegemonic power in Latin America are two different things—a fact that is becoming more evident as time goes by.

For its part, Latin America is wary of the unilateral exercise of U.S. power. Skeptical of revived hegemony, it struggles, vainly thus far, to find its own regional alternatives to U.S. intervention. The Central American peace initiative of the late 1980s points the way to cooperation without U.S. blessing. Still, the life span of such ambitious efforts at multilateral cooperation is frightfully short. The impact on the peace process of obstinate forces, irreconcilable interests, and asymmetries of power *within* Central America could prove fatal.

During the 1980s, the United States became alarmed about the widening cracks in its hegemonic armor. Its actions in the economic realm had mixed success. On the one hand, the economic crisis of the 1980s served to increase the gap between Latin America and the United States in terms of economic productivity and growth without bringing the whole system down. On the other hand, the turbulence in economic affairs further eroded the confidence of Latin American governments in U.S. leadership. The debt crisis served notice that the United States had forsaken hegemonic benevolence in favor of the narrow protection of its own strategic and private interests.

In the security realm, the United States fixated on the Left and revolution during the 1980s. Strategic intrusion and revolutionary de fection were dual threats to hegemonic security. The coming to power of the Sandinistas at the beginning of the decade was a rebuff to U.S. domination of Nicaraguan affairs. This sounded alarm bells in Washington, D.C. "Another Cuba" was not going to be tolerated on the mainland of the continent; the Reagan Doctrine had its main target. At first, the failure to make the Sandinistas "say Uncle" fueled the perception of growing U.S. decline. The policy of intervention through exile insurgency, CIA operations, and economic war did not defeat the Sandinistas militarily; it did not rid outside forces from the conflict; it did not have great support in the United States; and it may have even encouraged the independent efforts of Central America to settle the conflict through the peace plan. U.S. policy toward the Sandinistas was questioned more than ever before. Unilateral interventionism fed insecurity throughout Latin America. However, after years of bleeding the Sandinista regime, the revolution cracked under the pressure. The contra war and economic blacklisting of Nicaragua had turned the country into a basketcase. An anti-Sandinista coalition came to power and, after a decade of hegemonic policy, the United States once again had a more friendly ally in Managua.

Although intervention during 1980s evoked memories of the early years of U.S. involvement, it has not revived the hegemony of the past. But it has polarized the region and eroded the subjective hegemony of the United States. Consequently, Latin Americans are more reluctant than ever to accept U.S. unilateralism in their affairs, and resentment and doubts have committed them more than ever to the idea that regional negotiation and cooperation are political alternatives to U.S. military intervention for dealing with security problems in the hemisphere. However, until the United States also accepts this view, a pax Latina is utopian. And until it accepts détente with its adversaries, a pax Americana will be inadequate.

Latin America has scored even fewer successes on the economic front. Having suffered significant reversals during the interregnum of recession and debt in the 1980s, it is at a serious disadvantage with the United States during the last decade of the twentieth century. But reviving the economic growth necessary to increase the diffusion of economic power to the south will not come easily to Latin America. And though growth is a hallowed value in both the north and south, it may prove illusive. Without this southward shift in resources, hegemony may be prolonged because, if the 1980s provided a lesson about hegemony, it is that economic distress in the south and economic recovery in the north arrests the decline of hegemony.

The Empire Strikes Back

The Reagan administration left a bold imprint on inter-American relations. It embraced U.S. resurgence as a goal and insurgency as a strategy. It advocated unilateral confrontation, rather than multilateral negotiation, with foe and friend alike. It defined conflict in zero sum terms: Its losses were someone else's gains. And it railed against the intruders and heretics who dismissed or defied its hegemonic vision. But, for all the rhetoric, U.S. resurgence in Latin America during the 1980s was both limited and selective.

During this period, the United States preferred the stick over the carrot, something even its allies could testify to. The Mexicans were publicly chastized for corruption in drug enforcement. The Costa Rican president was browbeaten for his resistance to a wider war on Nicaragua. The Organization of American States was shortchanged by about one-third of its annual budget because the United States was in a cost-cutting mood and because the OAS lacked the ardor to confront communism in the Americas to the satisfaction of the Reagan administration.

The Reagan policy could also be fickle. Panama's Noriega was at one time the darling of the administration: He was showered with praise, awards, and a six-figure income annually from the CIA, and his collaboration against the Sandinistas was his main value to the United States. By 1988, however, he had become a blemish on U.S. policy and was therefore denounced as an drug-running thug to be cast aside.

Restoring hegemony during the Reagan years came to mean ridding the hemisphere of unrepentant and inconvenient regimes (mostly on the Left) and leaning heavily on allies to accept this understanding of the U.S. mission in the Americas. Making enemies quake and friends submissive was a short-term approach to U.S. resurgence, and restoring hegemony also called for force in expelling outsiders and overturning revolutionaries. But these were not long-term strategies for confronting the shift of economic power, the growing interdependence of Latin America with the world, and the emergence of regional activism. Consequently, the U.S. response to hegemonic decline during the 1980s was partial and problematic.

The Battleground

The U.S. mission was intended to reassert its power and restore its hegemony. However, it was also interwoven with more concrete goals, such as containing Soviet/Cuban advances, preserving democracy, stopping revolution in its tracks, or even repealing radical change in those few places where it found sustenance (e.g., Nicaragua).

Vanquishing the Sandinistas would not, of course, restore U.S. hegemony in Latin America or Central America. Beheading a government is not the same as killing a movement. Furthermore, the problems Nicaragua faces, some of which are a direct result of U.S. policy, could lead to a continuation of domestic conflict. Rather than blame the Sandinistas, Nicaraguans may find others to blame if national recovery is frustrated. In a broader vein, U.S. hegemony was on the line in Managua, but U.S. hegemony in the hemisphere was not. Long-term economic changes in the Americas, Latin American truculence about interventionism, and a host of other challenges await the United States beyond the borders of Nicaragua, a country the size of Maine.

Hegemonic outrage was sometimes more bark than bite. Though not unique to the Reagan years, this gap between word and deed, this preaching of hegemonic restoration above and beyond the practicing of it, was a glaring inconsistency in the administration's policy toward Latin America. The Iran-contra affair simply confirmed that it entertained goals far more ambitious than its means could support.

The failure of U.S. foreign policy to pursue hegemony to the fullest during the 1980s was a testament to durable, and especially domestic, constraints. Key Reagan strategists understood the barriers to building a consensus with inadequate resources, but this did not stop them from trying to hurdle or circumvent the barriers of congressional skepticism and public indifference. It created a secret, internationalized, and privatized alliance from within the White House itself to outflank overt constraints. Once exposed, this interventionist alliance ultimately collapsed, but without any guarantees that something like it would not happen again.

The Reagan policy of containing and vanquishing the Left dealt with the symptoms of hegemonic decline, not with the decline itself. The most that could be said in favor of this misreading of the forces of change is that

1. it slowed the revolutionary movement in El Salvador in the short term (although the antirevolutionary alliance there is not out of the woods in the long term);

2. it harassed and bled the Sandinistas and the Left in Central America;
3. it prevented a new status quo from emerging that would allow the adversary a safe haven.

The Reagan Doctrine

It was Latin America's destiny to be the turf for strategic confrontation under the Reagan Doctrine in the mid-1980s. This was nothing new. The Caribbean Basin, for example, has for decades been a regional laboratory for flexing hegemonic muscles and implementing strategies. In the early twentieth century, U.S. imperialism and occupation affected Caribbean states such as Nicaragua, Haiti, and the Dominican Republic; later, the United States adopted less direct forms of control such as installing the Somoza dynasty in Nicaragua. In principle, the Reagan Doctrine was a global crusade against Soviet inroads among the Third World regimes. In practice, it was largely an attempt to rid the Caribbean Basin of new and unconsolidated radical regimes.

The year 1981 had something in common with 1961. In both of these critical years, a newly elected U.S. president refused to accept the presence of a Marxist regime in his own backyard and attempted to dislodge it from power. President Kennedy approved the botched Bay of Pigs operation against Castro in April, 1961. Twenty years later, President Reagan started his long campaign against the Sandinista government. Tearing a page or two from Soviet insurgency manuals, the Reagan Doctrine used "their" methods to achieve "our" goals.

The Reagan Doctrine was also a strategic retort to the Brezhnev Doctrine. The latter pledged Soviet support to make sure no Socialist regime defected from the Soviet bloc; the Reagan Doctrine pledged to do whatever it could to accomplish just such a feat. The fact that the Soviets did not extend survival guarantees to the Sandinistas in Nicaragua as they have to their Eastern European bloc members may have emboldened the United States to launch the longest war in its history.

The Reagan Doctrine was containment-plus. This meant keeping the Sandinistas bottled up and contained in Nicaragua, but it also meant going one step further to liquidate the regime altogether. The doctrine's advocates refused to accept the status quo in Central America by allowing the Left to stay in power. Containment-plus, which goes beyond restraining the Left internationally and attempts to roll it back where it has gained a foothold, assumes Marxist regimes can and should be hounded from power. It was a strategy of rollback. A simple containment strategy would have accepted, if not legitimized, the status quo by letting the Sandinistas hold on to power.

The Reagan Doctrine's implicit hegemonic strategy faced four dilemmas:

1. Where should the Left be contained?
2. How should it be contained?
3. How much should be devoted to containment?
4. Who should contain the Left?[1]

The doctrine struggled with each of these dilemmas. It contended more successfully with the dilemmas of where and how to contain the Left, but was less convincing about how much and whom. Without doubt, the dilemma that most weakened the doctrine was that of how much because limited means generally have not matched the goals of containment and rollback.

On the dilemma of where to contain the Left, the doctrine was pragmatic, adopting a strong-point defense. By applying the doctrine to Nicaragua and the Caribbean area, the United States followed a well-trod path of anti-Communist interventionism close to home where its chances of success are better. If it cannot prevail in its own backyard where it is strongest, where can it? Ironically, though, the strong-point defense was risky. If it cannot work where it has the best chance to succeed, then the United States loses credibility as a great power.[2]

On the dilemma of how to contain the Left, the use of military means prevailed over political, economic, and diplomatic ones. This was to be expected, given that the goal was rollback, rather than simple containment. True, the trade embargo against Nicaragua that was imposed in the mid-1980s reflected an economic dimension, but it was part of the war rather than part of a strategy to contain Nicaraguan influence in Central America. The "two-track" policy toward the Sandinistas was never convincing. The military or paramilitary track, using the contras and the CIA, always dominated the negotiating track, which, in turn, was often used to gain domestic support for the military track.

The question of who should contain the Left was answered with U.S. unilateralism. The Reagan Doctrine sought a U.S. answer, with a little help from some friends; it relied on low-intensity war to attain pax Americana. Without the CIA, there would have been no significant armed resistance to the Sandinistas. Using Nicaraguan opponents to fight the war obviates the need for U.S. troops, but the home-grown insurgents were incapable of carrying the burden of the fighting effectively to the Sandinista defense forces. Nonetheless, the contra forces attacked civilians and economic targets in an attempt to wear down support for the Sandinista regime.

The United States virtually stood alone on this strategy. No major ally of the United States endorsed the contra war. No major Latin American power, except for Argentina under the generals in the early 1980s, endorsed it publicly. No ally (or client state) in Central America supported the cause of the contras or gave them support and bases without also arguing that other alternatives must also be explored.

Unable to enlist overwhelming support from major allies, the Reagan administration turned to others for help. It invented a subterranean network of private and public figures to channel $14 million to the contras, some of which they claim they never received. By subcontracting covert operations, the administration was still largely going it alone. The Reagan Doctrine aspired to pax Americana, but, with divisions at home, it came closer to pax Reagan. When Reagan left power, the Bush administration did not breathe new life into the doctrine.

The amount of military resources available to contain the Left was critical to the doctrine. The Reagan administration pushed for the largest military buildup in peacetime, especially during the first five years. But it came with a trade-off. Expanded military spending increased indebtedness and reduced private investment, and it became the hallmark of the Reagan strategy. Overreach is a clear sign of hegemonic decline.

Faced with limits, the Reagan Doctrine was insurgency on a lean budget. It was orchestrated and privatized by the U.S. government to wage "low intensity" warfare with limited funds. Given public skepticism and the memories of Vietnam, Reagan reassured everyone early on that the cost of fighting the good fight would be affordable—in other words, U.S. troops would not be dispatched to Nicaragua to realize the doctrine's goals.

How much was actually expended is anyone's guess. Off and on, Congress appropriated $154.5 million in military and nonlethal aid from 1983 until 1987 to conduct the war against Nicaragua,[3] and the CIA undoubtedly spent millions more. Less directly, U.S. military exercises in Honduras, such as the Big Pine manuevers, left behind large sums of aid in the form of five airstrips and other facilities.

Reviving hegemony for the Reagan administration by and large meant implementing the Reagan Doctrine; if the United States could rid the hemisphere of pests, then everything would be allright. The longer-term issues of *why* the hemisphere was going in such alarming directions were never addressed, except when they were laid at the feet of Soviet/ Cuban malevolence.

Nicaragua, Grenada, and Panama are chapters in this tale of hegemonic intervention during the 1980s and the storyline points to both success and failure. The successes involved U.S. intervention against regimes that were politically weakened or isolated. In any event, hegemony and intervention were linked very directly in the 1980s.

Grenada

The Reagan Doctrine was, at the most, a policy of rolling back Soviet client states; at the least, it was a policy of containing them to their point of origin. In Grenada, the doctrine worked because the leftist regime was deposed by a U.S. invasion, called a "pre-dawn vertical incursion" by the U.S. State Department. The risks of failure were low; and the results were clear and immediate. Public support of—and ignorance about—the invasion was high.

Why did the doctrine work in Grenada? Basically, Grenada was a military operation with few of the political complexities surrounding Nicaragua. The target was unprepared, unpopular in its own country, and it lacked broad contact with the international community. This was a textbook case of choosing a target in such a way that ensured the doctrine could not fail. A quick, low-cost, secretive invasion against a shaky government in a neighboring microstate is almost a sure-fire formula for success.

Most U.S. citizens were poorly informed about the domestic politics of an island country the size of Grand Rapids, Michigan. They were also kept in the dark about the details of the invasion itself, and information about losses led them to believe that the operation was a success. And the U.S. populace needed a success because, just a few days before the Grenada invasion, U.S. Marines died from a truck bomb in Beirut.

As with the U.S. invasion of the Dominican Republic in 1965, protecting U.S. citizens was held up as the ostensible goal of the "rescue mission." Concern for the safety of 1,000 U.S. men and women, including a few hundred medical students, was intended to legitmize the use of force in a country most people in the north had never even heard of or confused with Granada, the Spanish city. The U.S. government also used aerial photography of Grenada to "prove" the threat posed by new construction to accommodate large aircraft, much as it had done in publicizing the existence of Soviet intermediate missiles in Cuba during the crisis of October 1962. Unilateral intervention was also given a patina of legitimacy by the Organization of Eastern Caribbean States (OECS). Donating only 300 constables to the effort, these island neighbors of Grenada still made a valuable contribution because they had formally requested that the United States intervene in its neighbor's affairs to dislodge the leftist "thugs" from power, a public plea that allowed the Reagan administration to wear the crown of backyard redeemer.

The dilemma of how much manpower should be committed was avoided in Grenada. Inadequate means to accomplish ambitious goals was not a strategic problem here. U.S. forces, totalling 7300 marines, paratroopers, and Army Rangers, far outnumbered the 40 Soviet advisers and more than 600 Cubans.[4] Eighteen Americans died; 116 were wounded. Grenadian casualties were three times greater.[5]

The deadly feuds between Marxist factions on the island had provided the opportunity to invade against a government that was unable to maintain itself and was unpopular with most of its own people. Six weeks after the invasion, President Reagan proclaimed that the United States had been vindicated as a great power.

In reality, Grenada was a military exercise, pure and simple. Its success rested upon a traditional U.S. advantage: overwhelming superiority of military resources, manpower, and equipment. Grenada had "all the makings of an ideal setting for a successful yet inexpensive display of American military prowess."[6] This triumph was devalued somewhat. Very few radical states are so vulnerable and so easily dealt with, and very few of the factors constraining the Reagan Doctrine in Central America were present in Grenada. Put simply, Grenada worked because Grenada is not Nicaragua.[7] Restoring U.S. influence there was far easier than it would ever be almost anywhere else in the hemisphere.[8]

Nicaragua

U.S. intervention in the 1980s rested on a classic presumption of hegemony: Maneuverings in Washington, D.C., could shape Nicaragua as the United States wanted it to be rather than allowing the Nicaraguans to decide what they wanted Nicaragua to be.[9] But, unlike the early days, dilemmas of containment afflicted the Reagan Doctrine in Nicaragua. Although the Reagan administration made Nicaragua a high priority as soon as it came into office, it ruled out using U.S. troops. The CIA spearheaded the operation out of Honduras; it supplied, advised, and trained the contras, led by former Somocistas and Sandinistas. It conducted economic war against Nicaragua with the mining of harbors and with the trade embargo. However, the dilemmas of *how* and *how much* were thorny ones. When Congress's support for the policy waned, the Reagan administration responded with attempts to circumvent Congress. The policy fallout from these dilemmas frayed the fabric of consensus in the United States about how to deal with the Nicaraguan problem.

The Reagan administration wanted consistent funding to enable the contras to conduct a war on Nicaragua, if not on the Sandinista army itself. Yet this ran up against widespread domestic opposition. Two-thirds of the U.S. public preferred to give no aid at all or only nonlethal aid to rebel groups fighting Communist-supported governments; forty-two per cent were opposed to any aid whatsoever. The public feared the idea of a military quagmire more than U.S. leaders did and abhorred any long-term, messy, and inconclusive military intervention with open-ended costs.[10] Given these realities, Congress oscillated between reluctance and forbearance: It would turn on the spigot at one point but turn it off at another. This meant that Congress had to walk a very fine line. It did not want to appear to favor the Sandinistas, especially when they cracked down on opponents in Managua or when President Ortega visited the Soviet Union. But it was also leery about the policy and was engaged in a struggle with the administration over foreign policy prerogatives. To complicate things even more, Congress itself was divided. For example, the U.S. Senate in 1987 narrowly approved $36 million in contra aid but the House, in a close vote, torpedoed it.

Unable to resolve these dilemmas, the Reagan administration plodded ahead on its own. The contras were not militarily successful against the Sandinistas but they were able to bleed Nicaragua. The Sandinistas were unable to defend the people and the economy effectively from the U.S.-sponsored war, despite and even because of a large defense commitment in the Nicaraguan budget. Isolated at home and abroad, the Reagan administration resorted to a bizarre coalition of lesser states to sustain the contras.[11] Brunei, Saudi Arabia, Israel, Iran, and others had a hand in the subterfuge known as the Iran-contra affair. But the pygmies were not much help to the giant.

By 1987, two trends had become obvious: Politically, the interventionist policy was falling into disrepute, but so was the Sandinista regime. Congress was reluctant to approve any aid to the contras, and the peace process in Central America had seized the initiative away from the United States on the Nicaraguan question. Pummeling Nicaragua without serious negotiations was no longer viable: It was time to use more diplomatic tactics to deal with the Sandinistas and their reluctance to share power with their opponents. *Coercing* the Sandinistas into liberalizing was too limited; *convincing* them to liberalize was the alternative to war as embodied in the Central American peace plan. However, hegemonic intervention had taken a severe toll on the Sandinistas by the late 1980s. Nicaraguan mothers were opposed to the draft; wage earners had less to spend and consumers had less to buy; the unarmed opposition seemed more credible, and the Sandinistas seemed to be on the defensive. Although many Nicaraguans had little use for the contras as an alternative government, they were desperate to end the war. In the eyes of many, the Sandinistas were to blame for failing to protect the country against war and impoverishment.

The Reagan Doctrine did not topple the Sandinistas, but it made it harder for them to survive as a government. It helped create the intolerable conditions for which the Sandinistas had no cures. With one hand tied behind its back, the hegemonic power to the north had for a decade used a sporadic proxy war against the Left. But it was the concessions on democratization that the Sandinistas made to its neighbors, not to the United States, that made possible the liberalizing of Nicaraguan politics.

U.S. intervention may have helped to defeat the Sandinistas at the polls, but Nicaragua has also lost a great deal from a decade of hegemonic intervention. When the Sandinista revolution came to power, it tried vainly to reconstruct the economy after fighting Somoza. Now that anti-Sandinistas have come to power, they will ironically face the same ordeal. That is why the United States ended the trade embargo and offered economic assistance shortly after the 1990 election. The United States must deal with the more long-term challenge to its role in Nicaragua. Rather than intervening against revolution, the hegemonic state may have to confront the problems that produced this revolution in the first place.

Panama

Graham Greene penned a brief memoir describing his warm friendship with the former leader of Panama, General Omar Torrijos, entitled *Getting to Know the General.* The general was a popular nationalist who defended his country's interests in the Panama Canal treaty negotiations. A couple of years after his death in 1981, Torrijos' successor, General Manuel Antonio ("Tony") Noriega, inspired a quite different feeling—one of growing abhorrence both in Panama and in the United States.

The Reagan Doctrine had been devised to expel the Left from the Caribbean Basin. But, by the late 1980s, the Reagan administration also resurrected the idea that the United States had the right and the power to make its *allies* knuckle under. The unprincipled narcomilitarists in the Panama Defense Forces (PDF) were chosen as the next villains. The U.S. government had known since 1968 that the Panama Defense Forces (PDF) were in the drug business. But it was not until the judicial process in the United States put Panamanian narcomilitarism in the glare of the public spotlight during 1987–1988 that the Reagan administration had to "just say no" to General Noriega, commander of the PDF and the dictator of Panama. Clearly, leftists were not the only ones who had to be wary of intervention.

In the world as seen from the Potomac, Noriega had become the focus of what was wrong in Panama and what symbolized U.S. ineffectuality. He used the PDF to turn Panama into his base of operations and defied U.S. wishes. But trying to rid Panama of the general could also exacerbate the conditions that led to his rule in the first place. Noriega was seen as the cause rather than the symptom,[12] and U.S. policy became focused on Noriega as the cause.

Panama occupies a special place in the hegemonic strategy of the United States, for obvious reasons. The canal still holds a powerful grip on the U.S. imagination and retains some of its former luster as a strategic prize. And, for a time, Noriega was the U.S. agent in the isthmus. The United States conferred upon Noriega the trappings of a valued friend because he was willing to support U.S. goals in Central America. An unsavory friend is better than no friend. A traditional axiom of hegemonic policy in the Americas is that an unprincipled ally was still useful. "[I]t was preferable to have someone in power like Noriega with no discernible principles than to have such posts filled by leftists."[13] But extending an *abrazo* to the general also punctured U.S. credibility in combatting drug trafficking and in fostering democracy. An anecdote circulating in Panama was that General Noriega had three boxes on his desk: one for incoming mail, one for outgoing mail, and one for blackmail.[14]

Eventually, it became impossible to sweep Noriega's narcomilitarism under the rug. For more than two years, the United States used economic, diplomatic, and finally military means to topple the general. But, at first, Noriega had been greatly underestimated. Not only had the United States invented Panama in the early twentieth century but it had meddled off and on (and successfully more often than not) in the country's affairs ever since. It had thwarted the populist bid of Arnulfo Arias for the presidency in 1968, and it helped the defense force to consolidate its control over the government during the years that followed. The United States also played ball with the military by turning a blind eye to General Torrijos' warts as a leader in order to extract a canal treaty from the Senate in 1977.

Its past domination of Panama may have deluded the United States into thinking that it could easily both make and break the ruling elite and it would be able to do this without resorting to direct armed intervention. If United States could not prevail here, in this U.S.-created country, it could not prevail anywhere. The credibility trap was therefore set once again.

The Reagan administration declared economic war on Noriega in 1987. First, the United States halted economic assistance. Then, it suspended the quota for the sale of Panama's sugar to the United States.

Upping the ante, it then withheld payments of canal revenues and blocked transfers from U.S. banks to Panama. The theory behind this war is familiar to another adversary, the Sandinistas. U.S. measures are designed to sow dissension in the bosom of the enemy, and unable to withstand an aroused opposition from within and without, the enemy capitulates, giving the United States what it wants. But, in Noriega's case, the theory was severely tested—and found lacking. Economic pressures did, indeed, put Panama through a wringer but, in this case, the United States overestimated the upper and middle class opposition to Noriega and underestimated the cohesion of the Panama Defense Forces. And although Noriega was the target of this strategy, the casualties were the people of Panama.

The invasion of U.S. troops in December 1989 was both a success and a failure. Its main goal—to capture Noriega—was successful when, realizing he could not escape, Noriega turned himself over to the U.S. military for trial in the United States. According to President Bush, the United States achieved its other objectives: It installed the democratic leaders denied power after an election held earlier in 1989; it protected U.S. interests concerning the canal; it protected, and perhaps avenged, the lives of U.S. personnel. In other words, the intervention in Panama was in some ways a more elaborate replay of the Grenada operation. On the other hand, the invasion was a tacit admission of failure. Acting virtually as a proconsul in Panama immediately after the invasion, the United States showed that it had failed to foster a stable, democratic, antileftist regime in the country it created in 1903. Furthermore, the long-term prospects for Panama are cloudy, to say the least. And, once again, the United States was denounced by Latin America for its armed intervention in Panama.

The Latins React to the Doctrine

Latin America is confronted by the problem of how to counteract hegemonic intervention. The 1980s' interventionism proved that the region will go along with the United States reluctantly for a time, but, sooner or later, it will find its independent voice to pursue alternatives to U.S. policies.

The Central American peace plan of the late 1980s revealed that Latin America can offer but not impose an alternative to U.S. interventionism. It also showed how U.S. and Latin interests coincide and, unfortunately, how they diverge over the management and resolution of conflict, a key problem in the posthegemonic future of the hemisphere. The Reagan Doctrine is a response to hegemonic decline; the Central American peace plan, however, was the result of activism among the region's own states. Taking an independent approach to the problem, even small states can undercut the unilateral interventionism of the hegemonic state through initiative and cooperation. The peace plan provided a glimpse of what posthegemonic cooperation might look like; it also warned that, although cooperation without hegemony is possible, solving problems without the hegemonic state may not be.

How did the peace plan reflect an alternative to hegemonic restoration through the Reagan Doctrine? How has it fared? And is a pax Latina possible?

In Tune or at Odds?

The Central American peace plan and the Reagan Doctrine conflicted over several issues. Taken together, they represent how Latin American and U.S. approaches to solving problems may manage conflict in a posthegemonic hemisphere, but they also show how they may lead to or perpetuate conflict.

The peace plan, named Esquipulas II after the place in Guatemala where it was signed, advocated compliance with measures that would stabilize and tranquilize the region from one end to the other. Such political healing throughout the region was to be advanced through cease-fires, dialogue, and amnesty. Pacification would come from disarming insurgents, denying them bases from which to launch attacks, and banning outside military aid. Democratization and elections would enhance domestic pluralism within countries at the same time that it narrows the political differences among countries in the region.[15]

Both the Reagan Doctrine and the peace plan attempted to deal with the "Nicaragua problem." Both wanted to check and even undo the domestic shift to the Left in the Sandinista regime because both prefer democratic answers to the Central American crises. However, they differed in significant ways as well. The Reagan Doctrine sought "to remove (the Nicaraguan government) in the sense of its present structure"[16] and called for U.S. intervention until the Sandinistas surrendered to the contras. In contrast, the Central American peace plan sought, among other goals, a more pluralistic system in Nicaragua through negotiation rather than through U.S. intervention. The Reagan Doctrine pursued its objectives through confrontation, intervention, and interminable pressure on the Sandinistas, but the peace plan preferred a mix of multilateral concessions, pressure, and compliance. The doctrine sought the end of the Sandinistas; the peace plan sought to liberalize them. In other words, the Reagan Doctrine and the peace plan parted company over *how* to contain the Sandinistas while the U.S. and its

Central American allies agreed that an unrepentant Sandinista regime was a plague on the isthmus.

The Reagan administration's response to the peace plan was enlightening. The plan had shifted the initiative and leadership in the region away from the United States. The administration had stated for years that if the Sandinistas would embrace "democracy" then it could find a way to live with them. Yet the Reagan administration claimed that the peace plan was "fatally flawed" because it did not guarantee Sandinista compliance with provisions about democracy *before* the contras surrendered their arms and became assimilated into the body politic of the war-torn country; only if the contras were able to apply military pressure to the Sandinistas, contrary to the treaty, would the regime in Managua be forced to comply with the provisions about democratization. This theory proved flawed because the Sandinistas liberalized the regime, and lost power to the opposition, although the contras had not thrown down their arms.

But U.S. support for the contras was never seriously connected to any realistic strategy for negotiating with the Sandinistas. And the implementation of the Reagan Doctrine was outside the intent of the peace plan. The doctrine stipulated that the only negotiable issues were the terms under which the Sandinistas would be willing to surrender power; realistic negotiations that presumed the continued existence of the Sandinistas were never placed on a par with the goal of dislodging them from power. Thus, the Reagan administration regarded negotiations as a tool to deflect criticism and to support the military side of the policy, rather than to achieve U.S. interests with its enemies. For example, a confidential National Security Council document during the first term of the Reagan administration boasted how the United States had been able to derail a draft of the Contadora treaty, the forerunner of the Central American peace plan.

Although the Reagan Doctrine and the peace plan were two sides of the same coin, the doctrine would ultimately have negated the plan. Aiding the contras was the unilateral thrust of the doctrine, but this was clearly at odds with the plan's call for demobilizing insurgencies throughout Central America. If the plan itself avoided a slow death from implementation failures, steps towards compliance could further erode the legitimacy and effectiveness of the contra strategy. The peace plan could not work without U.S. acquiescence, but the Reagan Doctrine was a distasteful reminder of U.S. interventionism in Latin America.

Esquipulas II

The peace accord offered an indigenous solution for a very difficult problem. Esquipulas II was more successful than the Contadora process as an alternative to U.S. policy because the latter was seen in Central America as an open-ended plan imposed upon the region from its larger Latin American neighbors. It did not insure the establishment of democracy throughout the region, a key objective of the Central American plan. Nicaragua's neighbors also detected a bias toward Managua among the Contadora countries, especially Mexico, and Central Americans were skeptical about the democratic credentials of Mexico and Panama, two of the four Contadora members. Meanwhile, leading dailies in the region lampooned democracy in Panama during the mid-1980s. One cartoon depicted a Panamanian president as a puppet on the hand of General Noriega. (Noriega later "fired" the president after *he* tried to fire Noriega.)

The original version of the peace plan (Esquipulas I) set things in motion. All five Central American republics were expected to comply because all signed the accords, and others were asked to comply even if they had not signed. The United States did not sign the accords and has not complied with them.

The terms of Esquipulas I

1. provided for a *general amnesty* within sixty days of signing. Dialogue was to take place between all governments and the unarmed opposition to these governments. A cease-fire was to go into effect when the dialogue began.
2. called for *suspending military aid* to rebel forces from foreign governments. Rebels were to refuse such aid, if offered.
3. required the five countries to *deny the use of their territory to groups seeking to destabilize neighboring governments* and to deny them any support.
4. called for *disarming of rebels* and irregular forces sixty days after signing.
5. made provision for a committee to *verify compliance.*
6. called for authentic *democratization* and enumerated steps to bring this about. Within sixty days of signature, freedom of the press, association, media, and expression were to be proclaimed and practiced in all signatory countries.
7. set forth provisions for *elections.* A Central American parliament was to be chosen in the first half of 1988, and countries were to conduct national and local elections as provided for in their constitutions. All five countries (including Nicaragua) were to schedule elections for no later than 1990.

The original version contained no provisions on penalties for non-compliance or about simultaneity of treaty provisions.

Signed in August 1987, Esquipulas II differed slightly from the first. The period for establishing various freedoms was extended to ninety days, and there were additional provisions on follow-up and verification. Other nations, including some of the Contadora group, were given the task of conducting negotiations on force levels and disarmament of rebels. Like the original version, the modified peace plan called for deactivation of rebel forces before full democratization.

The peace plan received mixed reviews. It was greeted more warmly throughout Central America and in Europe than it was in Washington. Some in the U.S. capital believed that Nicaragua had gotten the better of the deal. They would have preferred an accord that would have forced the Sandinistas to abandon the emergency law, hold elections sooner, grant amnesty to the contras, and guarantee them a place in Nicaraguan politics. Yet for many in Central America, the plan was a source of some comfort. Above all, it was *their* plan, for better or worse. U.S. policy had not brought peace nor the downfall of the Sandinistas, and the plan was an alternative to endless conflict.

Unable to derail Esquipulas II, the United States tried to preempt it. A bipartisan peace proposal from the United States, announced just two days before the Central American peace plan was signed in August 1987, proved to be too little, too late. In fact, it may have spawned a sense of resentment in Central America and perhaps hastened the signing of the agreement by some of regional Washington's allies, such as President Duarte of El Salvador.

Esquipulas II promised relief; the Reagan Doctrine promised more of the same. But war is a viable policy only as long as it holds out the hope of achieving goals with bearable costs. An expensive stalemate faced the war-torn countries of Central America, and many were disheartened at the prospect of an endless war with escalating costs. Meanwhile, the insurgency in Nicaragua showed no sign of a conclusive victory for either side. It is ironic that the contra war, designed to topple the Sandinistas, actually led them to accept a plan that the United States opposed. In El Salvador, the Farabundo Martí National Liberation Front and the Democratic Revolutionary Front (the FMLN-FDR) can still wage, but not win, the war, as was proved once again in their late-1989 offensive. In Guatemala, the war of attrition waged by the guerrillas in the highlands has not attracted widespread popular support, but the military is unable to suppress these forces entirely.

The peace plan was a break with U.S. policy, and, consequently, was denounced in Washington. Contrary to U.S. wishes, the terse accord left some rather critical details to be worked out later.[17] The treaty deferred steps needed to implement the plan on certain points. Tough issues, such as a timetable for democratization and provisions for compliance, were not dealt with clearly. And, again, the Reagan administration wanted democratization before deactivating the contras.

The peace plan has also proved difficult to live by. The Sandinistas have vacillated between liberalization and repression, making negotiations with the contras as called for in the plan very difficult. And living next door to a revolutionary government can be discomforting. Nicaragua, for example, broadcast strident views to its neighbors over standard-wave radio signals, and music programs are laced with messages designed to inspire insurrection in adjacent countries. Another example is regional bus service, a major leg of interurban transportation in Central America. Such service used to extend all the way from Guatemala in the north to Panama in the south, but the link was severed and service north of Costa Rica was canceled during the late 1980s.

Despite such irritations, however, the peace plan was supported by those most affected by the war. The pursuit of détente with the Sandinistas is Central America's way of relieving tensions, promoting democracy, and ending the fighting. As the Reagan administration proved in late 1987 when it signed the intermediate nuclear forces agreement with the Soviet Union, you can deal with your adversary without necessarily trusting him. Central America took this lesson to heart and, in its own way, the peace plan has tried to put it into practice.

Making Peace

The peace plan was by no means a definitive response to the Reagan Doctrine, for a number of reasons. First, the United States cannot be discounted. Second, wariness and suspicion within Central America may impale the peace plan, and popular skepticism and the trials of compliance may poison the prospects for peace. Clearly, the unilateralism of the Reagan Doctrine was proven to be unavailing, but, on the other side of the ledger, the signers of the peace plan must vindicate their faith in negotiation and détente.

Unfortunately, skepticism has been justified to some extent by what has happened since August 1987. By early 1988, the record on compliance was mixed; depending upon one's perspective, the glass was either half empty or half full. It is true that the five countries have complied— up to a point. Some have merely complied formally with some provisions and sidestepped others.

Without its own insurgency to deal with, Costa Rica had little to do except encourage others to do better. President Arias had already closed down CIA and contra bases; however, allowing even a few contra representatives to be politically active within Costa Rica could be seen a possible breach of the treaty. So, in January 1988, they were "invited" to leave.

The Salvadoran government took a number of steps towards compliance. It stopped logistical support to the contras in Nicaragua, engaged in direct talks with the FMLN-FDR (which eventually broke down), encouraged Guillermo Ungo and other rebel leaders to return from exile, declared an amnesty and a fifteen-day unilateral ceasefire, allowed the FMLN-FDR to open political offices in government-controlled areas, and permitted some 4,000 refugees to return to rebel-controlled areas. On the negative side, political killings and other human rights abuses still stain the Salvadoran record. The rebels have not stopped fighting and still carry out sabotage against the country's infrastructure. Furthermore, the Salvadoran military complained that the peace plan hindered the war effort. The future of peace in El Salvador is uncertain.

Honduras did not comply with either the spirit or the letter of several provisions in the accord during the year following the treaty signing. For example, it did not deprive the contras of area, bases, and other support called for under the accord. In fact, Honduras refused to admit for a time that the contras even operated in its territory. Neither did it cut off supplies being sent to the contras. The treaty calls for signatories to create commissions of national reconciliation, but, in Honduras, the commission is weak and ineffective. Amnesty in Honduras means very little because the army does not take many prisoners.[18] Political and civil rights do exist, however, as stipulated in the peace accords.

With its first elected civilian president in many years, the Guatemalan government met briefly with rebel guerrillas in Spain. When nothing came of the meeting, government troops opened up a major offensive against them. The rebels have also refused to keep the peace. Still, basic freedoms, such as speech and press, were more protected under the civilian presient in the late 1980s than than they were in the early 1980s.

The Sandinistas were indispensable for compliance because they were the only Leftists in power and because a more skeptical eye was perhaps cast toward Managua than toward San Salvador, Tegucigalpa, Guatemala, and San Jose. In effect, the Sandinistas were guilty until proven innocent. And, in the beginning, this wariness seemed all but justified. The Sandinistas formally complied with some provisions of the peace plan but were not consistent; for example, they vacillated for years on how to deal with the independent media, allowing *La Prensa* to operate more or less freely and then closing it down. In the past, political parties complained of harassment and unfair rules, but the 1990 election was the fairest election held in all of Central America, except for Costa Rica. The UNO was well financed and operated as freely as possible. Amnesty was also a concern. The Sandinistas gradually relented, first releasing one thousand political prisoners from Nicaraguan jails in the late 1980s and then releasing still other prisoners, including some members of the infamous National Guard who had fought the Sandinistas during the Somoza dynasty. Talks with the rebels never did lead to a lasting peace before the electoral defeat in 1990. The peace talks broke down and President Ortega, in the fall of 1989, created a political uproar when he cancelled the official cease-fire due to continuing contra attacks. However, the campaign went ahead as scheduled. The Sandinistas also admitted publicly that they had aided the leftist rebels in El Salvador and had planned to create a huge reserve army.[19] Like many of the signatories, Nicaragua had sidestepped some of the spirit and a few of the letters of the treaty.

However, democratization was the most basic issue of compliance. There was pervasive skepticism about the willingness of the Sandinistas to surrender the power for which they had fought long and hard. Would the Sandinistas be willing to hold a fair and free election in which anti-Sandinista opponents could vie for control of the government? For years, Nicaragua's neighbors had harped on Sandinista noncompliance; charges of bad faith were levelled at Ortega at the San Jose summit of Central American presidents. President Oscar Arias had often lectured Ortega on democracy, but it was by no means clear just how well the pupil had taken the lesson to heart. At about the same time, in a meeting with Sandinista labor unions, Ortega publicly speculated about how far the Sandinistas would be willing to liberalize. He said they would be unlikely to lose to an opposition party in an election, but added that, if they did, the Sandinistas would surrender the government but not the power. The Sandinista Front and the people, he said, would ensure that the government would not turn the country over to the capitalist and *somocista* elements.[20] The 1990 electoral campaign, called for in the peace treaty, did much to answer Ortega's skeptics. Not only was the election widely regarded as fair, but the Sandinistas accepted their defeat at the polls. In an ultimate sense, they had complied with the treaty and paid a high price. Compliance had led to power-sharing, even without an official end to the war.

A de facto end to the war did not come before democratization because the United States did not want it. The truce and cease-fire in 1988 between the Sandinistas and the contras, which never really held firm, was opposed by the Reagan administration; a cease-fire prior to Sandinista concessions on democracy and power-sharing was unwise, the administration insisted. But holding a fair election during the war actually hurt the Sandinistas at the polls. So although the United States may have gotten what it wanted in Nicaraguan by dislodging the

Sandinistas from power, it had opposed many of the negotiated concessions that helped bring the Sandinistas down.

The problems inherent in Esquipulas II do not obscure its significance.
It remains an alternative to interventionism, from the Latin view, because
it stresses the independent, regional management of conflict. It does
coincide with some U.S. interests (i.e., democratization), but it also
relies upon measures that the Reagan administration largely opposed.
Fundamentally, the Reagan Doctrine called for intervention and hegemony as the way to manage the crisis. The peace plan called, instead,
for the Latin Americanization of the solution. Whether this really is an
effective way to reconcile national interests remains to be seen. The
1980s have shown that the Reagan Doctrine was too selective and
limited to restore U.S. power and credibility throughout Latin America;
it is too soon to tell if the peace plan will meet a similar fate. A pax
Latina may be illusive if the United States objects to its terms or if
these terms would threaten the claims to power of determined adversaries. The truth may be hard to accept: Neither the United States nor
Latin America have the exclusive power to invent a way to manage
conflict.

Currently, the United States and Latin America exercise countervailing
influences, and the U.S. will to intervene has stimulated Latin American
activism. But, alone or together, they have yet to take the initial steps
towards managing the hemisphere by minimizing the sources of discord
and enhancing the bases of cooperation. Until this is done, they will
be held hostage to, rather than transcend, the ordeal of hegemonic
decline. The stalemate between U.S. interventionism and Latin American
activism underscores a need to develop a new approach to management
of the hemisphere in an era of diminished hegemony.

9

Beyond Hegemony

In the shadow of a slowly fading giant, the hemisphere has no coherent way to manage conflict or to erect a stable order for a posthegemonic era. If the 1980s are an indicator of the future, then the Americas are still far from a utopian millennium of enduring peace, balanced growth, and hemispheric cooperation. Instead, diffusion of power, revolutionary defection, strategic intrusion, Latin American activism, and the inconsistent will of the United States to be hegemonic promise a turbulent and fluid situation in inter-American relations. What must be done to transcend these changes and to reconstruct the Americas after hegemony?

The ordeal for the Americas in the years to come is to adjust to a complex, new reality in which hegemony lingers but may not flourish. The United States is the military Goliath of the hemisphere, but no country feels all that secure, even the United States. It is the faltering economic colossus, but it has emerged from the adversity of the "lost" decade better than Latin America and retains impressive advantages in economic power. These paradoxes characterize the troubled interlude between hegemony and another order that has yet to crystallize.

As hegemony gradually proves to be less workable in the future, what will come next? What will become of hemispheric management? The declining hegemonic state still exerts great influence; an emerging but divergent Latin America seeks to exert more influence. And neither can dictate the rules for the Americas. This transition from hegemony, the greatest challenge facing the Americas, may last a long, long time.

Managing inter-American relations in a posthegemonic era is a formidable task. States often are guided by leaders who think in the short term and in the narrow framework of national advantage. If everyone insists on acting like a "rational egoist," cooperation may be sacrificed. It is possible that Latin America might be better off if the United States was less influential in the hemisphere—a little distance may, indeed, make better neighbors. History shows that cooperation overtakes discord in those rare cases when working together overwhelms the recent trend of assertive nationalism in the hemisphere. What the discord of the 1980s proves is that the United States and Latin America have pursued parochial interests and forsaken the longer-term benefits of cooperation.

Despite the policies of the Reagan administration and the changes in the 1980s which muted the decline of U.S. hegemony, the Americas now confront a future in which neither the United States nor Latin America can manage their hemisphere independently. North American edicts will rarely carry the day; Latin American pleas will not do so either.

The United States must secure its interests in Latin America while accepting the decline of U.S. hegemony. This means that it must "move from a stance of dominance to one of cooperation,"[1] although its influence will continue to be great, if not always decisive in hemispheric affairs.

Dominance and cooperation coexist uneasily in the Americas, and irreconcilable interests and zero sum conflict pervade all corners of the hemisphere. Dependency theory is not alone in arguing that inherent inequalities of affluence and the asymmetries of power are perpetuated by powerful states and nonstate actors. In this hardened view of irreconcilable conflict, national interests clash on the fundamental issues of power and the distribution of benefits from the structure of power. Cooperation would therefore be superfluous if the power asymmetries are so pronounced that the United States could have its way without Latin American cooperation. But this is not true of the Americas. Failure to cooperate today means that no country gets exactly what they want from inter-American relations.

The decline of hegemony brings a good deal of discord, often obliterating any vision of possible cooperation. Stable hegemony surrenders to the fluidity of asymmetric interdependence. And interdependence often makes for more, not less, conflict. Change places new burdens on both the United States and Latin America, and in attempting to shift the burdens onto others, the states of the region adopt incompatible policies, leading to further discord. In the 1980s, the United States did little to foster cooperation; the Reagan administration relied instead upon measures inimical to consensus and conflict management.

U.S. policies toward Latin America have been interventionistic politically, often protectionistic in economic terms, increasingly restrictive of immigration, patronizing in style and unilateral in implementation.[2]

By defining interests in zero sum terms, the United States precludes greater cooperation at the same time that it compels Latin America to find new ways to manage conflict and challenge U.S. policy. It has virtually discarded the regional arrangements for conflict resolution that it helped to define and refine in the immediate post–World War II era. Rather, it pursues sectarian and parochial interests over those that are more characteristic of a hegemonic state in full bloom.

Latin America has explored some new ways of cooperating through the Esquipulas II accords, the Cartagena group, and other efforts. But it has also had trouble overcoming discord within its own ranks. For one thing, the sheer diversity of the region makes it exceedingly difficult to find common ground on security problems, the debt crisis, and other pressing matters. The emergence of democracy in the 1980s has been of some help in this regard, but regional pluralism has so far fed conflict rather than cooperation in the hemisphere. Deliberately and out of necessity, it excluded the United States from some cooperative endeavors. In the 1970s, the Latin American Economic System (SELA) was created without the United States. In the 1980s, the Contadora group sought a negotiated settlement in Central America without the U.S. involvement. And the signatories of Esquipulas II took their own path toward a settlement, even as they implicitly acknowledged the power of the United States to undermine it.

A nostalgia for unilateralism on the part of the United States and a tendency toward selective multilateralism on the part of Latin America are signposts of inter-American relations under stress. Both trends threaten the chances for sustained cooperation across a whole host of security and economic issues.

Cooperation After Hegemony

Although hegemonic decline fosters conflict, cooperation after hegemony *is* possible. Furthermore, it is in the long-term interests of the United States and Latin America to narrow the scope of conflict and broaden the scope of cooperation whenever possible; the asymmetric interdependence of the Americas gives them no other choice. Increasingly, the United States cannot "win" without Latin American cooperation, and Latin America cannot "win" without U.S. cooperation. Although growing discord suggests that relations are often a "win-lose" proposition in the Americas, the way out of this stalemate requires a realization by both parties that security and prosperity are ultimately indivisible.

In an era of decline and change, what is *at a minimum* necessary for building cooperation in the Americas? To answer this, we must look at (1) the *common ground* of mutual interests and (2) the *international institutions* sustained by states.

Common Ground

Sharing this hemisphere is exasperating; finding enough in common to manage conflict in this contentious community of states can be overwhelming. In the old days, it was easier to govern the hemisphere because ideological hegemony made cooperation possible. Latin American leaders could agree that the United States did what was good for both the United States and sometimes what was good for them as well. In addition, the United States had the power and the interest to help things along.

But the scenario has changed. Ideological hegemony has crumbled, and the legitimacy of many U.S. actions has been impugned throughout the hemisphere. What the United States seeks may not be what Latin America seeks or the ways in which it would achieve broadly shared goals may be out of sync with Latin preferences. Today, Latin America no longer accepts U.S. leadership unequivocally. Stephen Krasner offers a viewpoint that is helpful here. He believes, as any realist would, that differences in power among states go a long way toward accounting for their different interests. More to the point, they account for the discord in North-South relations.[3] A realist view of interests in the Americas would, therefore, stress that conflict arises from asymmetries of national power.

There are complications, though. National interests and power are not necessarily so clear or straightforward.[4] If interests come from power, then what are we to make of the weak countries going along with—even taking advantage of—the opportunities of the international economic system? And how do we account for different interests within Latin America over the debt issue, for example? The poor and weak states are not poor and weak to the same extent.

Finding common ground in the Americas also recalls the issues of Latin American autonomy and U.S. power. What Latin America seeks is to calm its own anxieties about political vulnerability vis-à-vis the United States and the international system. Maximizing autonomy or increasing power is the overriding goal of countries seeking to reduce such threats. In fact, seeking power may even eclipse growth and prosperity as a priority.[5] Thus, common ground exists, but it is circumscribed by how the power of states affects their interests and how these interests are perceived. A black-and-white version of inter-American interests perpetuates the belief that there is little common ground, yet a narrow band of common interests can be found on some security and economic issues.

Let us touch upon peace, democratization, and economic issues as possible areas of common ground. The conventional wisdom is that the United States and the Sandinistas had irreconcilable differences due to the East-West overtones to the conflict.[6] The protagonists were painted in starkly contrasting hues: The United States was implacably intrusive and Nicaragua was committed to spreading revolution.

The Esquipulas II peace plan offered another lesson in building mutual interests. By excluding the United States and Contadora countries, the five remaining states of Central America built upon the peace plan of President Arias of Costa Rica. Broad agreement may have been helped along by a growing desperation and exhaustion in the small countries in Central America, as the rising costs of conflict forced a search for mutual interests where few had existed before.

Consensus emerged on broad points among those most keenly affected by the conflict. The resultant plan incorporated a cease-fire, elections, "democratization," and a ban of outside military support. Yet the key to the agreement may have been its breadth. For cooperation to flourish, agreement must survive the difficult process of translating general terms into concrete realities. It is at this critical juncture that consensus is most threatened. A negotiated settlement of conflict must protect the security interests of all major parties in the short term. But only if all parties are willing to talk to each other is it possible to envision mutual interests and gain. Yet what comes first? Must the insurgents in El Salvador and in Nicaragua first throw down their weapons? Or must they accept the situation they are trying to change before serious negotiations can take place?

Mutual interests may exist on the issue of democracy. Strengthening democracy may involve the protection of individual rights and socio-economic progress. And this, in turn, might necessitate a reinvigorated commitment to growth and distributive justice. It is, for example, myopic to attack the drug trade without addressing the economic and social reasons behind it in Bolivia, Peru, Colombia, or elsewhere. Economic issues also raise opportunities and challenges for developing mutual interests. Security issues are often portrayed in stark terms, but economic issues may hold out the possibility for greater (though still guarded) cooperation. To find mutual interests and build cooperation on these interests, states must deal with issues over which there may be winners, not just winners and losers. Among the specific economic issues that hold out hope for common ground are increasing the economic growth, expanding trade, sharing the burden of debt relief, infusing the region with new capital, adjusting the flow of international migration to national needs, and reducing drug trafficking.[7] But here, another truth comes into play: Common ground is easier to find on the broad issues, rather than on specific solutions.

Institutions

Although having some common ground is indispensable to cooperation in the posthegemonic future of the Americas, it is not enough. Cooperation through international institutions and less formal arrangements must also be achieved.

The Third World has relied upon international bodies to advance their interests and sustain individual members since the 1960s. Many of these institutions were created with the enthusiastic support of the United States. But by the time the United States lost control of them in the 1960s, such international bodies had come to be perceived as political clubs used by the Third World to assert its collective power against and to make claims on the developed world. However, there is no doubt that these institutions were vital to the drive for a new international economic order in the 1960s and 1970s. A fairly coherent Third World ideology and the decline of U.S. power also helped to strengthen the Third World's challenge to the economic liberalism of the hegemonic order.

Institutions foster cooperation by bringing governments together, legitimating behavior, limiting uncertainty, promoting common interests, and achieving the goals of states, including autonomy.[8] Ultimately, they make it possible to cooperate without the hegemony that created them in the first place.[9] What does this mean for the regional institutions of the Americas? What has happened to the venerable Pan-American Union, the Organization of American States, or the Rio Pact? Have they perpetuated cooperation on important matters for inter-American relations, or have they perished without receiving a formal burial?

The old inter-American institutions have survived, but just barely. They have not flourished and, in fact, many have even atrophied. For most practical purposes, they have been discarded or circumvented as mechanisms to promote intraregional cooperation. Take the Organization of American States as an example. It can trace its ancestry back one hundred years, but there are serious doubts about whether it will ever again be an important problem solver. U.S. financial support for the OAS is dwindling, and the Latin Americans have not rushed to its aid. More often than not, its principal mission in the peaceful resolution of conflict has been bypassed. In the Falklands/Malvinas War of 1982, the OAS sat on the sidelines as the United States helped Great Britain defeat Argentina. Seven years later, the involvement of the OAS in Noriega's Panama was unable to produce a collective solution just prior to the U.S. invasion.

New institutions in the hemisphere have been Latin American rather than inter-American. The Latin American Economic System, the Cartagena group, and others were organized to meet specific regional needs, rather than to deal with the most central problems facing U.S.–Latin American relations. These Latin-Americanized institutions have worked on the margins to foster cooperation among regional states. However, they have not confronted the essential questions of hegemonic power nor were they meant to. And they have left essentially unchanged the ways in which Latin American states interact with each other or with the world. Rather, they have been a response to a perceived need to manage technical, cultural, and economic relations among those Latin American countries that felt them to be useful, if only for modest purposes.

Discord

The bases for cooperation are skeletal, but they do exist. Unfortunately, however, the bases for discord are well entrenched and impressive. As hegemony ebbs, discord in the Americas is one of the few things to be found in ample supply.

Grievances, bombast, and breast-beating have filled the air of the Western Hemisphere for decades. U.S. *protectionism* is a grievance which is loudly protested by Latin American states for if they are to trade and grow out of debt and recession, the United States must relent on trade issues. On the other hand, the United States is concerned about Latin American states doing too little about *liberalizing economies* and *development strategies* as well as stemming the flow of illegal drugs and undocumented workers from their economies.

Latin America also objects to U.S.-supported *insurgency.* This recycled interventionism offends Latin American sovereignty and weakens regional efforts to conclude a negotiated settlement of the Central American conflict. But the United States took exception to any Nicaraguan peace plan developed by its Latin American neighbors that allowed the Sandinistas to survive without a major overhaul of their revolutionary state.

Latin America subscribes to the idea that the North, not just the South, should absorb some of the massive losses in *debt relief.* The United States, however, has yet to endorse such a view and may be reluctant to ever do so. Latin America also insists that the United States must do more to pump *capital* into Latin America at bargain rates to reignite growth—extraordinary needs require extraordinary measures. But the United States is more sanguine about the situation. It takes the view that the worst is over and that the best policy is to return to business as usual.

These discordant issues mar contemporary inter-American relations. But it is the deep-seated sources of discord that make such issues so difficult to solve to everyone's satisfaction. Five specific bases for discord impede the cooperative management of conflict. These are tied to the fundamentals of U.S.–Latin American relations and therefore help to explain why cooperation remains illusive.

1. A *divergence of perceived interests* permeates security and development issue areas;
2. *U.S. leadership* in the hemisphere has been openly assailed;
3. The United States and Latin America are at odds about the mix of *power and voice* in inter-American affairs;
4. There is a long-standing difference over who should carry the *burden of adjustment* for the economic and security crises besieging the Americas; and
5. The Americas are torn over the perennial issues of U.S. unilateral *interventionism* and Latin America's search for alternatives through *multilateralism.*

Irreconcilable Interests

Cold warriors in Washington, D.C., and Marxists in Latin America agree on at least one point: Their goals are irreconcilable because U.S. control and Latin American autonomy are polar opposites. The United States cannot feel secure unless it can pursue its own interests as it sees fit; Latin America cannot feel secure if the United States does just that.

The uncompromising U.S. view makes it clear that Latin Americans must be loyal foot soldiers in the larger war or be prepared to suffer the consequences. The United States must have its way, and its defense needs come first. As leader of the free world, it is in a larger, deadly conflict with the Soviet Union. For now, Latin America must accede to this view. According to the U.S. view, Latin America will be protected from Soviet expansion in the process. But, changes emanating from Moscow during the Gorbachev era may challenge this view in a more telling fashion than anything the Latin Americans themselves say or do.

The uncompromising Latin American view, sometimes described as "radical," also sees U.S. and Latin American security interests as implacably at odds. U.S. power, defiant and patronizing, poses a threat to Latin American independence and autonomy. It may not be realistic to exclude the United States from the region, but it is possible to tether or circumvent it to some extent. Having less to do with the

United States may be another strategy for maximizing autonomy. Although "radicals" call for an abrupt break, a more earth-bound strategy might be "selective delinking" of Latin America from the United States.[10] A lower profile and more self-reliance could reduce the intensity of the North-South conflict.

Leadership

Cooperation under hegemony happens because the hegemonic state desires it and has the power to make it happen and because the weak states accept the legitimacy of its leadership. In fact, Latin America looks to the United States for guidance and help even if it would prefer not to. If the hegemonic state does not want to underwrite cooperation, it will not happen; but it will also not happen if the small states go their own way by refusing to accept the legitimacy and benefits of hegemonic leadership. Leadership is dominance, but it also is cooperation based on the willingness to accept that leadership.

The erosion of ideological hegemony in Latin America is well advanced. The region has lost faith in the wisdom, good intentions, and competence of the United States to manage the Americas effectively. The debt crisis and events in Cuba, Nicaragua, the Malvinas, Grenada, and Panama go a long way to diminish the giant in the eyes of many in Latin America. Yet there may be no one else to turn to. Latin America laments U.S. leadership, but it also expects it. This ambivalence puts the United States in the awkward position of doing too much or not doing enough.

The problems of leadership and cooperation not only hound the United States but permeate Latin America, as well. The United States must learn to cope with its fading legitimacy on issues of hemispheric governance, and Latin America must help to create and rebuild legitimate structures of cooperation. Although Latin America has the advantage of extending its imprimatur to genuinely regional efforts in a way that unilateral U.S. initiatives cannot, a void left by the United States would be hard to fill.

Power and Voice

It used to be evident who did and should govern in the Americas. Now, however, the uneven and incomplete decline of U.S. power has seriously weakened simple verities about the distribution of power; it is unclear who should have a voice on the pressing issues of hemispheric governance.

No longer can the United States speak for Latin America. Indeed, it is not even certain that *any* single entity can speak for Latin America—

or even if there is one Latin America. Today, U.S. power is primarily the ability to assert its national interests in certain forums and in certain circumstances; less and less is it the ability to integrate interests throughout the hemisphere or to devise cooperative strategies. Its power to say no remains formidable; its power on questions of hemispheric governance—the power to say yes with others—is less impressive.

In the uncertain era of hegemonic decline, both the United States and Latin America claim more than their capabilities can accomplish. During the 1980s, the United States invoked the well-worn vision of the hemisphere as a U.S. domain, but in attempting to fulfill this vision, it did not always hit the mark. Similarly, Latin America's ambitions were more grandiose than its capacity to realize them. Unable to fill the void left by a less vibrant hegemonic state, Latin America could have aspired to a joint condominium with the United States, but instead had to settle for a less formidable role in hemispheric governance. Latin America and the United States are also at odds on how their interests should be represented. At present, neither a pax Americana nor a pax Latina is possible. Both desire a solution to the Central American imbroglio, but a solution acceptable to one may not be to the other.

Intervention

The one issue that has triggered the most discord in the Americas during the 1980s is U.S. interventionism. The way that the United States has inserted itself into Latin America has often driven a wedge into inter–American relations. Specific, short-term interests of the United States have, in other words, prevailed over broader questions of hemispheric governance. For its part, Latin America has not always staked out a coherent position. It rhetorically condemns intervention as contrary to the OAS Charter, but it has also been an occasional coconspirator in both U.S. interventionism and in homegrown interventionism within its own ranks.

U.S. intervention in the late twentieth century has unified Latin America while raising the level of dissonance between the United States and this region. Of course, the Reagan Doctrine devised an ideological and strategic test for intervention: If the regime is radical, pro-Soviet, or pro-Cuban, intervention, if not actual invasion, is by all means necessary. Such qualified intervention is not reserved only for the radical heretics in the Americas in the posthegemonic era.

Intervention has probably done more than anything else to sour the prospects for cooperation on inter-American issues. Yet for good reasons of its own, Latin America holds steady on a course for increased coordination. More affected by asymmetric interdependence than the

United States, the Latin American states have a direct interest in developing cooperative measures as an antidote for U.S. intervention. Cooperation is also a more satisfactory way to narrow the gap between their growing power and their ambitious national interests. But organization and coordination between states are hardly cost-free.

Although the United States was more inclined to practice intervention than cooperation during the 1980s, in the future it will have to view cooperation as a more viable option if it hopes to salvage its relations with Latin America. The record of the Reagan Doctrine certainly proved that trying to act like a diminished hegemonic state has its ups and downs. The underlying problem is that cooperation must somehow either reconcile diverse national interests or redefine them. If the United States will not accept anything less than the ouster of a regime, then cooperation may only be possible within Latin America, but not throughout the Americas. The prospect that the United States will be more interventionist in Latin America than the Soviet Union is in Eastern Europe is certainly not far-fetched in the Gorbachev era. Intraregional intervention is another problem for Latin America because a clash of interests in assertive states may nurture intrusion. On the other hand, consensus on interests for security and economic issues breathes life into cooperation as an alternative, rather than as a substitute, for intervention.

The United States and Latin America will likely continue to go their own ways. A new doctrine from the North will attempt to achieve U.S. interests in a hemisphere that is increasingly immune to unilateral and recycled policies. And Latin America will find unity in its opposition to U.S. policy, but it will have great difficulty in finding an acceptable alternative to it. The intrinsic diversity and differing ambitions of the states themselves present as great a challenge as does the United States.

Today, the United States is unable to restore the Americas of the past, and Latin America alone cannot reinvent the Americas for the future. These unequal partners must work *together* to redesign the Western Hemisphere by adjusting to the ordeal of hegemony, not by ignoring its significance. They must come to terms with their interdependence and find methods to manage the Americas jointly to ensure a stable peace. Only the twenty-first century will reveal how well they meet this challenge.

Notes

Chapter One

1. Lester D. Langley, *The United States and the Caribbean in the Twentieth Century* (Athens: University of Georgia Press, 1985), p. 14.

2. Richard McCall, "From Monroe to Reagan: An Overview of U.S.–Latin American Relations" in *From Gunboats to Diplomacy,* ed. Richard Newfarmer (Baltimore: The Johns Hopkins University Press, 1984), p. 16.

3. Walter LaFeber, *Inevitable Revolutions: The United States in Central America* (New York: W. W. Norton, 1984), pp. 80–81; G. Pope Atkins, *Latin America in the International Political System* (New York: The Free Press, 1977), p. 97.

4. Atkins, *Latin America,* pp. 90–91.

5. LaFeber, *Inevitable Revolutions,* p. 28.

6. E. Bradford Burns, *Latin America; A Concise Interpretive History* (Englewood Cliffs, N.J.: Prentice-Hall, 1972), p. 143.

7. Gordon Connell-Smith, *The Inter-American System* (London: Oxford University Press, 1966), p. 10.

8. Fernando Henrique Cardoso and Enzo Faletto, *Dependency and Development in Latin America* (Berkeley: University of California Press, 1979), p. 35.

9. D.C.M. Platt, "Dependency in Nineteenth-Century Latin America: An Historian Objects," *Latin American Research Review* 15 (1980): pp. 115, 116.

10. Michael J. Kryzanek, *U.S.–Latin American Relations* (New York: Praeger, 1985), p. 16; Atkins, *Latin America,* p. 96.

11. Jerald A. Combs, *The History of American Foreign Policy* (New York: Alfred A. Knopf, 1986), p. 186.

12. LaFeber, *Inevitable Revolutions,* p. 39.

13. Albert Fishlow, "The Mature Neighbor Policy," in *Latin America and the World Economy,* ed. J. Grunwald (Beverly Hills: Sage, 1978), p. 31.

14. Bryce Wood, *The Dismantling of the Good Neighbor Policy* (Austin: University of Texas Press, 1985), p. 194.

15. Dick Steward, *Trade and Hemisphere: The Good Neighbor Policy and Reciprocal Trade* (Columbia: University of Missouri Press, 1975), pp. 276, 280.

16. Quoted in ibid., p. 271.

17. James R. Kurth, "The United States and Central America: Hegemony in Historical and Comparative Perspective" in *Central America: International Dimensions of the Crisis,* ed. Richard Feinberg (New York: Holmes and Meier, 1982), p. 52.

Chapter Two

1. Jorge I. Dominguez, "Consensus and Divergence: The State of the Literature on Inter-American Relations in the 1970s," *Latin American Research Review* 13 (1978): p. 99.

2. Robert Gilpin, *The Political Economy of International Relations* (Princeton: Princeton University Press, 1987), pp. 77–78.

3. Bruce Russett, "The Mysterious Case of Vanishing Hegemony; or Is Mark Twain Really Dead?" *International Organization* 39 (Spring 1985): p. 211.

4. Susan Strange, "Still an Extraordinary Power: America's Role in a Global Monetary System," in *The Political Economy of International and Domestic Monetary Relations,* eds. Raymond Lombra and Willard E. Witte (Ames: Iowa State University Press, 1982), p. 82.

5. Robert O. Keohane, *After Hegemony: Cooperation and Discord in the World Political Economy* (Princeton: Princeton University Press, 1984), p. 218.

6. Abraham Lowenthal, "Ronald Reagan and Latin America: Coping with Hegemony in Decline," in *Eagle Defiant? U.S. Foreign Policy in the 1980s,* eds. Kenneth A. Oye, Robert J. Lieber, and Donald Rothchild (Boston: Little, Brown, 1983), p. 235.

7. Robert Wesson, *U.S. Influence in Latin America in the 1980s* (New York: Praeger, 1982), pp. 17–18.

8. Dominguez, "Consensus and Divergence," pp. 94–95.

9. Wesson, *U.S. Influence,* p. 7.

10. Robert Pastor, "Explaining U.S. Policy Toward the Caribbean Basin," *World Politics* 38 (April 1986) p. 493.

11. Dominguez, "Consensus and Divergence," p. 92.

12. Wolf Grabendorff, "Interstate Conflict Behavior and Regional Potential for Conflict in Latin America," *Journal of InterAmerican Studies and World Affairs* 24 (August 1982), p. 288.

13. Pastor, "Explaining U.S. Policy," pp. 509, 512.

14. Norman A. Graebner, *America as A World Power: A Realist Appraisal from Wilson to Reagan* (Wilmington, Del.: Scholarly Resources, 1984), p. 277.

15. Pastor, "Explaining U.S. Policy," p. 488.

16. Harold Molineu, *U.S. Policy Toward Latin America* (Boulder: Westview Press, 1986), p. 156.

17. Thomas H. Moorer and Georges A. Fauriol, *Caribbean Basin Security* (Washington, D.C.: Praeger Publishers and CSIS, Washington Papers XI, 1984), p. 11.

18. Molineu, *U.S. Policy,* p. 213.

19. Cole Blasier, *The Hovering Giant* (Pittsburgh: University of Pittsburgh Press, 1976), p. 223.

20. Molineu, p. 173.

21. Riordan Roett, "Does the United States Have a Future in Latin America?" in *Latin America, Western Europe and the United States: Reevaluating the Atlantic Triangle,* eds. Wolf Grabendorff and Riordan Roett (New York: Praeger, 1985), p. 230.

22. Jorge I. Dominguez, "The Foreign Policies of Latin American States: Retreat or Reform?" in *Global Dilemmas,* eds. Samuel P. Huntington and Joseph S. Nye (Boston: Harvard University Press, 1985), pp. 192–193.

23. Stephen Krasner, *Structural Conflict* (Berkeley: University of California Press, 1985), pp. 13–14.

24. Wesson, *U.S. Influence,* p. 223.

25. Ole R. Holsti and James N. Rosenau, *American Leadership in World Affairs* (Boston: Allen and Unwin, 1984).

Chapter Three

1. Abraham Lowenthal, "Ronald Reagan and Latin America: Coping with Hegemony in Decline," in *Eagle Defiant: United States Foreign Policy in the 1980s,* eds. Kenneth A. Oye, Robert J. Lieber, and Donald Rothchild (Boston: Little, Brown, 1983), pp. 311–335.

2. Edward J. Greene, "The Ideological and Idiosyncratic Aspects of U.S.-Caribbean Relations," in *The Caribbean Challenge: U.S. Policy in A Volatile Region,* ed. Michael Erisman (Boulder, Colo.: Westview Press, 1984), p. 41.

3. George C. Herring and Kenneth M. Coleman, "Beyond Hegemony: Toward a New Central American Policy" in *The Central American Crisis,* eds. Kenneth M. Coleman and George C. Herring (Wilmington, Del.: Scholarly Resources, 1985), p. 227.

4. Robert Gilpin, *U.S. Power and the Multinational Corporation* (New York: Basic Books, 1975); Robert Gilpin, *War and Change in World Politics* (Cambridge: Cambridge University Press, 1981).

5. George Modelski, "Long Cycles and the Strategy of U.S. International Economic Policy," in *America in A Changing World Political Economy,* eds. William Avery and David Rapkin (New York: Longman, 1982), pp. 97–118.

6. David Lake, "International Economic Structures and American Foreign Economic Policy, 1887–1934," *World Politics* 35 (July 1983): pp. 521–522.

7. Robert Keohane, "Hegemonic Leadership and U.S. Foreign Economic Policy in the 'Long Decade' of the 1950s," in *America in a Changing World Political Economy,* eds. William P. Avery and David P. Rapkin, p. 50; Robert Keohane, *After Hegemony: Cooperation and Discord in the World Political Economy* (Princeton: Princeton University Press, 1984), p. 40.

8. Arthur Stein, "The Hegemon's Dilemma: Great Britain, the United States and the International Economic Order," *International Organization* 38 (1984): p. 384.

9. Charles Kindleberger, "Dominance and Leadership in the International Economy," *International Studies Quarterly* 25 (1981), p. 247.

10. David Lake, "International Economic Structures and American Foreign Economic Policy, 1887–1934," *World Politics* 35 (July 1983), p. 540.

11. Robert Keohane, *After Hegemony,* pp. 182–216.

12. Abraham Lowenthal, "Ronald Reagan and Latin America," p. 325 (emphasis added).

13. Sergio Bitar, "United States–Latin American Relations: Shifts in Economic Power and Implications for the Future," *Journal of InterAmericana Studies and World Affairs* 26 (1984), pp. 5, 19.

14. Kenneth Boulding, *Conflict and Defense* (New York: Harper and Row, 1962), p. 231.

15. Abraham Lowenthal, "Ronald Reagan and Latin America," p. 326.

16. Sergio Bitar, "United States–Latin American Relations," p. 5.

17. Steve Lande and Craig Van Grasstek, "Trade with the Developing Countries: The Reagan Record and Prospects," in *U.S. Foreign Policy and the Third World: Agenda 1985–1986,* eds. John W. Sewell, Richard E. Feinberg, and Valeriana Kallab (New Brunswick: Transaction Books, 1985), p. 86.

18. David F. Ross, "The Caribbean Basin Initiative: Threat or Promise?" in *The Central American Crisis,* eds. Kenneth Coleman and George C. Herring (Wilmington, Del.: Scholarly Resources, 1985), p. 140.

Chapter Four

1. Nestor Sanchez, "The Communist Threat," *Foreign Policy* 52 (Fall 1983): pp. 43–44.

2. The President's National Bipartisan Commission on Central America, *The Report of the President's National Bipartisan Commission on Central America* (New York: Macmillan, 1983), p. 45.

3. Richard Fagen, "Revolution and Crisis in Nicaragua," in *From Gunboats to Diplomacy,* ed. Richard Newfarmer (Baltimore: The Johns Hopkins Press, 1984), p. 143.

4. Enrique A. Baloyra, *El Salvador in Transition* (Chapel Hill: University of North Carolina Press, 1982), p. 182.

5. Robert Pastor, "Our Real Interests in Central America," *Atlantic Monthly* 250 (July 1982): p. 28.

6. Lars Schoultz, *Human Rights and United States Policy Toward Latin America* (Princeton: Princeton University Press, 1981), p. 376.

7. Sergio Ramírez Mercado, "On Nicaragua's Resolve" (Interview), *World Policy Journal* 1 (Spring 1984): p. 675.

8. Guillermo Ungo, "The People's Struggle," *Foreign Policy* 52 (Fall 1983): p. 54.

9. Ralph Lee Woodward, "The Rise and Decline of Liberalism in Central America," *Journal of InterAmerican Studies and World Affairs* 26 (August 1984): p. 291.

10. Samuel P. Huntington and Joan M. Nelson, *No Easy Choice: Political Participation in Developing Countries* (Cambridge: Harvard University Press, 1976), p. 4.

11. John A. Booth, "Political Participation in Latin America: Levels, Structure, Context, Concentration and Rationality," *Latin America Research Review* 14 (1979): p. 47.

12. In Flora Lewis, "Roots of Revolution," *New York Times Magazine,* November 11, 1984, p. 86.

13. U.S. Department of State, *Democracy of Latin America* (Washington, D.C.: Bureau of Public Affairs, 1984), p. 3.

14. Walden Bello and Edward S. Herman, "U.S.-Sponsored Elections in El Salvador and the Philippines," *World Policy Journal* (Summer 1984): pp. 851–869.

15. Raymond Bonner, *Weakness and Deceit: U.S. Policy and El Salvador* (New York: Times Books, 1984), p. 305.

16. Ibid., p. 306.

17. Stephen Kinzer, "Nicaragua Can't Vote Away Pressures," *New York Times,* November 11, 1984, p. 4E.

18. Stephen Kinzer, "Nicaragua Enacts Rules for Voting," *New York Times,* March 17, 1984, p. 5.

19. Tom Barry, Beth Wood, and Deb Preusch, *Dollars and Dictators: A Guide to Central America* (New York: Grove Press, 1983), p. 122.

20. Allan Nairn, "The Guns of Guatemala," *New Republic,* April 11, 1983, p. 171.

Chapter Five

1. Margaret Daly Hayes, "U.S. Security Interests in Central America in Global Perspectives," in *Central America: International Dimensions of the Crisis,* ed. Richard Feinberg (New York: Holmes and Meier, 1982), p. 10.

2. Viron Vaky, "Reagan's Central American Policy: An Isthmus Restored," in *Central America: Anatomy of Conflict,* ed. Robert S. Leiken (New York: Pergamon, 1984), p. 252.

3. Michael Barnes, "U.S. Policy in Central America: The Challenge of Revolutionary Change," in *Third World Instability: Central America as an European-American Issue,* ed. Andrew J. Pierre (New York: Council of Foreign Relations, 1985), p. 71 (emphasis in original).

4. David Ronfeldt, *Geopolitics, Security, and U.S. Strategy in the Caribbean Basin* (Santa Barbara, Cal.: Rand, 1983), p. 51.

5. James Malloy, "Comment," in *Confrontation in the Caribbean Basin,* eds. A. Adelman and R. Reading (Pittsburgh: University Center for International Studies, 1984), pp. 229–230.

6. Wolf Grabendorff, "The Role of Western Europe in the Caribbean Basin," in *Confrontation in the Caribbean Basin,* eds. A. Adelman and R. Reading (Pittsburgh: University of Pittsburgh Press, 1984), pp. 278–279.

7. Ibid., p. 281.

8. John D. Martz, "Comments," in *Confrontation in the Caribbean Basin,* eds. A. Adelman and R. Reading (Pittsburgh: University of Pittsburgh Press, 1984), p. 59.

9. Rene Herrera Zuñiga and Mario Ojeda, "Mexico's Foreign Policy and Central America," in *Central America: The International Dimensions of the Crisis,* ed. Richard Feinberg (New York: Holmes and Meier, 1982), pp. 129–131.

10. Olga Pellicer, "Mexico in Central America: The Difficult Exercise of Regional Power," in *The Future of Central America,* eds. Richard Fagen and Olga Pellicer (Stanford: Stanford University Press, 1983), pp. 120–121.

11. Susan Kaufman Purcell, "Demystifying Contadora," *Foreign Affairs* 64 (Fall 1985): p. 75.

12. Morris Rothenberg, "The Soviets and Central America," in *Central America: The Anatomy of Conflict,* ed. Robert S. Leiken (New York: Pergamon, 1984), p. 131.

13. Enrique Baloyra Herp, "Internationalism and the Limits of Autonomy: Cuba's Foreign Relations," in *Latin American Nations in World Politics,* eds. H. Muñoz and J. S. Tulchin (Boulder, Colo.: Westview Press, 1984), p. 169.

14. George Schultz, "Nicaragua: Will Democracy Prevail?" Current Policy #797 (Washington, D.C.: U.S. Department of State), p. 2.

Chapter Six

1. Ruth Sivard, *World Military and Social Expenditures 1985* (Washington, D.C.: World Priorities, 1985), pp. 10–11.

2. Jack Child, *Unequal Alliance: The Inter-American Military System, 1938–1978* (Boulder, Colo.: Westview Press, 1980), p. 159.

3. Cole Blasier, "Security: The Extracontinental Dimension," in *The United States and Latin America in the 1980s,* eds. Kevin Middlebrook and Carlos Rico (Pittsburgh: University of Pittsburgh Press, 1986), p. 525; James R. Kurth, "The United States, Latin America and the World: The Changing International Context of U.S.–Latin American Relations," in ibid., p. 64; Sergio Bitar, "Economics and Security: Contradictions in U.S.–Latin American Relations," in ibid., p. 596.

4. Cole Blasier, "The Soviet Union," in *Confronting Revolution: Security Through Diplomacy in Central America,* eds. M. Blachman, W. LeoGrande and K. Sharpe (New York: Pantheon Books, 1986), p. 259.

5. Bitar, "Economics and Security," p. 600.

6. Lars Schoultz, *National Security and U.S. Policy Toward Latin America* (Princeton: Princeton University Press, 1987), p. 11.

7. Blasier, "Security," p. 547.

8. Howard Wiarda, *In Search of Policy: The United States and Latin America* (Washington, D.C.: American Enterprise Institute for Public Policy Research, 1984), pp. 88–90.

9. Heraldo Muñoz, "The Latin American Policy of the Reagan Administration," in *Latin American Views of U.S. Policy,* eds. Robert Wesson and Heraldo Muñoz (New York: Praeger, 1986), p. 13.

10. For comparative figures (1982) on military spending, see Ruth Leger Sivard, *World Military and Social Expenditures 1985* (Washington, D.C.: World Priorities, 1985), p. 55.

11. Ibid., p. 35.

12. International Institute for Strategic Studies, *The Military Balance, 1984–1985* (London: IISS, 1985), p. 114.

13. Calculated by the author from Arms Control and Disarmament Agency, *World Military Expenditures and Arms Transfers, 1985* (Washington, D.C.: USACDA, August 1985), Table III, p. 133.

14. James Wilkie and Adam Perkal, eds., *Statistical Abstract of Latin America* (Los Angeles: UCLA Latin American Center Publications, 1984), Vol. 23, Table 1106, p. 211.

15. Richard Halloran, "Language School a Chart of U.S. Military Ties," *New York Times,* August 20, 1986, p. 7.

16. Harold Molineu, *U.S. Policy Toward Latin America* (Boulder, Colo.: Westview Press, 1986), p. 213.

17. Kenneth Coleman, "The Political Mythology of the Monroe Doctrine: Reflections on the Social Psychology of Hegemony," in *Latin America, the United States and the Inter-American System,* eds. John Martz and Lars Schoultz (Boulder, Colo.: Westview Press, 1980), p. 111.

18. U.S. Department of Defense, *Soviet Military Power 1985* (Washington, D.C.: U.S. Government Printing Office, 1985), pp. 116, 120.

19. Ibid., p. 121.

Chapter Seven

1. *New York Times,* October 4, 1988.

2. Paul R. Krugman, "U.S. Macro-economic Policy and the Developing Countries," in *U.S. Foreign Policy and the Third World: Agenda 1985–1986,* eds. John W. Sewell, Richard E. Feinberg, and Valeriana Kallab (New Brunswick: Transaction Books, 1985), p. 32.

3. Albert Fishlow, "Revisiting the Great Debt Crisis of 1982," in *Debt and Development in Latin America,* eds. Kwan S. Kim and David F. Ruccio (Notre Dame: University of Notre Dame Press, 1985), p. 127.

4. Latin American Economic System, *Latin American–United States Economic Relations, 1982–1983* (Boulder, Colo.: Westview Press, 1984), p. 77.

5. ECLAC, *External Debt in Latin America: Adjustment Policies and Re-negotiation* (Boulder, Colo.: Lynne Rienner Publishers, 1985), p. 8.

6. Chris C. Carvounis, *The Foreign Debt/National Development Conflict* (New York: Quorum Books, 1986), pp. 75–76.

7. Fishlow, "Revisiting the Great Debt Crisis," p. 103.

8. Paul R. Krugman, "U.S. Macro-economic Policy and the Developing Countries," in *U.S. Foreign Policy and the Third World: Agenda 1985–1986,* eds. John W. Sewell, Richard E. Feinberg, and Valeriana Kallab (New Brunswick: Transaction Books, 1985), pp. 38–39.

9. Carvounis, *The Foreign Debt,* p. 88.

10. Ibid., p. 172.

11. ECLAC, *External Debt,* p. 7.

12. Carvounis, *The Foreign Debt,* p. 147.

13. Ibid., p. 171.

14. Steven Sanderson, "Recasting the Politics of Inter-American Trade," *Journal of Inter-American Studies and World Affairs* 28 (Fall 1986): p. 88.

15. InterAmerican Development Bank, *Economic and Social Progress in Latin America: External Debt: Crisis and Adjustment* (Washington, D.C.: IDB, 1985), p. 7.

16. Alan J. Stoga, "If America Won't Lead," *Foreign Policy* 64 (Fall 1986): p. 81.

17. Richard E. Feinberg, "American Power and Third World Economics," in *Eagle Resurgent? The Reagan Era in American Foreign Policy,* eds. Kenneth A. Oye, Robert J. Lieber, and Donald Rothchild (Boston: Little, Brown, 1987), p. 153.

18. Sanderson, "Recasting the Politics," p. 90.

19. David Rockefeller, "Let's Not Write Off Latin America," *New York Times,* June 5, 1987, p. E15.

20. Carvounis, *The Foreign Debt,* pp. 105–106.

21. European Community, *The European Community and Latin America* (Brussels: Commission of European Communities, June–July 1986), pp. 3, 5.

22. Christine A. Bogdanowicz-Bindert, "World Debt: The United States Reconsiders," *Foreign Affairs* 64 (Winter 1985/1986): p. 264.

23. Fishlow, "Revisiting the Great Debt Crisis," p. 102.

24. Rockefeller, "Let's Not Write Off," p. E15.

25. ECLAC, *External Debt,* p. 47.

26. Rockefeller, "Let's Not Write Off," p. E15.

27. Charles F. Meissner, "Debt: Reform Without Governments," *Foreign Policy* 56 (Fall 1984): p. 83.

28. European Community, *The European Community and Latin America,* p. 4.

29. Carvounis, *The Foreign Debt,* p. 75.

30. InterAmerican Development Bank, *Economic and Social Progress,* p. 12.

31. Riordan Roett, "Peru: The Message from Garcia," *Foreign Affairs* (Winter 1985/1986): p. 283.

32. *Economist,* June 27 1987, p. 21.

33. *Washington Post National Edition,* June 15 1987, p. 21.

34. Sanderson, "Recasting the Politics," p. 91.

35. Ibid., p. 90.

Chapter Eight

1. These four dilemmas are restatements of John Lewis Gaddis, *Strategies of Containment: A Critical Appraisal of Postwar American National Security Policy* (New York: Oxford University Press, 1982), Chapter 2.

2. Eldon Kenworthy, "Grenada as Theater," *World Policy Journal* 2 (Fall 1984): pp. 181–200.

3. E. Bradford Burns, *At War with Nicaragua: The Reagan Doctrine and the Politics of Nostalgia* (New York: Harper and Row, 1987); *New York Times,* September 26, 1987, p. 1 and November 29, 1987, p. 1.

4. Congressional Quarterly, *Almanac* (Washington, D.C.: Congressional Quarterly, 1983), p. 135.

5. Eldon Kenworthy, "Grenada as Theater," p. 637.

6. Ibid., p. 649.

7. Walter LaFeber, *America, Russia and the Cold War, 1945–1984* (New York: Alfred A. Knopf, 1985), p. 307.

8. Abraham F. Lowenthal, *Partners in Conflict: The United States and Latin America* (Baltimore: The Johns Hopkins University Press, 1987), p. 46.

9. Robert Pastor, *Condemned to Repetition: The United States and Nicaragua* (Princeton: Princeton University Press, 1987).

10. John Reilly, "America's State of Mind," *Foreign Policy* 68 (Fall 1987): 52–53.

11. "Report Deals Another Blow to Reagan Record," *Congressional Quarterly Weekly Report,* November 17, 1987, pp. 2847–2853.

12. Richard Millett, "Looking Beyond Noriega," *Foreign Policy* 71 (Summer 1988): p. 47.

13. Ibid., p. 53.

14. Ibid., p. 50.

15. Susan Kaufman Purcell, "The Choice in Central America," *Foreign Affairs* 66 (Fall 1987): pp. 114–117.

16. E. Bradford Burns, *At War,* p. 26.

17. Susan Kaufman Purcell, "The Choice," p. 116.

18. *New York Times,* January 10, 1988, pp. 1, 8Y.

19. Ibid., p. 1.

20. "FSLN 'Entregaría' el Gobierno, no El Poder," *La Nación* (San Jose), December 14, 1987, p. 22A.

Chapter Nine

1. Abraham Lowenthal, *Partners in Conflict: The United States and Latin America* (Baltimore: The Johns Hopkins University Press, 1987), p. 47.

2. Ibid., p. 199.

3. Stephen Krasner, *Structural Conflict* (Berkeley: University of California Press, 1985).

4. David Lake, "Power and the Third World: Toward a Realist Political Economy of North-South Relations," *International Studies Quarterly* 31 (1987): p. 226.

5. Stephen Krasner, *Structural Conflict,* p. 26.

6. Mark Falcoff, "Nicaragua and Its Neighbors," in *Conflict in Nicaragua: A Multidimensional Perspective,* eds. Jiri Valenta and Esperanza Durán (Boston: Allen and Unwin, 1987), p. 173.

7. Abraham Lowenthal, *Partners in Conflict,*, pp. 184–185; Bela Balassa, Gerardo M. Bueno, Pedro-Pablo Kuczynski, and Mario Enrique Simonsen, *Toward Renewed Economic Growth in Latin America* (Mexico City: El Colegio de Mexico, 1986).

8. Robert O. Keohane, *After Hegemony,* p. 245.

9. Ibid., p. 246.

10. Stephen Krasner, *Structural Conflict,* pp. 301–302.

Bibliography

Arrighi, Giovanni. "A Crisis of Hegemony." In *Dynamics of Global Crisis,* edited by Samir Amin et al. New York: Monthly Review Press, 1982.

Atkins, G. Pope. *Latin America in the International Political System.* New York: The Free Press, 1977.

Bitar, Sergio. "United States Latin American Relations: Shifts in Economic Power and Implications for the Future." *Journal of Inter-American Studies and World Affairs* 26 (1984): 3–32.

––––––. "Economics and Security: Contradictions in U.S.–Latin American Relations." In *The United States and Latin America in the 1980s,* edited by Kevin Middlebrook and Carlos Rico. Pittsburgh: University of Pittsburgh Press, 1986.

Blachman, Morris, Douglas C. Bennett, William M. LeoGrande, and Kenneth E. Sharpe. "The Failure of the Hegemonic Strategic Vision." In *Confronting Revolution: Security through Diplomacy in Central America,* edited by Morris Blachman, William LeoGrande, and Kenneth Sharpe. New York: Pantheon Books, 1986.

Blasier, Cole. *The Hovering Giant: U.S. Responses to Revolutionary Change in Latin America.* Pittsburgh: University of Pittsburgh Press, 1976.

Coleman, Kenneth. "The Political Mythology of the Monroe Doctrine: Reflections on the Social Psychology of Hegemony." In *Latin America, the United States and the Inter-American System,* edited by John Martz and Lars Schoultz. Boulder, Colo.: Westview Press, 1980.

Dominguez, Jorge I. "Consensus and Divergence: The State of the Literature on Inter-American Relations in the 1970s." *Latin American Research Review* 13 (1978): 87–126.

––––––. "The Foreign Policies of Latin American States in the 1980s: Retreat or Reform?" In *Global Dilemmas,* edited by Samuel P. Huntington and Joseph S. Nye. Cambridge: Harvard University Press, 1985.

Durán, Esperanza. *European Interests in Latin America.* London: Routledge and Kegan Paul, 1985.

––––––. "Contadora: A Next Phase?" In *Conflict in Nicaragua: A Multidimensional Perspective,* edited by Jiri Valenta and Esperanza Durán. Boston: Allen and Unwin, 1987.

Feinberg, Richard E. "American Power and Third World Economics." In *Eagle Resurgent? The Reagan Era in American Foreign Policy,* edited by Kenneth A. Oye, Robert J. Lieber, and Donald Rothchild. Boston: Little, Brown, 1987.

Fishlow, Albert. "Revisiting the Great Debt Crisis of 1982." In *Debt and Development in Latin America,* edited by Kwan S. Kim and David F. Ruccio. Notre Dame, Ind.: University of Notre Dame Press, 1985.

Frieden, Jeffrey A. "The Brazilian Borrowing Experience: From Miracle to Debacle and Back." *Latin American Research Review* 22 (1987): 95–131.

Gilpin, Robert. *War and Change in World Politics.* Cambridge: Cambridge University Press, 1981.

———. *The Political Economy of International Relations.* Princeton: Princeton University Press, 1987.

Grabendorff, Wolf. "Interstate Conflict Behavior and Regional Potential for Conflict in Latin America." *Journal of InterAmerican Studies and World Affairs* 24 (August 1982): 267–294.

———. "The Role of Western Europe in the Caribbean Basin." In *Confrontation in the Caribbean Basin,* edited by A. Adelman and R. Reading. Pittsburgh: University Center for International Studies, 1984.

Griffith-Jones, Stephany, and Osvaldo Sunkel. *Debt and Development Crises in Latin America: The End of an Illusion.* Oxford: Clarendon Press, 1986.

Hayes, Margaret Daly. *Latin America and the U.S. National Interest: A Basis for U.S. Foreign Policy.* Boulder, Colo.: Westview Press, 1984.

Kenworthy, Eldon. "Central America: Beyond the Credibility Trap." *World Policy Journal* 1 (Fall 1983): 181–200.

———. "Grenada as Theater." *World Policy Journal* 2 (Spring 1984): 181–200.

Keohane, Robert O. *After Hegemony: Cooperation and Discord in the World Political Economy.* Princeton: Princeton University Press, 1984.

Kindleberger, Charles. "Dominance and Leadership in the International Economy." *International Studies Quarterly* 25 (1981):242–254.

Klaveren, Alberto Van. "The United States and the Inter-American Political System." In *Latin American Views of U.S. Policy,* edited by Robert Wesson and Heraldo Muñoz. New York: Praeger, 1986.

Krugman, Paul R. "U.S. Macro-economic Policy and the Developing Countries." In *U.S. Foreign Policy and the Third World: Agenda 1985–1986,* edited by John W. Sewell, Richard E. Feinberg, and Valeriana Kallab. New Brunswick: Transaction Books, 1985.

Kryzanek, Michael J. *U.S.–Latin American Relations.* New York: Praeger, 1985.

Kurth, James R. "The United States and Central America: Hegemony in Historical and Comparative Perspective." In *Central America: International Dimensions of the Crisis,* edited by Richard Feinberg. New York: Holmes and Meier, 1982.

LaFeber, Walter. *Inevitable Revolutions: The United States in Central America.* New York: W. W. Norton, 1984.

Lake, David A. "Power and the Third World: Toward a Realist Political Economy of North-South Relations." *International Studies Quarterly* 31 (1987):217–234.

Lande, Steve, and Craig VanGrasstek. "Trade with the Developing Countries: The Reagan Record and Prospects." In *U.S. Foreign Policy and the Third World: Agenda 1985–1986,* edited by John W. Sewell, Richard E. Feinberg and Valeriana Kallab. New Brunswick: Transaction Books, 1985.

Langley, Lester D. *The United States and the Caribbean in the Twentieth Century.* Athens: University of Georgia Press, 1985.

LeoGrande, William M., Douglas C. Bennett, Morris J. Blachman and Kenneth E. Sharpe. "Grappling with Central America: From Carter to Reagan." In *Confronting Revolution: Security through Diplomacy in Central America,* edited by Morris Blachman, William LeoGrande, and Kenneth Sharpe. New York: Pantheon Books, 1986.

Lowenthal, Abraham. "Ronald Reagan and Latin America: Coping with Hegemony in Decline." In *Eagle Defiant? United States Foreign Policy in the 1980s,* edited by Kenneth A. Oye, Robert J. Lieber, and Donald Rothchild. Boston: Little, Brown, 1983.

_____ . *Partners in Conflict: The United States and Latin America.* Baltimore: The Johns Hopkins University Press, 1987.

Mertes, Alois. "Europe's Role in Central America: A West German Christian Democratic View." In *Third World Instability: Central America as a European-American Issue,* edited by Andrew Pierre. New York: Council on Foreign Relations, 1985.

Millett, Richard. "Looking Beyond Noriega." *Foreign Policy* 1 (Summer 1988): 46–64.

Modelski, George. "Long Cycles and the Strategy of U.S. International Economic Policy." In *America in a Changing World Political Economy,* edited by William Avery and David Rapkin. New York: Longman, 1982.

Molineu, Harold. *U.S. Policy Toward Latin America.* Boulder, Colo.: Westview Press, 1986.

Moorer, Thomas H., and George A. Fauriol. *Caribbean Basin Security.* Washington, D.C.: Praeger Publishers, and CSIS, Washington Papers XI, 1984.

Muñoz, Heraldo. "The Strategic Dependency of the Centers and the Economic Importance of the Latin American Periphery." *Latin American Research Review* 16 (1981): 3–29.

_____ . "The Latin American Policy of the Reagan Administration." In *Latin American Views of U.S. Policy,* edited by Robert Wesson and Heraldo Muñoz. New York: Praeger, 1986.

Oye, Kenneth. "Constrained Confidence and the Evolution of Reagan Foreign Policy." In *Eagle Resurgent? The Reagan Era in American Foreign Policy,* edited by Kenneth A. Oye, Robert J. Lieber, and Donald Rothchild. Boston: Little, Brown, 1987.

Pastor, Robert. "Explaining U.S. Policy Toward the Caribbean Basin." *World Politics* 38 (April 1986): 483–515.

_____ . *Condemned to Repetition: The United States and Nicaragua.* Princeton: Princeton University Press, 1987.

_____ . "The Reagan Administration and Latin America: Eagle Insurgent." In *Eagle Resurgent? The Reagan Era in American Foreign Policy,* edited by Kenneth A. Oye, Robert J. Lieber, and Donald Rothchild. Boston: Little, Brown, 1987.

Platt, D.C.M. "Dependency in Nineteenth Century Latin America: An Historian Objects." *Latin American Research Review* 15 (1980): 113–146.

Purcell, Susan Kaufman. "Demystifying Contadora." *Foreign Affairs* 64 (Fall 1985): 74–95.

———. "The Choice in Central America." *Foreign Affairs* 66 (Fall 1987): 109–128.

Roett, Riordan. "Does the United States Have a Future in Latin America?" In *Latin America, Western Europe and the United States: Reevaluating the Atlantic Triangle,* edited by Wolf Grabendorff and Riordan Roett. New York: Praeger, 1985.

Rupert, Mark E., and David P. Rapkin. "The Erosion of U.S. Leadership Capabilities." In *Rhythms in Politics and Economics,* edited by Paul M. Johnson and William R. Thompson. New York: Praeger, 1985.

Russett, Bruce. "The Mysterious Case of Vanishing Hegemony; or Is Mark Twain Really Dead?" *International Organization* 39 (Spring 1985):207–232.

Sanderson, Steven E. "Recasting the Politics of Inter-American Trade." *Journal of Inter-American Studies and World Affairs* 28 (Fall 1986):87–124.

Schoultz, Lars. *National Security and U.S. Policy Toward Latin America.* Princeton: Princeton University Press, 1987.

Strange, Susan. "Still an Extraordinary Power: America's Role in a Global Monetary System." In *The Political Economy of International and Domestic Monetary Relations,* edited by Raymond Lombra and Willard E. Witte. Ames: Iowa State University Press, 1982.

———. "The Persistent Myth of Lost Hegemony." *International Organization* 41 (Autumn 1987):552–574.

Vaky, Viron. "Positive Containment in Nicaragua." *Foreign Policy* 68 (Fall 1987):42–58.

Wesson, Robert. *U.S. Influence in Latin America in the 1980s.* New York: Praeger, 1982.

Wiarda, Howard. "Changing Realities and U.S. Policy in the Caribbean Basin: An Overview." In *Western Interests and U.S. Policy Options in the Caribbean Basin,* edited by The Atlantic Council's Working Group on the Caribbean Basin. Boston: Oelgeschlanger, Gunn and Hain Publishers, 1984.

———. *In Search of Policy: The United States and Latin America.* Washington: American Enterprise Institute for Public Policy Research, 1984.

Index

Accommodation, 3, 11, 13, 14–19
Adams, Brooks, 12
Africa, 117
ALADI. *See* Latin American Integration Association
Alfonsín, Raul, 130, 148
Allende, Salvador, 37
Americanization, 14
Americas Watch, 79
Amnesty International, 79
Andean Group exports, 60–61(table)
Arab states, 87, 110
Araña, Carlos, 78
Arbenz, Jacobo, 19, 22, 104, 157
ARDE. *See* Democratic Revolutionary Alliance
ARENA. *See* Republican National Alliance
Argentina
  air force, 115
  arms industry, 111, 115
  debt, 130, 145, 146(table), 148, 151
  economy, 131, 136, 137, 145
  exports, 60–61(table), 111
  GDP, 52(table), 54(table), 55, 56–57(table), 138(table)
  income, per capita, 137
  military, 100(table), 115, 116(table), 117, 118(table)
  military spending, 112–113(table), 115, 118(table)
  navy, 115
  and nuclear power, 117
  and Soviet Union, 143(table)
  and United States, 119, 120, 121(table), 143(table), 164
  U.S. investment in, 141, 142(table)
  and U.S. trade, 58–59, 62–63(table), 139
  See also Malvinas/Falklands War
Arias Sanchez, Oscar, 75, 175, 177, 183
Arms industry, 111, 114, 115
Arms traffickers, 77
Arms transfers, 119, 123, 125
Austerity, 134, 135, 138, 147
Authoritarian rule, 70

Bahamas, 138(table), 142(table)
Baker Plan (1985), 150
Balance of payments, 134
Baloyra Herp, Enrique A., 69
Bananas, 6
Barbados, 56–57(table), 112–113(table), 138(table)

Batista, Fulgencio, 36, 104
Bay of Pigs (Cuba) invasion (1961), 162
Belgium, 117
Belize, 56–57(table), 100(table)
Bermuda, 142(table)
Big Four
  global, 55
  regional, 55, 56–57(table), 58, 60–63(tables), 137, 141, 145
Big Pine maneuvers (Honduras), 164
"Big Stick" policy, 12
Bitar, Sergio, 53
Blaine, James, 7, 8, 14
Bolivia
  debt, 146(table), 149
  drug trade, 183
  economy, 136, 137
  exports, 60–61(table)
  GDP, 52(table), 56–57(table), 138(table)
  military, 100(table), 118(table)
  military spending, 112–113(table), 118(table)
  and Soviet Union, 143(table)
  and United States, 37, 121(table), 143(table)
Booth, John A., 72
Brazil, 3, 33
  air force, 115
  arms industry, 111, 115
  debt, 107, 144, 145, 146(table), 149, 150
  economy, 53, 134, 137, 145
  exports, 6, 60–61(table), 64, 111, 139
  GDP, 52(table), 54(table), 56–57(table), 138(table)
  income, per capita, 137, 147
  inflation, 147
  military, 100(table), 114, 115, 116(table), 117, 118(table)
  military spending, 112–113(table), 115, 118(table)
  navy, 115
  and nuclear power, 117
  raw materials exports, 6
  as regional power, 50
  and Soviet Union, 143(table)
  unemployment, 147
  and United States, 119, 121(table), 141, 143(table)
  U.S. investment in, 141, 142(table)
  and U.S. trade, 58, 62–63(table), 64–65, 67, 139
Brezhnev Doctrine, 162
Brunei, 87, 167

Bryan-Chamorro Treaty (1916), 13
Bush, George, 31, 164, 170

Calero, Adolfo, 93
Canada, 88, 112–113(table), 117, 153(table)
Capital
    and debt, 147
    inflow, 132, 135, 153, 183
    markets, 134
    transnational movement of, 32
Capital goods, 58
Capitalism, 13, 24, 27, 71
Caribbean Basin, 3, 25
    economies, 50
    exports, 65
    and Great Britain, 6, 7, 9
    individual rights, 77
    instability, 50
    Left, 84, 165
    regional associations, 38, 165
    and Soviet Union, 34, 106. *See also under*
        Cuba
    Spanish, 5, 7, 8
    and United States, 3, 4, 6, 7, 9, 10, 11, 12,
        16, 18, 21, 24, 25, 28, 31, 34, 36, 50, 85,
        86, 162, 163
    U.S. investment in, 141, 142(table)
    and U.S. trade, 21, 59, 64, 65, 139
    See also individual countries; under
        Security
Caribbean Basin Economic Recovery Act, 65
Caribbean Basin Initiative (CBI) (1983), 65
Cartegena group, 150, 181, 184–185
Castro, Fidel, 33, 104, 121, 157, 162
Catholic church, 71
CBI. *See* Caribbean Basin Initiative
Central America, 2, 3, 25, 28, 34, 37, 39, 90
    cash crop exporting economies, 68–69
    civil wars, 75, 76, 79
    crisis, 67–69, 70, 71–73, 81, 82, 83, 88–89,
        99
    debt, 69, 146(table)
    democracy in, 74–81
    democratization, 92, 168, 171, 173, 174–175,
        177–178, 183
    development, 70
    economies, 70, 71
    and Great Britain, 6
    industrialization, 70
    inflation, 69
    injustice, 70
    instability, 67, 69, 70
    Left, 71, 73, 74, 75, 77, 81, 83, 84–87, 88, 89,
        90, 97, 104, 106, 157, 159, 161–162, 163,
        171
    military, 70, 71, 73, 74, 81
    modernization, 70, 71
    neodependency, 28
    political participation, 71–74
    poverty, 70, 77
    states, 67–68
    unemployment, 69
    and United States, 3, 4, 6, 18, 21, 22, 25, 35,
        36, 40, 42, 44, 67, 81–82, 83, 84, 94, 96–
        97, 103, 125, 173, 185, 188. *See also*
        Containment strategies
    U.S. investment in and trade, 85
    See also individual countries; under Latin
        America
Central American Common Market exports, 60–
    61(table)
Central American Defense Council
    (CONDECA), 21
Central American peace plan (1987), 46, 74,
    79, 86, 88, 92, 94, 158, 167, 170–175, 181,
    183
    compliance, 175–178
    original version (Esquipulas I), 173
Central Intelligence Agency (CIA), 86, 157,
    159, 160, 163, 164, 166, 175
Cerezo, Vinicio, 78
Chamorro, Violeta Barrios de, 76
Chile
    arms industry, 115
    counterrevolution (1973), 37
    debt, 146(table), 151
    economy, 137
    exports, 60–61(table)
    GDP, 52(table), 55, 56–57(table), 138(table)
    income, per capita, 147
    Marxists, 157
    military, 99, 100(table), 118(table)
    military spending, 112–113(table), 118(table)
    and nuclear power, 117
    and Soviet Union, 143(table)
    and United States, 37, 119, 121(table),
        143(table), 157
    U.S. investment in, 142(table)
Christian-based community, 72
CIA. *See* Central Intelligence Agency
"Cinderella" of Central America. *See* Honduras,
    economy
Citibank, 149
Civil War (U.S.), 4, 7
Clark memorandum (1928), 15
Class interests, 27, 72, 73
Clayton-Bulwer Treaty (1850), 6
Cleveland, Grover, 14
Client states, 96, 103, 165
Coalitions, 16
Coffee, 6, 132
Cold-war internationalists, 40, 186
Coleman, Kenneth, 123
Colombia
    and Central America, 90
    debt, 146(table)
    drug trafficking, 108, 183
    exports, 60–61(table)
    GDP, 52(table), 55, 56–57(table), 138(table)
    military, 100(table), 118(table)
    military spending, 112–113(table), 118(table)
    and United States, 6, 119, 121(table),
        143(table)
    U.S. investment in, 142(table)
    See also Contadora process
Communications, 105, 115
Communist bloc, 32, 46, 58, 85, 94, 96, 107,
    114, 123, 162

Communists, 77
Conciliatory default, 149–150, 151
CONDECA. *See* Central American Defense
   Council
Conflict management, 42, 45, 121, 125–126,
   158, 179, 181, 186
   common ground, 182–183
   and international institutions, 184–185
   multilateral, 125–126, 170–171, 178, 181
   and U.S. containment policy, 83–84, 87–92
Consumer goods, 58
Contadora process, 46, 84, 88, 90–92, 94, 122,
   172, 173, 174, 181
Containment strategies, 83–96, 157, 161–162.
   See also Reagan Doctrine
Contra war (Nicaragua), 40, 79, 80, 86, 87, 90,
   93–95, 157, 159, 163–164, 166–168, 172,
   174, 175
   cease-fire, 177, 183
   force size, 94
   See also Central American peace plan; Iran,
   contra affair
Cooperation, 42, 50, 86, 158, 171, 178, 179–
   180, 181–185, 187, 188–189
Cooperatives, 72
Corporatism, 72
Corruption, 135, 160
Costa Rica
   and Central American peace plan, 175–176
   and Contadora process, 92
   contras in, 175–176
   debt, 146(table)
   economy, 81, 136, 137
   elections, 75
   exports, 60–61(table)
   GDP, 52(table), 56–57(table), 138(table)
   insurgency, 175
   living standards, 81
   militarization, 77
   military, 100(table)
   military spending, 112–113(table)
   and Nicaragua, 77, 86, 122, 125, 160, 175
   political stability, 72–73
   and United States, 25, 77, 121(table), 160,
   175
Counterinsurgency, 123. *See also*
   Counterrevolution
Counterrevolution, 36, 37, 77, 125
   containment policy, 84, 85, 92–96
   privatized, 87
Credibility, 35, 85, 86, 89, 106, 107, 169
Credit, 18
Crisis management, 45, 104
Cristiani, Alfredo, 76
Cuba, 36, 123, 150, 187
   exports, 6, 60–61(table)
   GDP, 56–57(table)
   and Great Britain, 7
   Left, 84
   military, 99, 100(table), 110, 114, 115,
   116(table), 117, 118(table), 123
   military spending, 111, 112–113(table), 115,
   118(table)
   and Nicaragua, 92, 93, 95, 96

   and nuclear power, 117
   raw materials exports, 6
   revolution (1959), 33, 35, 37
   and Soviet Union, 25, 34, 36, 68, 85, 93, 95–
   96, 103, 106, 119, 123, 143
   and Spain, 8, 9
   and United States, 8, 9, 10, 11, 13, 16, 25,
   37, 53, 85, 95, 103, 104, 106, 121, 157, 161,
   162, 164
Cuban Missile Crisis (1962), 101, 103, 165
Current accounts, 133

Debt. *See under* Central America; Latin
   America; *individual countries*
Debt for equity swapping, 151
Debtor cartel, 149, 150, 151
Debt repudiation, 149, 150
Debt service ratio, 144
Defection thesis. *See under* Revolution
Demilitarization, 125
Democracy, 13, 16, 26, 73, 74–81, 147–148, 161,
   172, 173, 181
Democratic Coordinadora (Nicaragua), 76
Democratic Revolutionary Alliance (ARDE)
   (Nicaragua), 94
Democratic Revolutionary Front (FDR) (El
   Salvador), 71, 174, 176
Democratization. *See under* Central America
Dependencia, 27
Dependency perspective, 27, 28, 29, 135, 180
Destabilization, 104
Development. *See under* Central America; Latin
   America
Development doctrine, 36
Discounting, 151
Distributive justice, 183
Dollar diplomacy, 10, 12, 13, 14
"Dollars and Dictators" alliance, 16, 67
Dominguez, Jorge I., 24, 38
Dominica, 56–57(table)
Dominican Republic
   debt, 146(table)
   exports, 60–61(table)
   GDP, 52(table), 56–57(table), 138(table)
   military, 100(table), 118(table)
   military spending, 112–113(table), 118(table)
   and Spain, 7
   and United States, 8, 11, 21, 104, 121(table),
   143(table), 162
   U.S. intervention in (1916–1934, 1965), 13,
   21, 22, 157, 165
Drago Doctrine 1904), 12
Drug trade, 100, 108, 168, 169, 183
Duarte, José Napoleon, 75, 76, 78, 87, 91, 174

East-West relations, 34, 68, 89, 108, 109, 183
EC. *See* European Community
Economic asymmetry, 15, 16, 18, 19, 20, 24,
   53, 55, 58, 66, 70
Economic Commission for Latin America, 70
Economic efficiency, 47
Economic exploitation, 27
Economic growth, 51, 52(table), 53, 55, 66, 70,
   129, 130, 131, 134, 136, 137, 139, 146, 147,
   159, 160, 183

Economic instability, 43, 44, 45, 47, 48, 49, 50
Economic interdependence, 25, 132. *See also*
    Interdependence
Economic nationalism, 17
Ecuador
    debt, 146(table)
    exports, 60–61(table)
    GDP, 52(table), 138(table)
    military, 100(table), 118(table)
    military spending, 112–113(table), 118(table)
    and United States, 121(table), 143(table)
    U.S. investment in, 142(table)
EEC. *See* European Economic Community
Elections, 26, 74, 75–76, 81, 171, 173, 183
Elites, 71, 72, 73, 83
El Salvador, 38, 71, 91
    and Central American peace plan, 176
    civil war, 75, 80
    and Contadora process, 92
    crisis, 69
    death squads, 78
    debt, 146(table)
    economy, 80, 137
    elections, 75–76
    exports, 60–61(table)
    GDP, 52(table), 56–57(table), 138(table)
    individual rights, 77, 78, 176
    insurgents, 108, 161, 174, 176, 177
    Left, 25, 71, 119
    military, 100(table), 115, 118(table), 176
    military spending, 112–113(table), 118(table)
    political participation, 73
    politics, 71, 72, 74
    poverty, 80
    rightist coalitions, 71
    and United States, 25, 80, 87, 104, 117, 119,
        121(table), 161, 174
    U.S. ambassador to, 78
    See also Nicaragua, and Salvadoran rebels
Esquipulas II. *See* Central American peace
    plan
Eurocentric world, 1
Eurocurrency, 134, 144
European Community (EC), 140, 154
European Economic Community (EEC), 65
Exchange rates, 135
Export-led growth, 135

Farabundo Martí National Liberation Front
    (FMLN) (El Salvador), 174, 176
FDN. *See* Nicaraguan Democratic Force
FDR. *See* Democratic Revolutionary Front
Federal Republic of Germany
    arms transfers, 119
    and Central America, 88
    economy, 55
    exports, 60–61(table)
    GDP, 54(table)
    GNP, 153(table)
    See also under United States
Figueres, José, 77
Fishlow, Albert, 130, 134
FMLN. *See* Farabundo Martí National Liberation
    Front

Foreign aid, 141. *See also* Military, transfers;
    individual countries, and United States
Foreign exchange, 136, 147
France, 7
    arms transfers, 119
    and Central America, 88, 89
    economy, 55
    GDP, 54(table)
    GNP, 153(table)
Free riders, 64
Free trade, 14, 17, 45, 59, 64, 65–66
Free Trade Area (FTA), 65
Frente Sandinista de Liberación Nacional
    (FSLN), 94. *See also* Nicaragua, Sandinista
    government
FSLN. *See* Frente Sandinista de Liberación
    Nacional
FTA. *See* Free Trade Area

Gallup poll (1985), 86
García, Alan, 130, 148
GATT. *See* General Agreement on Trade and
    Tariffs
GDP. *See* Gross domestic product
General Agreement on Trade and Tariffs
    (GATT), 64
General System of Preferences (GSP), 64, 65
Germany, 12. *See also* Federal Republic of
    Germany
Getting to Know the General (Greene), 168
Global recession (1980s), 26, 59, 130, 131–132,
    133, 136. 137, 138, 139, 152, 154, 155,
    158–159
GNP. *See* Gross national product
Good neighbor policy, 15–16, 17, 18, 19
Gorbachev, Mikhail, 96, 158, 186, 189
Grabendorff, Wolf, 29, 89
Gramsci, Antonio, 30, 44
Great Britain, 6–7, 8, 9–10, 12, 20, 23, 45, 48,
    88, 89, 124
    economy, 55
    GDP, 54(table)
    GNP, 153(table)
    as world leader, 4, 5, 17
    See also Malvinas/Falklands War
Greene, Edward J., 44
Greene, Graham, 168
Grenada, 122, 187
    Cubans and Soviets in, 166
    GDP, 56–57(table)
    government, 158, 165, 166
    U.S. invasion of (1983), 21, 24, 25, 88, 104,
        114, 122, 157, 165–166
Gross domestic product (GDP), 51, 52(table),
    53, 54(table), 55, 56–57(table), 94, 137,
    138(table), 139
    and defense, 118(table)
Gross national product (GNP), 29, 129, 136,
    153(table)
    and defense, 110, 111
GSP. *See* General System of Preferences
Guatemala, 92
    counterrevolution (1954), 37
    coup (1954), 19, 37, 122

debt, 146(table)
economy, 80
exports, 60–61(table), 80
GDP, 52(table), 56–57(table), 138(table)
government, 176
income, 80
individual rights, *77*, 78, 176
insurgents, 108, 157, 174, 176
Left, 71, 157
military, 74, 78, 100(table), 115, 118(table), 174, 176
military spending, 112–113(table), 118(table)
political participation, 73
politics, 71, 72, 74, 78
Rightist coalition, 71
state terrorism, 78
and United States, 19, 21, 104, 121(table), 143(table), 157
Guerrillas, 76, 77, 78, 80, 102, 125, 174, 176
of the poor, 36
Gunboat diplomacy, 10, 12
Guyana
economy, 137
GDP, 138(table)
military spending, 112–113(table)
and nuclear power, 117

Haiti
debt, 146(table)
economy, 137
exports, 60–61(table)
GDP, 52(table), 56–57(table), 138(table)
individual rights, 77
military, 100(table)
military spending, 112–113(table)
and United States, 121(table), 162
as U.S. protectorate (1915), 13, 15
Hegemonic stability theory, 43, 45, 49, 50
Hegemony, 3, 8, 9, 10–19, 20, 23, 68, 69, 123, 127, 154, 165, 187
change, 22, 23–24, 25, 31, 46, 47–50, 67, 158
cultural, 30, 31, 44
decline, 31–42, 43, 44, 46, 48, 49, 50, 51, 58, 59, 66, 84, 97, 110, 125, 129, 143, 154, 158, 160, 164, 180, 188, 189
defined, 2, 29, 43, 44, 47
eclectic, 29–30, 31
economic, 12, 14–15, 18, 20, 45, 47, 51, 53, 58, 64, 67, 129, 130, 149, 152, 154
ideological, 30–31, 44, 46, 182, 187
and leadership, 187
military, 12, 14, 15, 18, 24, 111
modern ordeal, 1–2, 41, 82, 154–155, 179, 189
political, 10, 16, 18, 67, 69
post-, 171, 179, 181, 184, 188
pure, 29, 31, 41, 43, 44, 67
restoration, 44, 48, 85, 87, 99, 102, 122, 125, 153, 155, 160, 161
stable, 180
values and norms, 106, 107
See also Power relations; Security
Honduras
and Central American peace plan, 176
and Contadora process, 92
contras in, 176
debt, 146(table)
economy, 77, 80–81
exports, 60–61(table)
GDP, 52(table), 56–57(table), 138(table)
individual rights, 77, 176
Left, 77
military, 73, 77, 100(table), 118(table), 176
military spending, 112–113(table), 118(table)
and Nicaragua, 86
political participation, 73
poverty, 77, 80
and United States, 6, 25, 81, 87, 119, 121(table)
U.S. military exercises in, 164, 166
Hoover, Herbert, 15
Hull, Cordell, 17, 18
Human condition, 74, 79–81, 147–148
Human rights, 77, 176

IMET. *See* International military education and training program, U.S.
IMF. *See* International Monetary Fund
Imperialism, 3, 8, 10–14, 85, 162
Imports, 49, 64–65. *See also under* Latin America
Import substitution, 135
India, 64
Individual rights, 74, 76–79, 176
Industrial Revolution, 3
Inefficiency, 135
Instability. *See* Economic instability; Political instability; *under* Latin America; Security
Interdependence, 22, 25, 26, 68–69, 86, 131, 144, 189
asymmetric, 26, 180, 188
Interest rates, 132, 134, 135, 136
Intermediate nuclear forces agreement (1987), 175
International arbitration. *See* Drago Doctrine
International currency, 46
International division of labor, 68
International financial system, 49, 130, 131, 148, 149, 150, 151, 152–153
International League for Human Rights, 78
Internationalism, 7
International military education and training program, U.S. (IMET), 120
International monetarism, 135
International Monetary Fund (IMF), 133, 147
Interventionism, 8, 10, 11–12, 13, 14, 15, 21, 22, 24, 25, 42, 86, 103, 104, 106, 108, 121, 122, 123, 125, 157–158, 159, 161, 162, 164–170, 172, 178, 180, 186, 188–189
anti-, 31, 122
limited, 40
Iran
-contra affair, 122, 125, 161, 167
and United States, 87, 104
Isolationism, 7, 40
Israel, 110, 114, 167
Italy, 119

Jamaica, 56–57(table), 112–113(table), 138(table)
Japan, 23, 32, 33, 46, 53, 131
  and Central America, 88
  economy, 55
  exports, 60–61(table)
  GDP, 54(table)
  GNP, 153(table)
  trade, 58, 64, 140(table)
Jefferson, Thomas, 5
Jesuits, 78

Kennedy, John F., 73, 162
Keohane, Robert O., 23, 47, 49
Kindleberger, Charles, 49
Kissinger, Henry, 37
Kissinger Commission (1983), 68
Krasner, Stephen, 39, 182
Krugman, Paul R., 130
Kurth, James R., 19

Lackland Air Force Base (Texas), 120
Lake, David, 49
Latin America, 27–28
  autonomy, 109–110, 184, 186, 187
  cash crops, 6
  and Central America, 89–90, 125, 188
  debt, 12, 26, 42, 44, 45, 50, 109, 125, 129, 130, 131–136, 137, 139, 140, 143–153, 154, 155, 159, 183, 185, 187
  development, 3, 22, 59, 64, 109, 135, 147, 148, 185, 186
  dictators, 16
  economies, 3, 7, 18, 21, 33, 38, 45, 50, 51–55, 108–109, 129–130, 131, 132, 135–137, 139, 143, 147, 159–160, 183, 189
  elected governments, 26, 148
  European colonial powers in, 4, 5–6
  exports, 6, 15, 17, 18, 59, 60–63(tables), 117, 129, 132, 133, 136, 138, 139
  foreign investment in, 6–7, 32–33, 88, 136, 140, 147. *See also subentry* U.S. investment in
  foreign policies, 38
  GDP, 53, 54(table), 55, 56–57(table), 138(table), 139
  GNP, 129, 136
  and Great Britain, 5, 6–7
  imports, 15, 117, 139, 147
  income, per capita, 129, 136, 137
  industrialization, 18
  industry, 55
  instability, 45, 50
  interstate conflicts, 21, 29, 83–84, 99–100, 108, 126, 178, 181, 188
  military, 21, 100(table), 110, 111, 114, 115, 117, 120, 126
  military spending, 110, 112–113(table)
  monetary policies, 135
  multilateralism, 181, 186
  nationalism, 31, 120, 180
  political stability, 4, 13, 14, 21, 50
  population increase, 129, 137
  security, 101, 102, 107–110, 126, 181, 186

  states, 31, 36, 37–39, 42, 45, 50–51, 106, 110, 124, 170–171, 181, 185, 189
  trade, 6, 8–9, 14, 15, 17–18, 32, 33, 45, 51, 53, 58–66, 111, 132, 136, 138–140, 143, 153, 185
  unemployment, 153
  U.S. investment in, 14, 15, 140–141, 142(table)
  See also Caribbean Basin; Power relations; *individual countries; under* United States
Latin American Economic System (SELA), 38, 181, 184
Latin American Integration Association (ALADI)
  exports, 60–61(table)
League of Nations, 17
Left, 106, 160. *See also under* Caribbean Basin; Central America; Political parties
Liberalism, 71
Liberal Party (Honduras), 73
Liberal perspective, 69, 70, 71
Libya, 107
Lomé III Convention, 65
Lowenthal, Abraham, 43, 50

Macroeconomic policies, 134, 146, 153
Malvinas/Falklands War (1982), 25, 91, 108, 123–124, 184, 187
Manifest destiny, 6, 9
Marcos, Ferdinand, 104
Market economy, 47, 49
Marxists, 157, 186. *See also* Left
Material resources. *See* Hegemony, defined
Mexico, 3, 33, 107
  and CBI, 65
  debt, 131, 144, 145, 146, 151
  and drug enforcement, 160
  economy, 13, 134, 137, 145
  exports, 60–61(table), 64
  and France, 7
  GDP, 52(table), 54(table), 55, 56–57(table), 138(table)
  and Great Britain, 7
  income, per capita, 137, 147
  inflation, 147
  military, 100(table), 115, 116(table), 118(table)
  military spending, 112–113(table), 118(table)
  and Nicaragua, 90–91, 173
  oil, 90, 133
  Revolution (1910), 13
  unemployment, 147
  and United States, 6, 13, 37, 90, 119, 121(table), 143(table), 160
  U.S. investment in, 141, 142(table)
  and U.S. trade, 59, 62–63(table), 67, 139
  See also Contadora process
Middle East, 33, 99, 117
Military, 110–120
  asymmetry, 24, 117
  bases, 105, 165
  Big Five, 115
  equipment, 114, 115, 119
  spending, 110–111, 112–113(table), 115

and United States, 22, 40, 104, 121,
143(table), 160, 168-170
U.S. invasion of (1989), 21, 24, 25, 31, 122,
157, 170
U.S. investment in, 142(table)
U.S. military training base, 120
See also Contadora process
Panama Canal
revenues, 170
security, 12, 85, 102, 105, 169, 170
treaty negotiations, 168
Panama Defense Forces (PDF), 168, 169, 170
Pan-Americanism, 14
Pan American Union, 7, 184
Paraguay
debt, 146(table)
economy, 137
exports, 60-61(table)
GDP, 52(table), 56-57(table), 138(table)
military, 100(table), 115, 118(table)
military spending, 112-113(table), 118(table)
and United States, 121(table)
Paramilitary forces, 115, 118(table)
Pastor, Robert, 29, 34
PDF. *See* Panama Defense Forces
Peasants, 72, 73, 78
People's war, 36
Perón, Juan, 120
Peru, 5
air force, 115
debt, 130, 146(table), 148, 149
drug trade, 183
economy, 137
exports, 60-61(table)
GDP, 52(table), 56-57(table), 138(table)
income, per capita, 147
military, 100(table), 115, 118(table)
military spending, 112-113(table), 115,
118(table)
navy, 115
and United States, 119, 121(table), 143(table)
U.S. investment in, 142(table)
See also Shining Path
Petrodollars, 134
Philippines, 104
Platt Amendment (1901), 8, 16
Pluralism, 40, 72, 73, 121, 124-125, 171, 181
tolerance of, 125, 126
Political instability, 67, 70
Political participation, 68, 71-74, 77, 81, 82
Political parties, 73, 76
center, 70, 73, 75, 76, 78
left, 71, 73, 74, 75, 77, 81
left-of-center, 70
right, 74, 75, 76, 81
Populism, 72, 73
Poverty. *See under* Central America; El
Salvador; Honduras
Power relations, 3, 27, 46, 47, 69, 85, 106-107,
180, 182, 186, 189
asymmetry, 28, 31, 129, 180, 182
and change, 1, 2-3, 15, 22-23, 26-29, 41, 42,
48, 66, 115
diffusion, 31, 32-33, 42, 43, 44, 46, 48, 50,
53, 55, 67, 148, 152, 154, 159-160, 179

distribution, 4, 5, 20, 22, 33, 38, 41, 44, 46,
107, 117, 121, 143, 160, 187-188
economic, 129, 130, 148, 152, 154, 160
use, 24, 25, 30, 44, 85
See also Hegemony; United States, decline
Prensa, La (Managua), 176
Price distortions, 135
Private lending, 134, 135, 144, 145, 149, 150,
151-152
Proconsularism, 35, 170
Protectionism, 8-9, 45, 64, 135, 180, 185
Protectorates, 13, 14, 15

Radical perspective, 69, 70-71, 84, 187. *See
also* Revolution
Raw materials, 6, 58, 105, 106
Reagan, Ronald, 26, 40, 41, 68, 86, 87, 110,
160, 161, 164, 166, 172, 180
peace plan (1985), 94
Reagan Doctrine, 157, 158, 159, 162-169, 170,
171, 172, 174, 175, 178, 188, 189
Recession. *See* Global recession
Reciprocal Trade Agreements Act (1934), 17-18
Reformism, 70, 71, 73
Regional associations, 38, 60-61(table), 158,
165, 181, 184-185. *See also* Central
American peace plan; Contadora process
Regional bus service, 175
Regional détente, 87-88, 159, 175
Relative productivity, 47, 58
Republican National Alliance (ARENA) (El
Salvador), 76
Retrenchment, 40, 48, 49
Revolution, 25, 28, 36, 70, 71, 73, 92-93, 104-
105, 106, 124, 125, 161, 162, 183
defection thesis, 31, 35-37, 42, 45, 67, 157,
159, 179
Rio Pact (1947), 19, 21, 25, 184
Robelo, Alfonso, 94
Roett, Riordan, 38
Roosevelt, Franklin D., 17
Roosevelt, Theodore, 11, 12

Sandinistas. *See* Nicaragua, Sandinista
government
San Jose (Costa Rica) agreement (1984), 91
Sapóa truce (1988), 95
Saudi Arabia, 87, 167
Sea lanes, 102, 105
Security, 21, 27, 28, 36, 85, 99, 121-127, 181,
183
assistance, 117
of Caribbean Basin, 12, 28, 34, 35, 50, 65,
68, 102, 105-106
concept, 101
consensus, 101-102, 124, 126, 183, 189
global, 49, 102, 103
instability, 43, 45, 46, 49, 50, 104-105
political, 124-125
and stability, 102
of Western Hemisphere, 4, 8, 9, 10, 11, 20,
25, 34, 42, 45, 91, 95, 100-101, 102-107,
109, 117, 121, 122-124, 126, 127, 157, 159,
186

training programs, 119–120
transfers, 117, 119–120, 164
treaties, 120, 121(table)
See also under Central America; Latin
America; *individual countries*
Miskito Indians (Nicaragua), 79
Modernization, 70
Molineu, Harold, 37
Monetary system, 49, 135
Monroe, James, 5
Monroe Doctrine (1823), 5, 7, 8, 9, 15, 85,
122, 123, 124
Roosevelt Corollary (1904), 10, 11, 12, 15,
122
Most favored-nation treatment, 17
Multipolar world, 3, 22

NAMUCAR (Caribbean shipping firm), 38
Napoleonic Wars, 5
Narcomilitarist. *See* Noriega, Manuel Antonio
National Guard (Nicaragua), 177
Nationalism, 4, 31, 45, 120, 180
National Opposition Union (UNO)
(Nicaragua), 76, 159, 176
National Security Council (U.S.), 87, 172
NATO. *See* North Atlantic Treaty Organization
Neoconservative perspective, 69–70
Neodependency, 28
Neomercantilism, 17
Netherlands, 8
Netherlands Antilles, 142(table)
Neutrality, 4
New Deal, 17
Nicaragua, 34, 36, 38, 71, 107, 108, 160, 187
anti-Sandinista coalition. *See* Democratic
Coordinadora; National Opposition Union
anti-Sandinista government (1990), 25, 74,
76, 158, 159, 168, 176, 177–178
death squads, 79
debt, 146(table)
economy, 80, 161, 167, 168
elections, 76, 79, 176, 177
exports, 60–61(table)
GDP, 52(table), 56–57(table), 138(table)
GNP, 94
income, 80, 167
individual rights, 77, 78–79
labor unions, 177
Left. *See subentries* Revolution; Sandinista
government
military, 94, 100(table), 117, 118(table), 163
military spending, 111, 112–113(table),
118(table)
political parties, 176
political participation, 73
political prisoners, 177
Revolution (1979), 25, 28, 35, 37, 45, 84
and Salvadoran rebels, 93, 177
Sandinista government (1979–1990), 22, 70,
76, 78–79, 80, 83, 84, 87, 88, 90, 91, 92,
93, 94, 96, 104, 159, 162, 163, 167–168,
171, 175, 176, 177, 183
security, 125–126
social conditions, 80, 167

and Soviet Union, 36, 69, 92, 93, 94, 95, 96,
107, 123, 162, 167
state of emergency, 79
and United States, 6, 11, 13, 16, 22, 37, 53,
76, 83, 84, 86, 87, 91–92, 94, 103, 104,
106, 119, 121, 157, 159, 161, 162, 163–164,
166–168, 171, 172, 183, 185
See also Central American peace plan;
Contra war; *under* Costa Rica; Cuba;
Mexico; Venezuela
Nicaraguan Democratic Force (FDN), 93
Nixon, Richard M., 37
Nonintervention, 16, 18, 19
Noriega, Manuel Antonio, 22, 31, 40, 104, 107,
121, 160, 168–170, 173, 184
North, Oliver, 87
North Atlantic Treaty Organization (NATO),
105
North-South relations, 34, 39, 43–44, 99, 108,
109, 126, 148, 158, 160, 185, 187
Nuclear weapons, 117

OECD. *See* Organization for Economic
Cooperation and Development
OECS. *See* Organization of Eastern Caribbean
States
Oil, 85, 132
bust (1980s), 89, 132–133, 137
credits, 91
imports, 105
prices, 133
shocks (1970s), 25, 49
Oligarchy, 14, 16, 69, 70, 71, 73
OPEC. *See* Organization of Petroleum
Exporting Countries
Open trade, 45, 53, 59, 64–65
Operation Just Cause (1989), 25
Opportunism, 103, 105
Order, 16, 70, 81, 104
Organization for Economic Cooperation and
Development (OECD), 88, 131, 132, 137,
139, 147, 151, 152, 154
Organization of American States (1948), 19,
160, 184
charter, 188
Organization of Eastern Caribbean States
(OECS), 165
Organization of Petroleum Exporting Countries
(OPEC), 32
Ortega, Daniel, 76, 79, 121, 167, 177

Pacification, 171
Panama, 90, 184, 187
debt, 146(table)
exports, 60–61(table), 169
GDP, 52(table), 56–57(table), 138(table)
government, 158, 168, 170, 173
income, per capita, 137
and Libya, 107
military. *See* Panama Defense Forces
military spending, 112–113(table)
as part of Colombia, 6
and Soviet Union, 107

Wesson, Robert, 24, 39
Western Europe, 23, 32, 33, 46, 53, 58, 83, 89, 114
Western Hemisphere
  discord, 185 189
  GDP, 54(table), 56–57(table), 137
  GNP, 153(table)
  See also under Security
West Germany. *See* Federal Republic of Germany

Wilson, Woodrow, 13, 14
Woodward, Ralph Lee, 71
Working class, 71, 147
World Bank, 150
World economy, 32, 47, 48, 51, 64, 182
  liberal, 45, 46, 49
World trading system, 49
World War I (1914–1918), 14, 16
World War II (1939–1945), 16, 18, 48, 101
Write-downs, 151

See also Conflict management; Military; *under* Latin America
SELA. *See* Latin American Economic System
Self-determination, 19
Semi-industrialized periphery, 32
Shah of Iran, 104
Shining Path (Peru), 108
Slave trade, 6
Smoot-Hawley Act (1928), 17
Somoza dynasty, 36, 67, 104, 106, 122, 162
Soviet Union, 2, 24, 37, 89, 90, 119, 123, 143, 162, 189
  geographical fatalism doctrine, 95
  See also Communist bloc; *under* Argentina, Bolivia; Brazil; Chile; Cuba; Nicaragua; Panama; United States
Spain, 5, 7, 8, 9, 12, 88, 89
Spanish-American War (1898), 9, 12
State, 27–29, 31
  activism, 37–39, 45, 170–171, 178
  evolution of, 4
Strategic intrusion, 31, 33–35, 162, 179
Strategic perspective, 26–28, 68, 157, 158, 159
Subsidies, 135
Sugar, 169
Surinam(e), 56–57(table), 77, 138(table)

Taft, William Howard, 12–13
Tariff policy, 15, 17. *See also* Protectionism
Technology, 2, 47, 111, 114, 115
Terms of trade, 132–133
Third World, 23, 38, 40, 85, 89, 101, 139, 150, 162, 184
Torrijos, Omar, 168, 169
Trade embargo, 86, 163, 168
Transisthmian traffic, 6
Treaty of Tlatelolco (1967), 117
Trinidad and Tobago, 112–113(table), 137, 138(table), 142(table)
Trujillo, Rafael, 104

Underdevelopment, 109
Ungo, Guillermo, 176
United Nations, 148
United States
  banks, 51, 144, 149, 154
  business interests, 12, 13, 14, 16
  and communism, 19, 105, 109, 160, 163, 164
  debt, 129, 134, 164
  as debtor/creditor nation, 145–146
  decline, 1, 2, 3, 23, 44, 45, 55. See also under Hegemony
  economy, 2, 3, 15, 16–17, 20, 21, 22, 44, 46, 51, 53–55, 99, 111, 129, 130, 136, 137, 179
  exports, 60–61(table), 111, 139
  and Federal Republic of Germany, 49, 89
  GDP, 53, 137
  GNP, 110, 153(table)
  income, per capita, 137
  industry, 7
  interdependency, 22, 25, 26
  -Latin American relations, 1, 2, 3, 4, 5, 6, 7–8, 9, 10–20, 21–22, 24, 26–29, 30, 99, 108, 114, 117. *See also* Conflict management;

Hegemony; Latin America, U.S. investment in; Latin America, trade; Security; *individual countries,* and United States
  manufactures, 55
  Marines, 11, 13, 15, 16, 24, 165, 166
  military, 2, 21, 22, 99, 100(table), 110, 111, 115, 116(table), 126, 164, 166
  military assistance from, 117, 119–120, 164
  military spending, 110, 111, 112–113(table), 164
  nationalism, 4
  national will, 31, 39–41
  nineteenth century, 3–9
  oil imports, 105
  peace plan (1987), 174
  policymaking, 40, 44, 83, 161, 180. *See also* Containment strategies
  political consensus, 3, 7, 157, 166–167
  and Soviet Union, 35, 40, 84, 85, 95, 103, 105, 106, 158, 161, 162, 164, 165, 175, 186. *See also* East-West relations
  unilateralism, 181, 186
  and Vietnam, 40, 114, 164
  as world power, 1, 2–3, 10, 19, 22, 23, 46–47, 157, 186
  See also Security; *under* Caribbean Basin; Central America; Iran; *individual countries*
UNO. *See* National Opposition Union
Uruguay
  debt, 146(table)
  economy, 137
  exports, 60–61(table)
  GDP, 52(table), 56–57(table), 138(table)
  military, 99, 100(table), 110, 118(table)
  military spending, 112–113(table), 118(table)
  and United States, 121(table)

Vargas Llosa, Mario, 73
Venezuela
  and CBI, 65
  debt, 145, 146(table), 151
  economy, 137, 145
  and El Salvador, 91
  exports, 60–61(table)
  GDP, 52(table), 54(table), 55, 56–57(table), 138(table)
  and Germany, 12
  and Great Britain, 8, 12
  income, per capita, 147
  military, 100(table), 118(table)
  military spending, 112–113(table), 118(table)
  and Nicaragua, 91
  oil, 137
  and United States, 90, 119, 121(table), 143(table)
  U.S. investment in, 142(table)
  and U.S. trade, 58, 62–63(table)
  See also Contadora process
Vietnam
  Syndrome, 40
  See also under United States
Virgin Islands, 8
Voluntary associations, 72